The
News
Twisters

The
News
Twisters

Edith Efron

Nash Publishing

Los Angeles

THE AUTHOR AND PUBLISHER WISH TO ACKNOWLEDGE SEP-
ARATELY THE FOLLOWING SOURCES:

Atheneum Publishers for granting use of quoted material from Theodore H. White's *The Making of the President, 1968,* copyright © 1969 by Theodore H. White.
Reprinted by permission of the author and Atheneum
Publishers.

Fortune Magazine for permission to quote from the
article "What's Wrong With the News? It Isn't New
Enough." Reprinted courtesy of *Fortune* Magazine; ©
1969 Time Inc.

Newsweek for permission to quote from the copyrighted
articles included herein.

The New York Times for permission to quote from the
copyrighted articles included herein.

Triangle Publications, Inc., for the free use of Miss
Efron's own articles and other copyrighted materials which
have appeared in *TV Guide* Magazine.

The Wall Street Journal for permission to quote from
their editorial of January 12, 1970.

Library of Congress Catalog Card Number: 72-167511
Standard Book Number: 8402-1206-2

Published simultaneously in the United States and
Canada by Nash Publishing, 9255 Sunset Boulevard,
Los Angeles, California 90069.

Printed in the United States of America

First printing

Acknowledgments

I thank the many people who assisted me in various ways, and at various stages of this project:

Carl, Guy, and Ann Chambers, who tape-recorded the programs;

Betsy Wells, Jerry and Linda Klasman, Bill and Jeanne Lawry, Ken and Judith Costello, and Jeanette Swiderski, who did such patient research;

Julia and Lynn Mulligan and Rita Quinn, who took seemingly endless dictation, typed a quarter of a million words of research, and several versions of the final manuscript;

Clytia Chambers, whose aid on all fronts and whose inventive organizational abilities kept this complex project from falling into chaos;

And the Board of Directors of The Historical Research Foundation, whose confidence in me, and whose financial generosity, made the entire undertaking possible.

To all, I express my gratitude.

Contents

Preface

On November 5, 1972, the people of the United States will once again go to the polls to elect their President. They will do so, guided in some significant measure by the political information they receive from the American press and, most notably, from network news—above all from the 7:00-7:30 prime-time nationwide news reports on ABC, CBS and NBC-TV which are the major source of political information for the whole country.

It is legally required of broadcasters that their political coverage be nonpartisan and neutral. The standards for such neutrality have been set forth in a Federal Communications Commission code known as "The Fairness Doctrine," and have been sanctioned as compatible with the First Amendment by the Supreme Court. Strangely, however, no analytical method has ever been devised which would permit either the FCC, or the networks, or any private citizen to check systematically on the neutrality of the nationwide network news services. Over the years, political storms have blown up over individual stories and individual programs which were charged with supporting one side of a political controversy. For lack of a coherent theory of bias and a simple analytical method, such cases have always been determined in favor of the networks, provided these programs included even a symbolic amount of "contrasting" opinion. In the theoretical void which prevails, the Fairness Doctrine is virtually unenforceable.

The dilemma engendered by an unenforceable standard of "fairness" has been the source of profound unrest in this country. Throughout the sixties—the decade during which I have been reporting professionally on the broadcasting industry—the conviction that network news is politically biased has grown rapidly in the body politic, and tends to rise to a peak during electoral periods.

During the election of 1960, most bias charges came from the far right. Rightist complaints moldered in the files of the Federal Communications Commission, and were flatly ignored by the networks as "lunatic fringe" opinion.

During the Presidential elections of 1964, repeated outbursts at the Republican convention revealed that this "lunatic fringe" opinion had swelled in four years to include former President Dwight D. Eisenhower and most of the Republican party. Again, the protests were ignored by both the Federal Communications Commission and by the networks—dismissed, this time, as "partisan."

By 1968, the network coverage of the race riots, of the antiwar riots in Chicago, and of both the Republican and Democratic conventions inspired protests against biased coverage from a majority of the country—including Democratic Presidential candidate Hubert Humphrey and a significant portion of the Democratic Party. These protests, too, were dismissed as invalid by the FCC. And network officials explained that they were generated by a collectively neurotic desire to evade "bad news."

In 1969, Vice President Spiro Agnew delivered his famous speech charging the networks with biased political coverage of certain issues during the campaign of 1968, and with a continuation of this bias during the following year. Predictably, the FCC supported the networks on one of his charges, and evaded the others. Network officials replied to none of his charges, and countercharged the Vice President with "fascistic" and "repressive" intentions. And when it was revealed that a majority of the country—all conservatives, most Republicans, a third of all Democrats—supported the Vice President's charges, network officials then declared that these Americans were all suffering from "selective perception" and a neurotic desire to "kill the messenger" who bore the "bad news."

What united most of these bias charges was the prevailing belief, in the majority of the country, that the networks were sanctioning, inflating, and sympathizing with the positions of the far left splinter of the spectrum. During this same period, however, the far left splinter itself frequently charged network newsmen with bias—a seeming contradiction which the networks seized upon as further proof that "selective perception" was operating in the body politic.

Since that time, poll after poll has revealed that a substantial part of the country continues to believe that network political coverage is biased. And each time such information is released, network officials deny the charges fervently and continue to offer the same remarkable explanations for such public reactions—explanations that boil down to the curious claim that from one-half to two-thirds of the nation is now a "lunatic fringe" whose perceptions of bias stem from mass cognitive malfunction.

Is half the nation or more suffering from such cognitive malfunction? Or is the political coverage of the networks biased? As we approach yet another Presidential election, it would be advisable to solve this problem.

There is only one way to solve it—and that is to arrive at a clear and demonstrable definition of political bias, to define a simple analytical method for ascertaining the presence or absence of such bias, to apply this method to the network product, and to arrive at a documented answer.

This book was written to report just such a solution.

The work began three years ago. In the summer of 1968—just before the last Presidential election—I was awarded a grant by The Historical Research Foundation, in New York City, for the express purpose of devising an analytical method for testing bias in news coverage and for the purpose of evaluating the tri-network coverage of the then upcoming 1968 presidential campaign. It took more than one year to solve the theoretical problem alone. It took another year to apply the results to the recorded transcripts, to subject these results to multiple checks, and to write the final study.

I hereby offer the results of these two years of research to the public. I offer it with five distinct intentions:

1) to report on how the last Presidential campaign and its issues were covered by the three network news departments, to offer concrete evidence that this 1968 coverage was severely biased, and to demonstrate that the subsequent nationwide charges of bias are not a function of cognitive malady;

2) to show how the charges from the right and from the left are both valid, are noncontradictory, and do not constitute evidence that the networks are politically neutral;

3) to issue a warning to all that if the same reportorial methods are still in use—and there is no known reason to suppose them changed—the coverage of the Presidential campaign of 1972 and its issues will again be severely biased;

4) to offer a coherent theory of bias and a simple analytical method which can be used to check on the fairness or bias of political coverage in broadcast news;

5) to inform the networks, the FCC, Congress and concerned private citizens at all points of the political spectrum that this analytical method exists and to propose that it be adopted immediately and applied to network coverage of the campaign of 1972.

The time has come for all good men, whatever their political affiliation may be, to take rational action before yet another Presidential campaign is handled in partisan fashion over the national airwaves. It is my profound hope that this book will inspire such action.

Edith Efron
New York City 1971

What Is Bias?

"Bias" is a concept which by now has become a loaded code-word—used as automatic invective by people who dislike the networks on political grounds and denied by those who are politically sympathetic to the networks, with few of the critics or defenders capable of saying what it is they are talking about.

In the few cases where attempts have been made publicly by network officials themselves to define the concept of bias, the results have been less than elegant.

As a case in point, on November 25, 1969, in a CBS broadcast called "60 Minutes," Walter Cronkite of CBS defended network news against the bias charges of Vice President Spiro T. Agnew, and in the course of this defense proffered definitions of "bias" and "objectivity." The definitions revealed little about either, except the fact that this eminent newscaster didn't know or didn't choose to know what they were.

"What is objective reporting?" asked Mr. Cronkite. "How [do] we define objective reporting? Well, we all have our prejudices, we all have our biases, we have a structural problem in writing a news story or presenting it on television as to time and length, position in the paper, position on the news broadcast. These things are all going to be affected by our own beliefs, of course they are. But we are professional journalists. This is the difference. We are trying to reach an objective state, we are trying to be objective. We have been taught from the day we went to school, when we began to know we wanted to be journalists, integrity, truth, honesty, and a definite attempt to be objective. We try to present the news as objectively as possible, whether we like or don't like it. Now *that* is objectivity."

In this desperate conceptual struggle with his subject, Mr. Cronkite merely ended up saying: "Objectivity is when one tries to be objective." It is rather circular as definitions go.

On November 24, 1969, on National Educational Television, in a program called "Mr. Agnew and the News," Fred Friendly, former President of CBS News and now Professor of Broadcast Journalism at Columbia University, made a similar stab at defining these issues. In answer to the moderator's question "What is fair play in the news?" Mr. Friendly said:

"Anybody that has to be told will never know. I like what Mr. Brinkley said a year and a half ago. I liked hearing him again when he said 'You try, you strive to be fair.' I think this whole debate, this whole climate that's been created, and I think it has been very carefully created, has been to create a climate, and I think the one man who could put everybody's fears to rest is the President of the United States, who has been silent. Look, three things bother the American people: the war in Vietnam, which the prior administration had tried to conceal; race; and what's happening to the youth. No President and few Governors are willing—and few Mayors—to put that all on the line. It's the journalist's job to do it. The broadcast journalist has got a very tough job, and I wish some of them were on this program, some of the broadcasters, to speak for themselves. To do it night after night, day after day, with the voices and sounds of the war in Vietnam, the people in the streets of Watts and Harlem and Chicago, and with the youth at the campuses in California, San Francisco State and New York. It's a tough job. They're never going to be loved for it. Sometimes they get killed. Sometimes they get rocks thrown at them. A few more correspondents have been shot at in Vietnam than there have been politicians shot at in Vietnam. They try to be fair. They try to be fair by doing interpretive journalism when it is required, not letting a Senator McCarthy—and I don't mean any odious comparison to anybody—say there are 205 Communists in the State Department, and letting an outrageous unsubstantiated charge like that go unidentified for what it is. The broadcast journalist today has got the job sometimes, although he doesn't want it that way, of having to do it when the event is going on, sometimes a day later, a week later. I think it ought to be labelled for—not for editorializing which I don't think broadcast journalists do, but for what it is—news analysis, as varying from straight reporting. I think it is fair to do that, and I think fairness is something you know in your gut you're doing."

Mr. Friendly's definition of "fairness" is even less sleek than Mr. Cronkite's. Ultimately, he knows it, mystically, in his "gut." And if someone else's "gut" disagrees . . . there isn't much that can be done about it.

In both men's "definitions" there is the clear intimation that they are helpless in the face of human "subjectivity." And "subjectivism" has become a fashionable network defense these days against bias charges. Indeed, on an NET broadcast on December 22, 1968, David Brinkley declared that to be "objective" was to be a "vegetable": "Objectivity is impossible to a normal human being," he said.

Similarly, publisher Bill Moyers—an ABC-TV commentator during the campaign period—said in mid-campaign (*Time,* September 20, 1968): "Of all the myths of journalism, objectivity is the greatest."

The formal meaning of this denial of "objectivity," of course, can be summed up by the old subjectivist bromides: "What's true

for me isn't true for you," "Man can't perceive real reality," etc.—
notions that abolish the possibility of any objectively demonstrable
facts and postulate the cognitive impotence of man. It's a curious
hypothesis to hear advanced by newsmen who covered man's flight
to the moon.

It is not worthy of debate, however, in this context, because
man's alleged incapacity to establish objective truths is hopelessly
irrelevant to the issue of bias on the airwaves. It is a philosophical
red herring. The major charges of bias against the networks do not
pertain to the objective truth or falsity of any statements made on
news programs—they pertain to the issue of according *preferential
status* to certain political positions and opinions.

There is nothing whatever subjective or mystically ungraspable
about the issue of preferential status. In fact the networks have repeatedly demonstrated a perfectly lucid understanding of every
aspect of it. When faced with a definite law requiring them to give
equal time to conflicting political opinions by candidates for office
and/or to people whose political opinions or positions have been
attacked, the networks have found no difficulty whatever in establishing:

   a) What a political position is.
   b) What a defense of that position consists of.
   c) What an attack on that position consists of.
   d) When a position has been attacked.
   e) Who represents any given "side" of the issue in-
      volved.
   f) What equitable treatment consists of.

At no time has a network ever declared that these issues were
beyond its ken by virtue of human "subjectivity." It is apparently
only where no hard law exists and where their own political positions are involved that network men suddenly experience mental
impotence on these identical questions and engage in philoso-
phizing about "objectivity" and "subjectivism."

It is nonetheless strange that they use this particular red herring
since there is a Federal Communications Commission regulation
which deals explicitly with these issues; and although it does not

have the status of a hard law passed by Congress, it has been in effect for 21 years, the networks claim to abide by it religiously and frequently invoke it in their own interests.

That regulation is the Fairness Doctrine.

This doctrine is a modification by the Federal Communications Commission of its own 1941 ruling known as the "Mayflower Decision." This historic decision forbade broadcasters to express their own thoughts on controversial issues, and had the inevitable effect of abolishing almost all thought from television. In 1949, the Fairness Doctrine was developed to rectify this situation. It granted the broadcaster the right to express his views—provided he also sought out and presented "all sides of controversial issues."

On June 9, 1969, Supreme Court Justice Byron White sanctioned the Fairness Doctrine as follows:

> To condition the granting or renewal of licenses on a willingness to present *representative community views* on controversial issues is consistent with the ends and purposes of those constitutional provisions forbidding the abridgment of freedom of speech and freedom of the press. *Congress need not stand idly by and permit those with licenses to ignore the problems which beset the people or to exclude from the airways anything but their own views of fundamental questions.* (Italics mine)

The Fairness Doctrine elaborates in some detail what is meant by "fairness" and by "bias." Its definitions pertain exclusively to controversy—to the realm of *opinion-coverage.* According to this ruling:

- The networks are required to select and broadcast contrasting and conflicting views on the major political issues—regardless of their truth or falsity.

- This selective process is to be "nonpartisan" and "non-one-sided," i.e., favoring neither side.

- And the selected opinion must be presented in an "equal" and "equally forceful" manner.

To do this, says the FCC, is *fairness*. To fail to do this, says the FCC, is *bias*.

The FCC's definition of bias is limited in that there can also be "partisan" selection of issues and facts, not just of opinion—as a hasty scanning of politically diversified publications will indicate. Nonetheless so far as it goes, the FCC's definition of bias as a "partisan" selection of opinion is valid.

The FCC definition—further elaborated on later in this essay—is the one formally used by this study.

SELECTIVITY: THE SOURCE OF BIAS

The FCC's definition roots bias in an editorial *selective process*. And Mr. Brinkley of all people should be able to defend this, for he is the man who once said:

> News is what *I* say it is. It's something worth knowing by *my* standards.

This statement, made to *TV Guide* on April 11, 1964, may well be one of the most revealing ever made by a contemporary journalist about the meaning and nature of news. Mr. Brinkley, at that time, did not give the reasons for this remarkable statement. And since these are precisely the reasons that must be set forth to ground any investigation of bias, I hereby present them.

"News" *is* what Mr. Brinkley and his colleagues say it is—because "news" is an entirely *chosen,* an entirely *selective* operation.

"News" merely means: "Something new" that has happened somewhere. The basic "news beat" is the Universe. The basic audience for "news" is Mankind. Any new event in the Universe of interest to or of importance to Man is "news," ranging from the birth of a new star in outer space to the sudden proliferation of a potent, invisible virus.

There are as many kinds of news-gathering and news-disseminating agencies as there are areas of human interest. There are special news services and publications for every branch of the arts and sciences, for every profit-seeking venture, for every pleasure-seeking activity of mankind. News is gathered for and disseminated to philosophers and philologists, to bacteriologists and sociologists, to students of facelifting and students of foreign policy. News is gathered for and disseminated to: producers of steel, and sellers of shoes, and feeders of chickens; to sports lovers, chess players, mountain climbers; to admirers of movie stars, to book lovers, photographers, child-rearers and chiropodists.

If something has happened in any one of these and numberless other specialized areas of existence—a discovery, an achievement, a triumph, a trend, a controversy, a problem, a disaster—it is "news."

In an essay in *Fortune* Magazine, October 1969, Max Ways, member of *Fortune*'s board of editors, writes:

> Journalism encompasses newspapers, newsmagazines, radio and television newscasts or "documentaries," press services, trade magazines, corporate house organs, labor-union periodicals—in short, the enormous variety of publications that describe or comment upon the current scene or some segment of it. Along with education and the arts, journalism is one of the three great information systems that account for the bulk of "the knowledge industry," the most rapidly expanding part of every advanced society.
>
> One reason why journalism expands is the amazing diversity of contemporary society. All the nonsense about regimentation to the contrary, there has never been a time when men varied so much in their work, pleasures, beliefs, values, and styles of life. In part, this growing diversity in life is a reflection of the specialization in knowledge and in education. To be "an educated man" no longer denotes participation in a common, circumscribed body of knowledge. Though the total of extant knowledge has multiplied many times, that part of it which "everybody knows" has increased much more slowly. Society cannot afford to imitate the university,

where communication between departments is either per-
functory or non-existent. Outside the university, the
world becomes smaller in terms of interdependence while
it becomes larger in terms of the difficulty of communicating between heterogeneous groups and diverse individuals . . . As the circles widen, the communication
difficulty increases . . . To deal with this difficulty, contemporary journalism had developed along a scale that
ranges from publications addressed to as few as a thousand readers up to television and magazine audiences
ranging around fifty million.

A general—as opposed to a specialized—news service or publication is one which engages in an almost incredibly selective operation: it is culling out from all the events in the universe every week
or every day those events which the editors believe to be of the
greatest importance and interest to *most* people.

A general prime-time daily news program on a network requires
an even more incredibly selective process. Here the editors are
culling out the events of the universe which they believe to be of
the greatest importance to most people and which they can pack
into 22 minutes.

But this choice of events to cover is not where the selective process stops. It continues through every other aspect of news-gathering and dissemination down to the minutest detail. In every single
news story, every element is a terrain of incessant choice.

To cite the major selective processes in one political news story
alone: the event selected for coverage is a matter of *choice;* the issues covered are a matter of *choice;* the facts isolated are a matter
of *choice;* the number and kinds of participants in the event who
are interviewed for the story are a matter of *choice;* the authorities
and experts cited in the story are a matter of *choice;* the number
and extent of their opinions included in the story are a matter of
choice; the interpretations and explanations of the event are a matter of *choice;* the theories offered about the causes of the event and
any proposed solutions to problems are a matter of *choice.*

And even this is not where selectivity stops. It is continued throughout the period in which the reporter sits down at his typewriter and writes the actual words of the story. His selection of vocabulary, his connotations, his implications, his associations, his dramatic structure, his logical organization and his emotional intellectual, moral and political stresses—all are a matter of *choice*.

News is indeed what Mr. Brinkley and his colleagues say it is. No facts and no opinions are broadcast to this nation on prime time network television which they have not *chosen*. And the facts and opinions that are not on the air they either do not know or have chosen to *leave out*.

Selectivity—the decision to include, or exclude information—is the essence of a news operation. It is the axiom of the Fairness Doctrine and of Justice White's defense of that doctrine.

BIAS: THE HIDDEN STANDARD

It is quite obvious that such continuous and complex acts of selectivity—usually performed at breakneck speed by contemporary news-gathering and disseminating agencies—require one or more standards of selectivity: implicit or explicit value-guides which tell the racing reporter what is and is not "important," "significant," "central," "essential," etc. If he had to stop dead in the face of each new event and figure out such a hierarchy of values at every instant, he would be mentally paralyzed and unable to work. The reporter can only select and exclude at top speed because he is applying deeply ingrained standards of selectivity which function as a screening agent for him, and help him to determine what is, or is not, "news."

As Mr. Brinkley puts it: "It's something worth knowing by *my* standards."

In political newscasting there are *political* standards of selectivity: There are a substantial number of selective standards in the political realm which are completely nonpartisan—and used by journalists, whatever their political convictions or sympathies.

The broadest ones emerge directly from the nature of politics itself: It doesn't matter what the individual's theory of government may be—*all* political persuasions agree that politics does involve government. And thus the major aspects of government operation —elections on national and state levels, and in the cities with greatest population concentration; the passage of laws; the decisions of the Supreme Court, etc.—are considered significant by all journalists regardless of political persuasion.

Similarly, *all* agree that major economic elements within a society are crucial components of its political life. Thus, the state of business and labor, general productivity, the stability of money, and economic trends, are subjects of universal choice, regardless of political persuasion.

Finally, any events which will have an impact on great numbers of people or are likely to have such an impact are identified by *all* as political phenomena. Thus any political-social-economic trends in the populace; any problems affecting large groups of people; any threats to the external security of the populace; wars, etc., are subjects of universal choice.

This indeed is a rough list of what stands for "political news"— and there is broad political agreement on *subject* selection within these areas.

However, these are universal choices in only the most restricted sense: the universal agreement is only on the *fact* of their significance. *What* they signify, *why* they signify it and what if anything to *do* about any problems that have arisen—all these are controversial political questions. And the standards of selectivity used in deciding which of a huge range of possible interpretations to transmit to the public are almost invariably partisan.

Newsweek Magazine has commented (November 10, 1969):

> One of the first things every journalism student learns is that a given fact can usually be contrived to mean many different things, *depending on who is interpreting it and how,* and that political facts are perhaps more susceptible to this phenomenon than others. (Italics mine)

The interpretive "Why?" in the political realm is the controversial question par excellence. It is the causal question that leads right to the most virulent moral, sociological and economic battles over the genesis and solutions of the socio-political problems of our era. "Why"—the reasoning that explains the "meaning" of a phenomenon—is the area where partisan selectivity reigns supreme, and where covert editorializing runs amok.

Where partisan selective standards do exist in political coverage, these standards, in our era, tend to cluster around liberal-left and conservative-right poles. This polarization is most familiar to us in terms of the differences in such publications as: *The New York Times* vs. *The Chicago Tribune; U. S. News and World Report* vs. *Time* Magazine; *The Wall Street Journal* vs. *The New York Post; The New Republic* vs. *Human Events; Ramparts* vs. *The National Review,* etc.

Historically the key issue dividing "conservative" and "liberal" is the relation of the individual to the state, and partisan selective standards spring from this seminal source. Generally the left-of-center spectrum is Marxist-influenced, advocates increasing state intervention into individual life, with the far left advocating total statism or dictatorship. Generally, the right-of-center spectrum is rooted in 19th-century liberalism, advocates decreasing and/or minimal state intervention into individual life, with the libertarian far right advocating virtually total state exclusion from all areas of existence.

These are the ultimate standards determining political positions and, of course, they generate innumerable substandards as they are applied to specific issues.

Characteristically it is the intellectuals and political theorists in both broad camps who alone are aware of these fundamental selective standards. Nonintellectuals and pseudo-intellectuals tend to learn and apply the substandards to specific issues—i.e., "race" or "the Vietnam war" or "the bombing" or "the Carswell nomination"—with little or no knowledge of the derivation of these positions. It is the collection of substandards at any given period which establishes the short-term conservative or liberal "party line" of that period.

Although a liberal publication and a conservative publication will both cover the "universally significant" issues, they tend necessarily to cover different secondary issues. And in the "universal" issues they often present different sets of political facts, cite the opinions of different sets of people, offer different causal interpretations and transmit different solutions. These differences emerge directly from their contrasting standards of political selectivity.

There can consequently be an enormous difference between a liberal news story and a conservative news story on the same subject, both in content and in the way it is actually written. And because this disparity is directly relevant to this particular study, I will illustrate this idea in some detail.

In Appendix A are two long news stories—each of which is obviously determined in all its details by an implicit standard of political selectivity.

Both are reports on conditions in Hanoi. One is from the liberal *New York Times* of December 16, 1969, under the headline: "In Hanoi, Leaders and the Public Seem Confident."

One is from the conservative *U. S. News and World Report* on December 22, 1969, under the headline: "North Vietnam: Plight of the Enemy . . . Buildings in Hanoi Crumbling . . . Haiphong is Ruined, Ravaged."

The story in the liberal *Times* begins like a poem: "At dusk, a mist settles over Thuyen Quang Lake in the southern section of Hanoi and young couples sit close on benches along the shores, their bicycles parked against trees.

"The sounds of a bamboo flute and a girl singing a heroic folk song drift across the lake from a loud speaker. At one end of the lake there are night food stalls selling bowls of noodles, fried chicken, green vegetables and red peppers. A few old women in black cotton trousers and padded jackets squat over baskets of tangerines and bananas, their wares lighted by tiny kerosene lanterns."

As the *Times* reporter portrays it, Hanoi sounds like one of the most delightful places in the world. And he tells us: "The mood of war time Hanoi is determined but surprisingly relaxed. There is no sense of panic or depression that the war has gone on for so many years." The morale, he says, is good.

The *Times* reporter then reports on a series of interviews with three members of the Politburo of the Communist party—mentioning, as an aside, that he was travelling with his grandfather, "Cleveland industrialist Cyrus Eaton." He does not mention that his grandfather has made a career of espousing Communist causes, and is far more famous for that than for being a "Cleveland industrialist." And the reporter relates that he found no signs of anti-American feeling; on the contrary, even the children are eager to shake hands with an American.

What he did find was anti-Nixon feeling. The Nixon administration, his Communist sources inform him, is regarded as "hostile and aggressive"—the children think so, too.

Only towards the very end of this very long story do we learn that "most buildings in Hanoi badly need a fresh coat of paint; few houses have more than one bare electric bulb showing at night, and many residents must draw their water from communal taps in the street."

The reporter mentions that, "strangely," he only saw two disabled men of military age during his week in Vietnam, and says that "few of the men . . . who march south every year return." He offers no explanation.

He ends with a remark about Vietnamese spirituality—"The people here do not seem to measure things in a materialistic way." And he quotes another Communist about the Vietnamese resolve to drive out the Americans.

By contrast, the *U. S. News & World Report* story presents a picture of devastation and want, a country "kept afloat" only by Russian and Chinese aid.

Under a photograph on the first page of the story, the caption reads: "Heart of Hanoi Teems with People—but War-Weariness, Low Morale are Evident." And *U. S. News* writes:

> Cumulative problems are telling. American bombing
> ended more than a year ago, but few basic industrial

plants have been rebuilt. Labor productivity is low. Repeatedly the regime complains openly about petty thievery, black marketeering and other crimes . . .

Morale has been hurt because the end of the bombing has not meant the end of the war. Young men still are conscripted and disappear.

War-weariness is growing among the people. One reason: last year, for the first time, wounded began to be sent home from the crowded field hospitals in Laos and Cambodia. For the first time Northerners began to see the lame, the halt and the blind—and to hear their tales of hardship in the South.

There is enough food, but it is mostly bad.

And the first part of the story concludes: "The enemy is suffering weakness that can be exploited," and says that if President Nixon is given time, North Vietnamese problems will grow worse.

The sources from which *U. S. News & World Report* draws its conclusions are not the high officials in the North Vietnam Communist party—but "U.S. experts" with access to "official intelligence" and other sources.

This section of the story is backed up with a lengthy interview—again, not with a Communist, but with French journalist Pierre Darcourt, who was born in Saigon, grew up in North Vietnam and went to college in Hanoi—and who has spent 32 years in the Far East. And Mr. Darcourt supports the dark picture painted by the earlier section of the story.

He says such things as "There isn't a single family in the North that hasn't lost a husband or a son . . . There is no industry to speak of . . . Electricity is rationed. . . . It's impossible to get the simplest items—buttons, safety pins, paper, pens, wire, wool, anywhere . . . North Vietnam is in ruins. I'd say the air war put the country back 20 years. It is almost entirely dependent on outside aid . . . With the economy at a sub-standard level, the only trade is barter in the villages."

And, after some discussion of the internal splits between North and South Vietnam, and within the North Vietnamese themselves, he concludes that "the longer Hanoi waits to negotiate, the more its options are narrowed."

Finally, in the *U. S. News* story, one does not learn about how "hostile and aggressive" the Nixon Administration is. One learns, instead, from Mr. Darcourt, about how criminal Ton Duc Thang, Ho Chi Minh's successor, is: He is a murderer and kidnapper who has spent a good part of his life in jails.

What *are* the conditions in Hanoi? Is it a poetic tourist paradise with flickering candles, romantic couples, delicious fried chicken, with few signs of physical devastation from years of U. S. bombing or of the human crippling that is war's legacy; and peopled by benevolent Communists, young and old, who love all Americans and hate only the wicked Nixon?

Or is it a war-torn, destroyed little world hanging on by virtue of Russian and Chinese aid, reduced to primitive barter and thievery, seeing its youth go South and "disappear" or return crippled and maimed?

Take your choice.

What is important about these two stories in the context of this study, however, is not their ultimate truth or falsity, but their method.

Each story is a skillfully woven tissue of *facts;* each story contains quoted opinions: neither story contains overt editorial opinion. Further, there is no particular reason to suppose that either the *Times* reporter or the *U.S. News* reporter fabricated any of the details or quotations.

What is overwhelmingly clear is that different political standards were guiding their choices of facts to relay and to exclude and of opinions to cite.

It does not require genius to deduce their respective attitudes to the U. S. war in Vietnam and to President Nixon. These underlying attitudes served as the standard of selectivity and determined the implicit political point of view in both stories.

In Appendix B are two other news stories—this time on the nomination of Judge Harrold Carswell to the Supreme Court:

Again one is from *U. S. News and World Report,* February 2, 1970, under the headline: "The Carswell Nomination—New Direction for High Court: A Change in the Balance of Power on the Highest Bench is in the Making Once More. Mr. Nixon's Nomination Could Tip the Scales to the Side of 'Conservatism.' "

And one is from *Time* Magazine of February 2, 1970, under the heading: "Once More, With Feeling,"—the lead sentence reading: "God Almighty, did I say that? It's horrible!"

Again, there is a considerable diversity in the choice of facts for the story, in the degree of detail accorded to certain points, and in the organization and dramatic structure.

The *Time* story, after its explosive lead about a "blatantly racist speech" made twenty-two years ago by Judge Carswell, devotes five long paragraphs to his former racist attitudes and then goes into consideration of his possible impact on civil rights decisions once on the Court. The only content of Carswell's conservatism as seen by *Time* is: racism.

The *U. S. News* story, on the other hand, leads off with complex considerations involving the possible reshaping of the Supreme Court into a more conservative mold—pitting conservatism against liberalism and "judicial activism" in a variety of political areas. It does not mention the existence of Carswell's former racist attitudes until the twenty-second paragraph of the story, where it is dealt with in six diplomatic lines and never mentioned again.

It is perfectly clear from the structure, stress, and detail alone, that to *U. S. News and World Report,* the "significant" news is the possibility of having a philosophical conservative on the Court. Indeed, it accompanies the story with a chart listing "liberal" and "conservative" judges. For this publication, the past racist expressions of Judge Carswell are an unfortunate detail to be rapidly glossed over and buried deep in the middle of a long story, if not absolutely evaded.

And it is equally apparent that to *Time* Magazine, the overwhelmingly "significant" news is that evidence exists that Carswell once made racist comments; indeed, for *Time,* the conflict between philosophical conservatism and liberalism scarcely exists.

Again, it does not require unusual deductive skill to know which publication considers it desirable to see the Court move in a philosophically conservative direction and which does not. Nor is it difficult to deduce which publication considers racism to be central to the concept of conservatism and which does not. These are the political attitudes which served as the implicit standards of selectivity.

I reiterate that in none of these four stories, on Hanoi and on Carswell, are there any grounds for challenging *factual accuracy*. The facts as selected are doubtless true. The opinions as selected and quoted were doubtless uttered. What is at issue in both sets of stories is the *standard of selectivity*. It is the selective (or exclusionary) process which is controversial.

Because these four can be described as liberal and conservative stories, they are in some significant sense *partisan* stories. The choices of issues, facts, opinions, definitions as well as the literary, structural and stress choices, convert each of these news stories into covert editorials.

Perhaps the most important thing that can be said of these four stories, however, is that they are in no way unique. They certainly should not be seen as special cases of "distortion." They are, on the contrary, *standard* stories in liberal and conservative publications.

The stories in the liberal and conservative press habitually serve as transmission belts for the current "party line."

In summary:

- There are nonpartisan standards of political selectivity and there are partisan standards of political selectivity.

- Nonpartisan standards of selectivity are numerically restricted.

- Factual accuracy is no guarantee that partisan selective standards are absent.

- Partisan selective standards are at least as numerous as issues of controversy and they are frequently present in political coverage.

- Where such partisan selective standards are in use, the
story is politically *biased*.

To seek to discuss and analyze political bias in network news—
let alone to resolve a nationally explosive concern over this issue—
requires a clear understanding of what political bias is and what
causes it.

No analysis of bias in political news has any meaning unless it is
grounded in the phenomenon of selectivity.

And, more specifically, no analysis of bias in political news has
any meaning unless it is grounded in a consideration of the different *types* of political selectivity that exist in the American political spectrum.

Political bias is a specific type of selective process in a *specific
political context*. It cannot be discussed in a political void. When it
is discussed in a political void—as in the statements by Mr. Cronkite and Mr. Friendly at the opening of this chapter—all that
results is conceptual gibberish and protestations of good faith.

*Liberal, Democratic and left-wing bias are contentless concepts
save in opposition to conservative, Republican and rightist bias.*

BIAS: PROTECTED BY THE FIRST AMENDMENT

It is precisely this political selective process which is sheltered by
the First Amendment to the Constitution of the United States.

It is because the press is free to select and interpret by any political standard it deems fit, because it is free to include and exclude
facts and opinion in accordance with freely chosen political values,
that we have a full spectrum of political publications in this country. It is the difference in political standards of selectivity which
generates this journalistic spectrum and which keeps the channels
open for new publications with new political points of view.

Because the press is free, such politically oriented publications
do not conceal their political standards. *The Times* and *The New
York Post* are liberal and describe themselves as liberal. *The Chicago Tribune* and *Human Events* are conservative and describe

themselves as such. It is commonly understood that their selective processes are different, that they offer different factual and opinion choices to their readers; and these publications do not pretend otherwise. *The Times,* out of traditional pretentiousness, may declare that it offers "All the news that's fit to print." But if one wants to know what conservatives are thinking, one had better buy *National Review* and *Human Events. The Times'* selective pattern is liberal and under the First Amendment, it is free to consider most conservative opinion as "unfit to print."

The First Amendment gives the press the right to be biased.

Press freedom is not commonly stated in this form, but such is the case. *The New Yorker Magazine* on December 6, 1969, summed up this aspect of the First Amendment with lucidity: "There is nothing in the Constitution that says the press has to be neutral. Nor, for that matter, is there anything that says it has to be objective, or fair, or even accurate or truthful, desirable though these qualities are. For who is to be the judge? The press is simply free, and its freedom, like any other freedom, has to be absolute in order to be freedom. It is free to print any information it wants to print, *and to write from any point of view whatever."* (Italics mine)

BIAS: FORBIDDEN BY THE FAIRNESS DOCTRINE

Broadcast news organizations are in a totally different legal situation. Despite the endless assertions that the First Amendment shelters broadcasters equally with the press, this is not true. *Broadcast news is explicitly denied the First Amendment right to be biased.*

The FCC regulation called the Fairness Doctrine intervenes into the heart of the selective process and instructs the broadcaster that he is to seek out and provide "non-partisan," "equal" and "equally forceful" coverage of contrasting opinions on controversial issues.

In effect the Fairness Doctrine seeks to convert broadcast news into a neutral debating forum when controversial issues are involved. FCC Commissioner Rosel Hyde, in fact, called the doctrine a vehicle for fostering "robust debate." (*Broadcasting,* April 13, 1970.)

The debate need not always be simultaneous according to this regulation, nor need it be included within each story on the controversial issue. One set of views may be cited on one day, another on the next day, etc. But over the period of time in which this controversy is being covered, the news broadcaster is supposed to be "non-partisan" and to give "equal" and "equally forceful" play to major contrasting or conflicting views.

This equity in the Fairness Doctrine does not mean precisely equal time. That legal proviso is restricted to free broadcast time given to political candidates during a campaign. The definition of "equal," and "equally forceful" is left loose. Nonetheless, the intent of both concepts is clear enough:

"Equal:"

If a broadcaster airs an attack on an issue or a set of ideas, he is expected to provide a "balance" by airing a defense or an affirmative analysis of that issue or set of ideas.

The exact number of words or the exact number of minutes it takes to speak those words is certainly of importance, since no intellectual equity is possible if one side is allowed, let us say, 5,000 words and the other 25 words!

The networks are quite aware of this. On December 10, 1969, ABC-TV released information of a study, boasting of its *temporal* equity in dealing with controversial issues; approximately the same number of hours and minutes, according to Elmer W. Lower, President of ABC News, was allegedly devoted to the pros and cons of the issues aired by the study. Mr. Lower, like the News Presidents of the other networks, was quite aware that *reasonable* temporal equity is logically entailed in the Fairness Doctrine, even if precise temporal equity is not essential.

"Equally Forceful:"

"Equally forceful" is actually the wider and more encompassing concept since it implies reasonable temporal equity and adds the important proviso that there be *equity of conceptual potency* as well.

This standard poses more difficulties since journalists cannot be held responsible for the intellectual potency of their interviewees. The only thing they can do is to give people on both sides of a controversy an equal opportunity to express their views and let potency take care of itself.

What they must *not* do is to seek in any way to *diminish* or *augment* the potency of one side or another by any act of selectivity or editorial stress.

Here is a practical illustration of what the Fairness Doctrine logically requires:

The character of Mr. Nixon was a controversial issue in the campaign of 1968. Let us assume that a network aired three attacks on Nixon, such as these:

> My observation of Nixon goes back a long way and I think it's important that people not forget the Tricky Dick that we used to talk about because there was significance in that phrase. It goes back to his behavior when he first entered politics, the kind of campaign he ran against Jerry Voorhis, against Helen Douglas. The fact that in the course of his whole career in politics he hasn't

seemed to follow any consistent line, that he has been a man who seemed much more interested in what public opinion polls were showing than in what basic principles were involved.

The public never sees the issues on which Mr. Nixon speaks, a man who deliberately misleads when trusted to lead. It's not too late for Mr. Nixon to tell us what he stands for, if anything. We know that he's playing a game. He tells us every day.

Actually, Nixon's Congressional tenure is remembered better for how he won his seats than for how he filled them. He entered the House by defeating a respected Democrat, Jerry Voorhis, in a campaign in which "Red" innuendo and misleading assertions about "pro-Communist" labor support figured prominently.

He won his Senate seat by beating his House colleague Helen Gahagan Douglas (who became "the pink lady") in a spectacular campaign that is still cited as a classic of underhanded campaigning. And in later years as he campaigned for Congressional candidates from the Vice Presidency—especially 1954—he acquired the aura of slick meanness and opportunism that he has not been able to shake to this day—even despite relative restraint in later years.

The network is then required by the Fairness Doctrine to air a defense such as this:

Nixon is not what [many] people say he is—a weakling posing as a warrior, a panicky opportunist trying to prove himself a heroic statesman, a chronic trickster reverting to form . . .

Mr. Nixon is a man who does not easily give way, whose political reputation was originally made by refusing to give way; by refusing to give way, moreover, to precisely those forces of political liberalism . . . which are today once again ranging themselves against him in furious condemnation.

The original occasion, of course, was the case of the American traitor Alger Hiss, hero of the American Establishment, whom Mr. Nixon singlehandedly exposed, defying the whole massed weight of "informed opinion" which was convinced of his innocence.

I was in Washington during those years. Richard Nixon was the victim of a sustained and vitriolic smear campaign. He was a social and political pariah, shunned and derided. Yet he refused to bend, and was eventually proved abundantly right, although never forgiven by those he proved wrong.

This was the beginning of the myth of "tricky Dicky." What is the point of recalling this story today? Because it shows Mr. Nixon to be the very opposite of what his detractors accuse him of being. It shows him to be determined to the point of obstinacy, thick-skinned, single-minded and, once convinced of the rightness of his cause, relentless and ruthless in his pursuit. He is a formidable figure who has to be taken seriously.

The first two attacks are by George Ball and Ramsey Clark and they were aired on network television. (NBC, September 27, 1968 and CBS October 16, 1968) The third attack comes from an advertisement for the Humphrey campaign that appeared in *The New York Times* (November 5, 1968). The defense, by Peregrine Worsthorne, a British journalist writing in the *London Sunday Telegraph,* was reprinted in *National Review* on August 11, 1970.

As will be seen, the number of words pro- and anti-Nixon are not identical. The defense is shorter than the combined attacks. And precise equity is not needed. On both sides of the issue very strong statements are presented and, most important, *they deal with the same points.* One side is the characteristic anti-anti-Communist assault on Nixon by the left; the other side is the characteristic conservative defense, praising Nixon for his anti-Communist attitudes and attacking the anti-anti-Communist attack.

It is obvious that a defense of Nixon as a golf player or as a good father or even as a hard worker would not be a defense at all, no matter how eloquent or impassioned.

Equity of forcefulness in controversial issues means forcefulness on the same issues—or it means nothing.

The simplest way to sum up the meaning of the Fairness Doctrine, then, is as follows:

1) Reasonable temporal equity is required to "balance" contrasting opinion.

2) Opinion on a set of issues should be "balanced" by contrasting opinion on that same set of issues.

This is the classical "debate" view of what is "fair" in situations involving a conflict of opinion.

Anyone who challenges this concept of fairness must be prepared to argue that it is "fair" to give one side of a controversy much more time than the other and that it is "fair" to leave major attacks and arguments unanswered.

The networks have never challenged this "debate" concept of fairness. On the contrary, they have repeatedly declared that they are in accord with it and that they apply it.

OPINION: ITS ROLE IN BIAS

The intervention of the Fairness Doctrine into the reporter's selective processes is incalculably important.

Although the choice of what opinions to include in a story is only one of many classes of decisions that must be made—the choices involved in opinion coverage have a unique significance. They are unique because it is the opinion element in a story that contains the *evaluative* element. It is the element in the story that states not just what *is,* but also what *ought to be;* that states what is *good* and *bad* about the situation being reported on; that takes positions pro and con. It is the most emotionally loaded of all the elements in a story.

The Fairness Doctrine's requirement that such evaluative elements be equitably "balanced" has a correspondingly unique significance. It abridges the reporter's freedom to be "partisan" at a most critical point—in the *moral* realm of his story.

This opinion-balancing requirement—if obeyed—virtually eliminates partisan coverage of controversial issues. It is important to know why:

When a political news service is free to select only the opinion it chooses, it might very well, and usually does, put predominantly the opinion of which it approves into its stories.

Thus, in the case of Nixon's character, a liberal-Democratic news agency might very well give a transcendent place to a series of attacks on Richard Nixon of the type made by George Ball and Ramsey Clark; give space (or time) to very few favorable appraisals of Nixon; and it would be likely to refrain from giving play to any opinion at all which attacked liberal morality, as in the Peregrine Worsthorne statement.

The resultant coverage of Nixon would be powerfully anti-Nixon —without the news agency itself having said one editorial word.

If, however, the same news agency is ordered by law to include equity in defense, and specifically is ordered to present an "equally forceful" defense—it must air the Peregrine Worsthorne statement or its equivalent in sufficient number to give reasonable balance.

If the news agency obeys this regulation honorably and gives "equal" and "equally forceful" coverage to both sides, *on the same issues*—it is no longer in control of the political context of the opinion it selects for transmission. Its anti-Nixon point of view has been neutralized.

The news agency has in fact lost its most powerful partisan weapon.

Freedom in the realm of opinion-coverage is the single most powerful weapon in the editorial armament, because it is the most hidden weapon. It is the only editorial device that allows a news agency or reporter to proselytize freely, even passionately, while saying nothing directly.

The only other alternatives are covert editorializing and overt editorializing in which the agency and/or the reporter reveal their own partisan positions.

OPINION AS AN INDEX OF BIAS

The key role of opinion-selectivity as a political indicator in the news is virtually bromidic.

If one goes to a library and asks a trained librarian where one can find New Left opinion, liberal opinion, and conservative opinion, she will automatically turn, respectively, to New Left publications, liberal publications, and conservative publications. To a very great degree, the existence of a particular type of opinion in its pages is what is meant by the political labels given to publications, journals, or publishing houses.

It is to *Ramparts* that one must go if one is to keep up with the political opinions on the major issues of the day by such men as Eldridge Cleaver, Rap Brown, Huey Newton, Jack Newfield, Herbert Marcuse, and Tom Hayden, because only a New Left publication so admires the wisdom of these men that it will report regularly on their opinions.

It is to *The Chicago Tribune* and *Human Events* that one must go if one wants to keep up with the political opinions of such men as Barry Goldwater, Senator Tower, Governor Ronald Reagan or J. Edgar Hoover—again because only a conservative publication so admires the wisdom of these men as to report regularly on their opinions.

And it is to *The New York Times, Time, Newsweek* and to liberal news agencies generally that one must go if one wants to keep up with the political opinions of ex-Vice President Hubert Humphrey, New York Mayor John Lindsay, Senator Edward Kennedy, Senators McGovern, Fulbright, et al—again only because liberal publications so admire the wisdom of these men as to report regularly on their views.

These groups of political figures are *only* considered to be repositories of intelligence and wisdom by certain political groups. They are not esteemed, indeed they are despised, by others.

One of the primal principles of free political journalism is that a political news agency does not give much *interpretive* house room in its pages or stories to its political foes. The foes are certainly covered but they serve as objects of *attack;* the major interpretive role, which is to say the opinion role, is safely placed and kept in the hands of political friends.

A parallel phenomenon lies in the readership of such publications. It is not liberals who flock to read *The Chicago Tribune* or *Barron's Weekly* or *U. S. News and World Report*—it is conservatives. Conversely, it is not conservatives who dash out to get the latest issue of *The Village Voice, Ramparts* or the assorted underground press.

Study after study has revealed that people buy publications with whose editorial views they agree. A substantial part of what they are seeking out and agreeing with is the *opinion-selectivity* of that publication—namely, the views of those political and moral leaders deemed important by the publication and quoted consistently in its stories and articles.

Because of the relationship between the political philosophy of a news agency and its opinion-selectivity, any pattern of political preference in the opinion-selecting process is an index of the political point of view of the news agency. It will reflect the standard of selectivity operating in other partisan areas of choice as well.

It is for this reason that although the FCC's definition of bias is limited, it is an efficient *key* to the identification of a total political pattern. To know the opinion-selectivity of a news service is to know its politics.

In prime time network news in particular, with its restricted 22 minutes a night, opinion-selectivity is necessarily the most crucial index of any existing bias.

Partisan opinion-selectivity is the most economic method of proselytizing for a reporter who has little time for editorializing—if the reporter wants to proselytize.

Supervising the pattern of opinion-selectivity, including editorial opinion, is the most economic way for the FCC to check on network bias—if the FCC wants to check.

And analyzing opinion-selectivity, including editorial opinion, is the most economic way to do a study of network bias.

It is the way this study was done.

"Equal . . . ?"

What, more precisely, is the method by which I conducted this study?

Logically dictated by the definition of bias itself, the method is essentially simple. It can be used by any citizen with full command of the English language, with the knowledge of the full repertoire of the opinions and arguments on the opposing sides of the contemporary political controversies, and with the conviction that freedom of expression is not the property of any one section of the American political spectrum.

Presented in great detail in Appendix C, my procedure is here described briefly:

1) I chose to restrict myself to the prime-time nationwide news broadcasts of ABC, CBS and NBC—those which are aired between 7:00 and 7:30 P.M.—because they are known to be the major source of political information for the whole country.

2) I selected a set of controversial issues, on which there were strong opposing positions taken by the Republican-conservative-right axis, and by the Democratic-liberal-left axis.

Specifically, I selected the three Presidential races of 1968, and a set of 10 related issues: The U.S. policy on the Vietnam war; the U.S. policy on the bombing halt; the Viet Cong; black militants; the white middle class; liberals; conservatives; the left; demonstrators; and violent radicals.

3) I chose the period of time during which these issues were being covered by network news—a period during which the networks were expected to be "fair." The exact time span of the study was determined by the nature and duration of the principal controversy itself.

Specifically: it was the critical latter two-thirds of the 90-day-long Presidential campaign period—the seven-week period starting on September 16, when the three Presidential campaigns moved into high gear, and ending on November 4, the night before the election. The electoral period provided its own cut-off date.

4) Between these polar dates, I tape-recorded the prime-time shows of each network, and had the resultant newscasts transcribed. All material was recorded, with certain exceptions noted and explained in Appendix C.

5) From the resultant body of about 100,000 words per network, I isolated all stories dealing with the chosen issues—and excerpted all "for" and "against" opinion on these issues.

The task is simpler than it may sound. Network news is an extremely nonintellectual commodity, and the opinion which it relays tends to be simple, short, highly partisan, and crudely "for" and "against." It is readily isolated.

It comes, invariably, from four sources: Presidential and Vice Presidential *candidates; politicians;* members of the *public;* and from the *reporters* themselves. In stories on the Vietnam war, there is also opinion from *foreign sources.*

The opinion appears in four clearly identifiable forms: *direct quotes,* in which an individual states his own opinion; *paraphrase,* in which a reporter condenses an individual's opinion; *narrative reports,* in which a reporter summarizes the position of a group of people; and *editorial opinion,* which appears either in separate commentaries and analyses, or within the body of a news story.

6) When all such opinion was isolated, and filed, I then counted the number of words of opinion "for" and "against," on each issue.

7) Finally, I totalled the number of words spoken on both sides of each issue.

This, in brief, was the method. It was simply calculated to reveal the pattern of opinion-selectivity by network reporters.

In the pages that immediately follow, I present the results in the form of bar graphs. Please note that two different scales are used for the candidates and for all other issues.

**The number of words spoken
for and against Richard Nixon
on the three networks combined.**

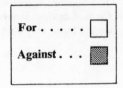

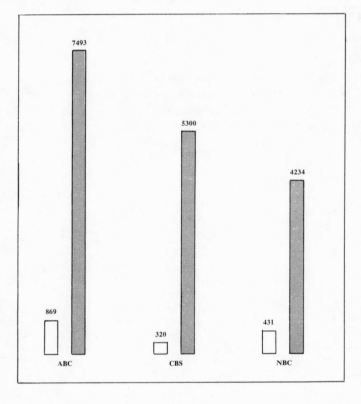

**The number of words spoken
for and against Hubert Humphrey
on the three networks combined.**

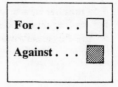

For . . . . . ☐

Against . . . ▨

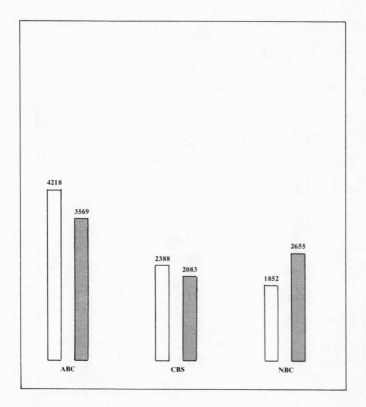

4218

3569

2388

2083

2655

1852

ABC   CBS   NBC

A comparison of the number of words spoken for Richard Nixon with the number of words spoken for Hubert Humphrey on the three networks combined.

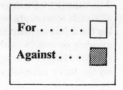

For . . . . . ☐

Against . . . ▨

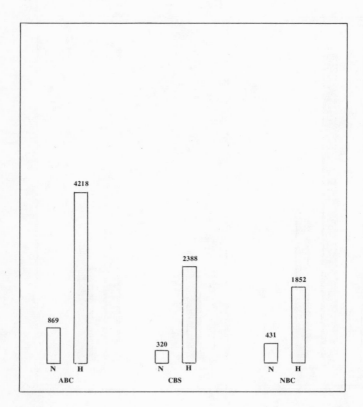

	ABC		CBS		NBC	
	N	H	N	H	N	H
	869	4218	320	2388	431	1852

A comparison of the number
of words spoken against
Richard Nixon with the
number of words spoken
against Hubert Humphrey
on the three networks combined.

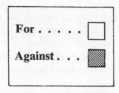

For . . . . . □
Against . . . ▨

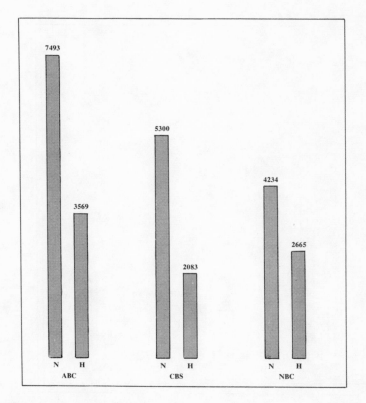

**The number of words spoken
for and against George Wallace
on the three networks combined.**

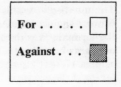

For . . . . . ☐
Against . . . ▨

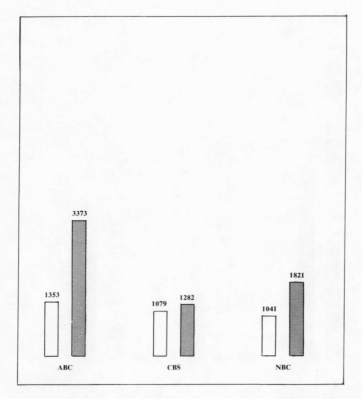

ABC   CBS   NBC

The number of words spoken for and against U.S. Policy on the Vietnam War on the three networks combined. [1]

For . . . . . ☐

Against . . . ▨

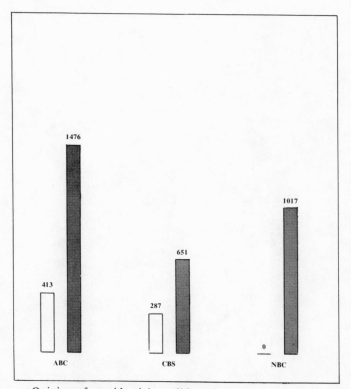

[1] Opinion of presidential candidates is not included. There was virtually no material from Mr. Nixon and Mr. Wallace, and Mr. Humphrey's statements could not be clearly classified as for or against.

**The number of words spoken for
and against U.S. Policy on the
Bombing Halt on the three
networks combined.** [1]

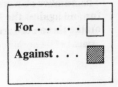

For . . . . . ☐
Against . . . ▨

904

814

407

165   147

                 36

ABC   CBS   NBC

[1]Opinion of presidential candidates is not included. See preceding
chart. Opinion is not tallied after October 31, 1968, when the bombing was halted.

**The number of words spoken
for and against the Viet Cong
on the three networks combined.** [1]

For . . . . . ☐
Against . . . ▨

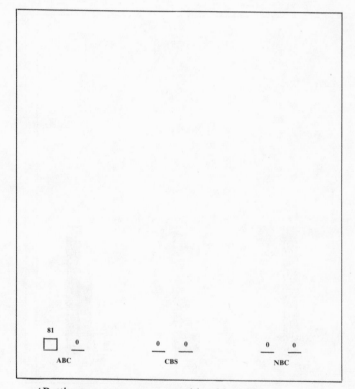

81
☐   0   0   0   0   0
ABC   CBS   NBC

[1] Battle reports are not covered by this study.

**The number of words spoken
for and against Liberals on
the three networks combined.**

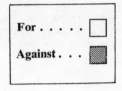

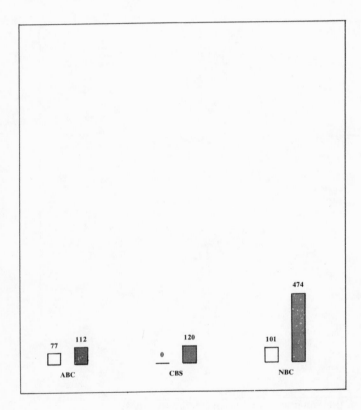

**The number of words spoken
for and against Conservatives on
the three networks combined.**

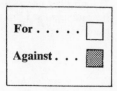

For . . . . . ☐
Against . . . ▦

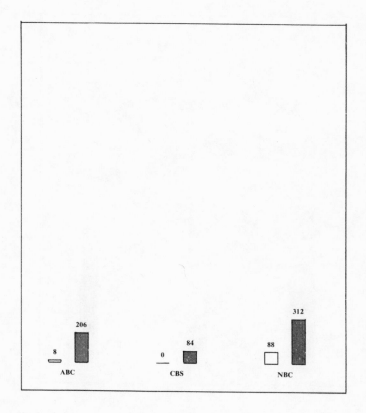

**The number of words spoken
for and against the Black Militants
on the three networks combined.**

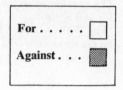

For . . . . . ☐
Against . . . ▨

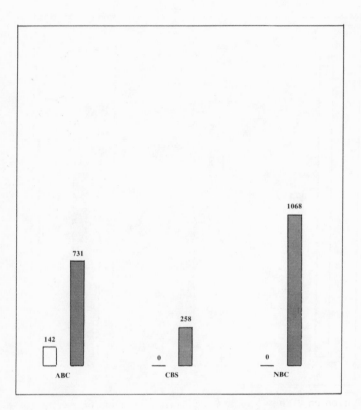

**The number of words spoken
for and against
"The White Middle Class"[1]
on the three networks combined.**

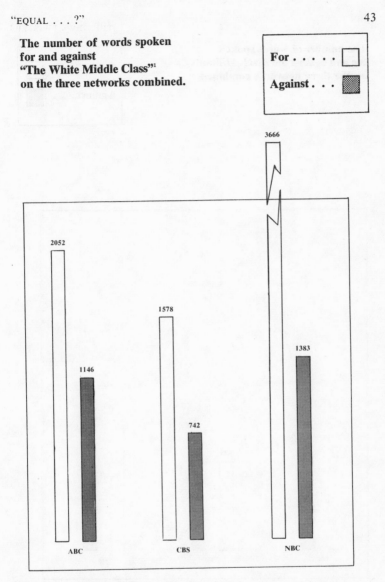

For . . . . . ☐

Against . . . ▨

[1]Opinion on "White Middle Class" includes opinion on "white America," "the white American majority," "white racist America," "the white middle-class majority," etc.

**The number of words spoken
for and against the Left
on the three networks combined.**

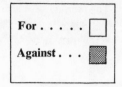

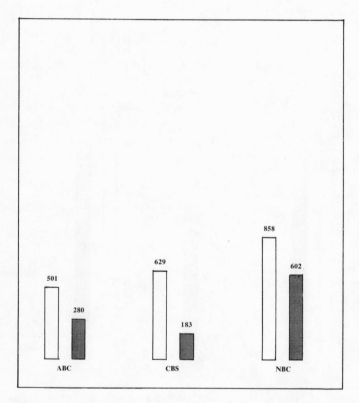

**The number of words spoken for
and against "Demonstrators"[1]
on the three networks combined.**

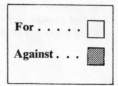

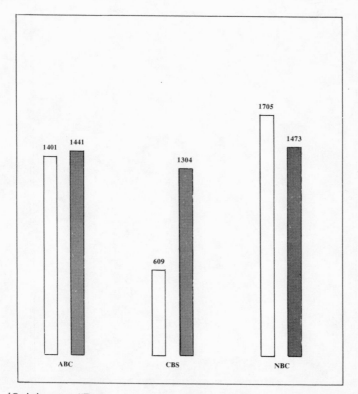

[1]Opinion on "Demonstrators" includes opinion on "activists," "militants," "students," "hippies," etc., provided these have no explicit political identification as leftists or radicals.

**The number of words spoken
for and against Violent Radicals
on the three networks combined.**

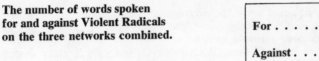

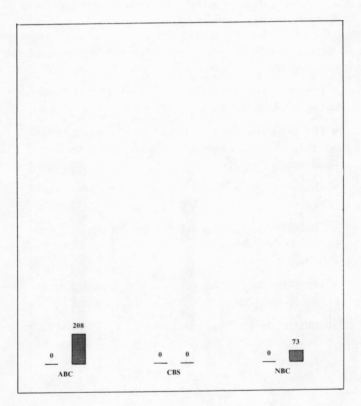

CONCLUSIONS

On the basis of these descriptive statistics, it is clear that network coverage tends to be strongly biased in favor of the Democratic-liberal-left axis of opinion, and strongly biased against the Republican-conservative-right axis of opinion.

The actual amounts of opinion on each issue vary considerably from network to network, and the degree of bias, and sometimes its direction, shifts both from network to network, and from issue to issue. The picture is not consistent.

But the preponderant opinion slant is unmistakable. Based on these figures alone, one can make these statements about this period of coverage:

- The networks actively slanted their opinion coverage against U.S. policy on the Vietnam war.

- The networks actively slanted their opinion coverage in favor of the black militants and against the white middle-class majority.

- The networks largely evaded the issue of violent radicals.

- The networks actively favored the Democratic candidate, Hubert Humphrey, for the Presidency over his Republican opponent.

- The networks actively opposed the Republican candidate, Richard Nixon, in his run for the Presidency.

In summary, the Presidential campaign of 1968 and its major issues were handled in a partisan fashion by all three networks.

"Equally Forceful. . . ?"

Given the descriptive statistics of the study, it is almost unnecessary to explore the qualitative issue of relative "forcefulness" of the opinion on the major campaign issues of 1968.

One can deduce that the "forcefulness" will be far greater on the Democratic-liberal-left side of most of the issues.

Nonetheless, the details of this heavily one-sided opinion-coverage are intensely interesting, and are highly revealing of network practices. This section of the study will report on the major findings on the opinion chosen for transmission on the various issues studied, their political content, and the relative "forcefulness" of the pro and con material.

Since the "forcefulness" of the interviewees does not lie within the control of reporters, the issue is examined in this section exclusively in terms of what does lie within reportorial control—namely, editorial choices to enhance or weaken one side of the controversy.

In each of the sections of this chapter that follow, the analyses are documented with references to statements of opinion in specific network stories. These are coded by month, day and numerical order in the transcripts, and under the heading under which each was filed in my own research. Thus: "9/16/4, Pro–Black Militants," or "10/15/20, Anti-Humphrey." My complete opinion files are available to the reader on payment of reproduction fees.

For readers who do not care to review a quarter of a million words of research but who wish to have a bird's eye view of the "for" and "against" opinion on each issue, I offer Appendices D-M. They contain summaries of this opinion. Even in summary form, the material is highly revealing, and readers are advised to turn to the summaries on each issue after reading the content analyses that follow.

CANDIDATES HUMPHREY AND NIXON

I have already said that there is one conclusion to be drawn from comparison of the opinion aired on Mr. Nixon and Mr. Humphrey: all three networks clearly tried to defeat Mr. Nixon in his campaign for the Presidency of the United States.

On the basis of quantitative differences between the Nixon-Humphrey figures alone, no other conclusion is tenable. And the qualitative nature of the opinion chosen for transmission about both men confirms this conclusion.

The opinion-selectivity of all three networks resulted in:

1) A portrayal of Mr. Humphrey as a quasi-saint.

2) A portrayal of Mr. Nixon as corruption incarnate.

Here is a summary of the personal praise received by Humphrey during the seven-week period:

> ON ABC: Hubert Humphrey is declared to be: able to
> lead and heal the world; a fighter and a patriot; endowed
> with courage, common sense and compassion; warm; en-
> thusiastic; a man of exacting qualities of mind and spirit,

of settled principles and clear vision; a man of perception and compassion; a man with understanding of the epic forces governing the world; a man with a capacity to lead us to peace; a good and honorable man; spontaneous; beloved by the poor and downtrodden of the nation; the last best hope of the unfortunate.

ON CBS: Hubert Humphrey is declared to be: a fighter and a patriot; a man with a passion for education; an intense, aggressive man; a humanitarian; an impressive man; a man of great political sensitivity, strength and leadership qualities.

ON NBC: Hubert Humphrey is declared to be: a man of perception, compassion, who can understand the epic forces at work in the world and will guide the country to peace; self-confident; understanding; imaginative; a man with a commitment to freedom; a man with a love of country; a man with a capacity to do good; a man who is likely to bring peace; a man who is for racial and economic justice.

In addition, on ABC: Mrs. Hubert Humphrey is said to be: confident, enthusiastic and exuberant; a woman in the great tradition of all Democratic First Ladies; a woman of strong personality and independent convictions.

Does Hubert Humphrey have any personal flaws at all? A few:

ON ABC: it is said or implied that he talks too much; that he is piqued with the demonstrators because they tried to interrupt him; and that he talks too much.

ON CBS: it is said or implied that he role-plays; that he talks too much; and that he harms well-written speeches by ad libbing.

ON NBC: it is said or implied that he talks too much;
that he postures.

Hubert Humphrey has flaws according to network TV but they are
minor flaws indeed for a man possessed of all earthly virtues.

What by contrast are the personal qualities of Richard Nixon?
What are his virtues as transmitted by network TV?

ON ABC: it is said that Nixon has fine powers as a de-
bater and extraordinary political astuteness.

ON CBS: it is said he is a man of great dimensions.

ON NBC: it is said that he is calm and serene in the face
of hecklers.

Mr. Nixon has virtues but clearly as far as network-transmitted
opinion goes, he suffers from a serious shortage of them in contrast
to Mr. Humphrey.

And what are the flaws of the Republican candidate?

ON ABC: it is said or implied that Mr. Nixon is: an un-
kind automaton; overconfident; attacker of liberals and
Communists; afraid of being interviewed; intellectually
intimidated by reporters; coldbloodedly intent on mar-
keting himself; a man who is lamentably lacking in qualities of mind and spirit; a man who lacks principles and
clear vision, who lacks compassion and does not understand the epic forces that govern the world; that he is
massaging the prejudices of the whites against the young,
the poor and the black; that he is unattractive to the
young and cannot communicate with them; that he is a
liar; overconfident; a posturer; a pseudo-statesman and
a pseudo-philosopher; that he is morally unprincipled; a
racist; that he is divisive, is trying to set Americans
against each other in mutual fear and suspicion; that he

is an obstacle to peace because of his anti-Communist background; that he is a mechanical, robotic man, calculating, posturing and without emotion; a man who talks in generalities, who is overconfident; a poseur; a man who inspires no confidence or enthusiasm; a man who is not big enough for the role of President; an untrustworthy man, a liar, a man from whom one shouldn't buy a used car; a cheerleader at his own rally; a man who is weak and fearful before hecklers, restless; a man who will not keep his campaign promises; a posturer, a man who experiences nagging fears, a failure; a racist, an anti-Communist; a man whose speeches are like freeze-dried bits of bland pap; whose oratory is uninspired and slick; a man who is in extreme conflict from holding in the desire to go for his enemy's jugular; a man whose nature it is to go after an enemy with a club or a meat axe, a man with the psychology of a murderer.

ON CBS: it is said or implied that Mr. Nixon is: a boring anti-climactic presence at his own rallies; overconfident; that he is unyoung, unhandsome and unsexy; that his own followers do not like him; that he is a man with a rancorous streak; overconfident; a liar, a man who lacks ability, character, principles; a man who is a danger to the country; a hard-core anti-Communist in the past; a man who is appealing to the race prejudice of young and old; a racist; cynical; irresponsible; an anti-Semite; a racist; a hypocrite; devoid of principles; a man who appeals to failures and malcontents; inhuman, a computing machine who is programmed by a programmer; a man who deliberately misleads Americans; a man who appeals to fear and hatred; who fabricates straw men; who stands for nothing; a game-player; a wrecker; an egotist; nonhuman; untrustworthy; an obstacle to peace; emotionally false; playing the hero; a man whose followers are indifferent to him; an anti-Communist who impugned the patriotism of opponents; a man who pretends to be supported by youth; a man who makes contradictory campaign promises; a man whose supporters are not convinced by him; a man who makes vicious and false accusations without taking responsibility for his words; an inhuman computer; a square who believes in heroes.

ON NBC: it is said or implied that Mr. Nixon: traveled the low road of anti-Communism; lacks perception and compassion; does not understand the epic forces that govern the world; that he is: tricky Dick, given to attacking liberals as Communist sympathizers; inconsistent, cynical, shallow, shockingly irresponsible; malicious, posturing as a winner; a man who uses commercial gimmickry and fakery to win his support; a man who utters bromides; a man whose followers are bored with him and don't like him, who only cheer him because his writers know how to write applause lines; a cruelly mocking man; a liar, a hypocrite, a name-caller, a man who appeals to fear and hate in the electorate; a man who fails to talk seriously to the public; a racist WASP who wants to hold Negroes down economically; a hater of Negroes; a man whose audiences don't like him and who are only responding to threatrical gimmicks; a lair; an opponent of racial and economic justice; a venal militarist.

In addition, on ABC it is implied that Mrs. Nixon is a charming robot without an individual mind; a cool, slightly false woman neurotically isolated from people—just like her husband.

It should now be said that none of these opinions include the views of opposing candidates. Neither Mr. Nixon's criticisms of Mr. Humphrey nor Mr. Humphrey's criticisms of Mr. Nixon are included in this array of alleged character attributes. Nor do these lists include public opinion or the running daily praise and attack on a variety of purely political issues. This contrasting portrait of the characters of Richard Nixon and of Hubert Humphrey is exclusively the result of the combined opinions of politicians and reporters.

Network reporters in alliance with Democratic-liberal politicians portrayed Hubert Humphrey as a talkative Democratic saint studded over with every virtue known to man. Deprived of reporters in league with Republican-conservative politicians, Mr. Nixon is not portrayed as a human being at all but is transmogrified into a demon out of the liberal id.

Given this loading of the political decks, there is no need to analyze the other types of pro and con opinion on Messrs. Nixon and Humphrey. The opinion in Appendix D is worth reading—particularly the one-sided editorial assault on Nixon as an evader of the issues, while Mr. Humphrey, whose ambiguities merited a similar charge, is spared. But when an assault of this magnitude is directed at the most crucial aspects of a human being and Presidential candidate—his mind, his morality and his character—nothing else is of much significance.

If Richard Nixon is President of the United States today, it is in spite of ABC-TV, CBS-TV and NBC-TV. Together they broadcast the quantitative equivalent of a *New York Times* lead editorial against him every day—for five days a week for the seven weeks of his campaign period. And every editorial technique was employed on three networks to render the pro-Nixon side less "forceful" than the anti-Nixon side. Indeed, to speak of "forceful" pro-Nixon opinion is impossible. It does not exist.

CANDIDATE WALLACE

In one sense, George Wallace was ignored by the networks. Most reporters did not bother to attack him very much editorially as they did Nixon, and when they did, it was brief.

Nor did the reporters load the "negative" opinion catastrophically against the "affirmative" as they did to Richard Nixon. A specific selective pattern was used instead.

As the summaries in Appendix E indicate, Wallace coverage consists largely of four elements:

1) Quotations from union men who were for Wallace;

2) Quotations from Democratic Party and union leaders who are appalled by the falling away of this Democratic vote to Wallace;

3) Violent indictments of Wallace by the Democratic establishment, with a little assistance from reporters;

4) Reports on verbal and physical assaults on Wallace.

The pattern of coverage, in other words, reflects the perspective of the Democratic Party. If the content of the "affirmative" opinion reveals that Democrats in large numbers support Wallace—the intent of most of the anti-Wallace opinion is to drive the Democratic voter back into the fold.

As the campaign progressed and Wallace's support rose, the reporters increasingly resorted to the 4th selective technique: they reported incessantly on physical assaults on Wallace by mobs. And they never named the assaulters politically or ideologically, although there are repeated references to "college students" and "black militants."

The selection of opinion on the very complex Wallace phenomenon is so stylized and so repetitious that it is clearly conscious. And, indeed, Theodore H. White in *The Making of the President 1968* (p. 424) describes this very tactic of "the media" to stop George Wallace. The description is an accurate one for network TV as well:

The polls, with their figures, had alerted the national media to the potential in Wallace. The media, trying to document the Wallace campaign in words and pictures, began to spread the image of a man not mastering disorder in the nation but provoking it where he went.

The headlines of his rallies, read from early October on, at random, thus: "Tennessee Mob Beats Boy Who Sassed Wallace"; "Wallace Was Target for Bomb"; "Hecklers Throw Eggs, Apple Core at Wallace in Oshkosh"; "Clashes Mar Wallace Rally in Detroit"; "Wallace Shakes the Garden"; "Police Club Leftists after Wallace Rally"; "Fights Break Out as Hecklers Disrupt Wallace Rally in Texas."

It was, says Mr. White, the "cumulative effect of this reporting" which turned the Wallace tide. The "pressure of the media and influence-makers and the liberal unions," says White (p. 467), reduced the Wallace vote far below its true potential.

If the newspaper stories elaborated on the details of these clashes that broke out at Wallace rallies, network TV's stories did not. Indeed network coverage of Wallace gradually came to consist largely of these "headlines"—"headlines" which, like those quoted by White, reported most often on provocations of and attacks *on* Wallace and Wallace followers, who frequently fought *back*—with the resultant violence attributed to the candidate. An NBC reporter (10/30/9, Anti-Wallace) was voicing the media "party line" when he referred to "the violence that has become the signature of the Wallace campaign."

The selective technique of increasingly giving air time to Wallace enemies and of focusing on the fights that broke out as the politically unidentified "hecklers" continuously disrupted his rallies, was dubious journalistic practice. There were valid concerns and anxieties on the side of the middle class that was fleeing the Democratic Party as well as valid reasons to oppose Wallace. The serious issues on *both* sides, however, were not explored by the networks either in the form of opinion or of general coverage. They increasingly focused their cameras and their words on fists and rocks. The physicalistic coverage was despairingly anti-intellectual.

When the violence was not caused by Wallace or by his followers, as often it was not, this technique was morally condemnable as well, for it constituted distortion.

But this calculated zeroing-in on violence, often provoked by unidentified leftists and black militants and attributed to the candidate, is not the only network misdemeanor in regard to Wallace coverage. There is a graver one by far. Network men covertly encouraged physical violence directed at Wallace.

They did so by a specific set of euphemisms. Language customarily used to describe those who engage in verbal protest was used to describe those who engage in physical assault. This was a tacit sanctioning of the assaultive conduct.

This linguistic device in use on all three networks is highly significant coming as it does from men with large and varied vocabularies and men who are well able to distinguish between a verbal criticism and an act of physical violence. Certainly, network men have never in a burst of collective imprecision referred to club-swinging policemen—or, more recently, fist-swinging construction workers—as men engaging in verbal expression or men simply manifesting their intellectual disagreements. And yet network reporters insistently described people as intellectual or verbal dissenters at the precise moment when these people were engaging in physical acts of violence—thus systematically blurring the existential, moral and legal distinction between physical attack and verbal dissent.

Here are all recorded examples[1]:

ABC

10/22/5 (Anti-Wallace): Opponents of Wallace threw

---

[1]These passages appear in my opinion files and statistics as anti-Wallace opinion by the *public*, not by reporters. The same passages could not be counted *twice*. It is only in this section, therefore, that this aspect of editorial opposition to Wallace is reported.

eggs, vegetables and fruit at Wallace. The reporter calls them *"hecklers."*

10/23/6 (Anti-Wallace): Opponents threw objects including eggs, vegetables, fruit and stones at Wallace. One stone strikes Wallace in the face. The reporter calls these opponents *"hecklers"* and says, amusingly, evoking an old folk rhyme, that they threw "sticks, stones and names" at Wallace. He thus equates physical violence and words.

10/31/6 (Anti-Wallace): A group disrupts a Wallace rally, throws rocks, and hits two girls on the head. The reporter calls the group *"demonstrators."*

CBS

9/30/4 (Anti-Wallace): The story states that an opponent of Wallace threw an egg at him. The reporter's description is: "The *dissenters* made their presence known."

10/22/6 (Anti-Wallace): Opponents threw rocks at George Wallace. The reporter calls them *"hecklers."*

10/23/4 (Anti-Wallace): Black-power opponents of George Wallace throw "objects" at him. The reporter describes this as Wallace's being *"heckled."*

NBC

10/17/8 (Anti-Wallace): Opponents of Wallace throw tin cans at him. The reporter refers to this as *"disruption"* of Wallace's speech—thus describing violence directed at a human being as if it were the interruption of a speech.

10/22/10 (Anti-Wallace): The reporter describes

George Wallace as being *"heckled* mercilessly" and as being hit with an "apple core" flung by the *"hecklers."*

10/23/3 (Anti-Wallace): The reporter says college students throw objects at Wallace. He sums it up as: "letting Wallace know what they *think* of him"—thus describing physical violence as if it were an expression of "thought."

10/31/8 (Anti-Wallace): Demonstrators hurl objects at Wallace. The reporter describes it as "they heckled and threw things." This is the only formulation that makes a distinction between speech and physical violence, but it is still a remarkably casual way of describing the phenomenon.

Over and over again, by this false equation of speech and force, these reporters were subtly, but repeatedly broadcasting the message that bodily assault and violence were just another form of "dissent" and that throwing cans and rocks was an accredited and constitutionally protected verbal form of expression . . . if the target was George Wallace.

In seven weeks, not one reporter expressed the view or quoted anyone as expressing the view that this outbreak of physical attacks on Wallace was assault, that it was *illegal,* that it was morally *wrong*—that these were not "hecklers" or dissenters, but hoodlums.

Many network reporters in the 1968 campaign made it eminently clear that they were not opposed in principle to political violence if directed at certain political targets—and this broader issue will be discussed elsewhere in this study.

As it applied to George Wallace, what emerges from editorial opinion is the clear-cut implication that violence from the left (never named as such) is legitimate if directed at the racist right— that it is the racist right, per se, which is the social evil—and that against it no ethics, no laws, need prevail.

A powerful and explicit expression of this very thesis is to be found in an editorial opinion which was delivered on ABC (9/20/8, Anti-"Demonstrators"). It is the *only* impassioned editorial on violence delivered by a reporter in seven weeks. In it, the reporter condemns "young militants," classifying them as poor and rich, white and black, educated and illiterate. The reporter then charges these ideologically anonymous "militants" with violating other people's rights, with physical destruction, and calls them "the apostles of violence and disruption." The reporter does not attack these actions as evil, per se. He attacks them for quite a different reason. The danger of this conduct, says the reporter, is that *while the violent militants' motives are good, they may "manage to elect George Wallace."*

Thus, in the *only* strong attack on "militant" violence from an editorial source during the seven weeks studied, the left goes protectively unnamed, the motives of all violent "militants" are proclaimed pure—and the real evil is identified as Wallace, symbol of the racist right. In this editorial opinion we find the standard of selectivity that determined Wallace coverage on all three networks.

It need hardly be said that, however one may condemn Mr. Wallace's rightism and racism, he is as entitled to the full protection of the law, as let us say, a Communist Black Panther arrested for threatening to murder President Nixon. It is a curious fact that this cardinal principle of American ethics and law totally vanished from the minds of network reporters during the Wallace campaign.

In sum: the coverage of opinion on George Wallace is heavily weighted against Wallace and editorially sanctions the physical attacks upon him. Editorial choices were repeatedly made to render the anti-Wallace side of the controversy more "forceful."

U.S. POLICY ON THE VIETNAM WAR AND THE BOMBING HALT; THE VIET CONG

If the quantitative imbalance of opinion on war-related issues suggests a conscious determination to slant coverage, the actual content of this opinion reinforces this suggestion.

The opinion-summaries in Appendix F reveal a steady drumbeat of antigovernment voices, united in an assault on the Vietnam war, and in a demand for a unilateral bombing halt by the United States.[1]

So crude is this drumbeat of synchronized opinion that there is almost nothing to analyze, no special documentation to isolate. All the reader has to do is to turn to the appendix, and contemplate the dramatis personae and its identical positions:

> 9/26 George Ball opposes the war
> 9/26 Students oppose the war
> 9/30 Senator Fulbright opposes the war
> 10/8 Senator Eugene McCarthy opposes the war
> 10/8 Nine pacifists oppose the war
> 10/15 Soldiers oppose the war
> 10/22 Japanese leftists oppose the war
> 10/23 SDS leader Tom Hayden opposes the war
> 10/28 The Communist Party opposes the war
> 10/31 Eldridge Cleaver opposes the war
> etc., etc.

and

> 9/23 U Thant opposes U.S. bombing
> 10/1 Humphrey aides oppose U.S. bombing

---

[1]The antigovernment opinion classified by this study does not include the two or three "hawk" attacks on government war policy expressed by Senator Barry Goldwater and candidate Curtis LeMay, since their opposition was on totally different grounds: they charged the government with fighting a "no-win war." To have included such opinion in the "antiwar" totals would have distorted their meaning. The controversy analyzed here is the LBJ vs. "dove" controversy exclusively.

It is worth noting that all three networks virtually ignored the pure "hawk" or conservative or "victory" position, although it had heavy support in the public. According to pollster Lou Harris, it was still a majority position one year after the period of this study—52%, on October 31, 1969, were willing to support the government in a last-ditch effort to win military victory.

10/1 Averill Harriman opposes U.S. bombing
10/25 Xuan Thuy opposes U.S. bombing
10/28 Soviet Premier Kosygin opposes U.S. bombing
10/30 Indira Ghandi opposes U.S. bombing
etc., etc.

All that need be said here is that this uniform outcry came from an editorially selected alliance of: a couple of "dove" Republicans and Democrats; domestic Communists and far-left organizations; politically unidentified "students" and "pacifists"; foreign leftists and "neutralists"; network reporters; and the enemy itself.

Enemy opinion and reporter opinion, in fact, constituted the majority of the opinion advocating a unilateral bombing halt. Out of 37 such endorsements aired by the networks in 6 weeks—the voices stilled on October 31, when President Johnson stopped the bombing—more than one-third came from enemy sources: 11 came from Xuan Thuy, chief negotiator for North Vietnam; from Hanoi; and from Soviet Premier Kosygin. And almost one-third, 9, came from reporters.

As portrayed on the air by the networks, the "dove" alliance was a curious one. On network TV, almost no antiwar or bombing halt opinion came from the political center, none came from the right of center, none came from anti-leftists and anti-Communists. The antiwar movement was construed by network TV to be almost exclusively a left-wing movement, and throughout the campaign, the voices of the left had a virtual stranglehold on opinion on the war.[1]

And what of opinion on the other side of the "dove" vs. LBJ controversy? It can best be described as a calculated void. Opinion in support of the Administration's war policy was flatly omitted by

---

[1]According to a study published in the *American Political Science Review* in December, 1969, the majority of those who were opposed to the war in 1968 were antagonistic to the leftist "protesters"—23% being extremely "hostile." The nature of the antiwar movement in the United States was severely distorted by portraying it as an almost exclusively leftist position.

NBC News. This network functioned as if there was only one side to the controversy. The pro-Administration side was covered, symbolically, on CBS and ABC, which relayed a few opinions from the Administration itself. Similarly, opinion supporting the Administration's demand for a conditional bombing halt was meager.

In general, those who might have supported the Administration's side of the controversy were not to be seen or heard. There was no public opinion in support of the war on any of the three networks. There was not a word of opinion from any of the Asian nations in whose interests the war was being fought. President Thieu of South Vietnam was almost totally silent during this period; he spoke a few sentences each on ABC and NBC—and none on CBS. The Administration's allies were, quite simply, kept off the air.

Finally, the nature of the enemy, the Viet Cong—revealed, a few months earlier, as the perpetrator of the mass murder of thousands —was the object of systematic evasion by the networks. Only once during the seven-week period did a political opinion appear on the subject of the Viet Cong: An ABC reporter justified Viet Cong "savagery" as the fault of the United States.

In sum, on the general subject of Vietnam, there was no attempt, on any of the three networks, to present "equally forceful" opinion. All "forcefulness" was reserved for opposition to administration policies.

RACE: LIBERALS VS. CONSERVATIVES

In terms of statistics, the liberal-conservative picture suggests a political paradox. The figures reveal both an anti-conservative bias and an anti-liberal bias. This suggests that network selectivity is antagonistic to both groups, in defiance of the general pro-liberal, pro-left pattern.

This paradox is promptly proved to be illusory when the content of the opinion on both groups—summarized in Appendix G—is examined.

If one starts with pro-liberal opinion, one sees that it is minimal. Only two expressions of it can be found on the air during this period, both editorial—once on ABC (9/27/2) and once on NBC (9/17/8). Both times, however, the reporters make identical points: they isolate liberals as nonracists. The clear implication, on both occasions, is that conservatives, by contrast, are racists.

When one turns to opinion on conservatives, one sees that this implication is fully substantiated. There is almost no pro-conservative opinion, while opinion critical of conservatives, explicit and implicit, runs as follows:

> ON ABC: they are criticized as violent; as racist advocates of law and order; as rude; as stupid.
>
> ON CBS: they are criticized as violent; and as racist malcontents.
>
> ON NBC: they are criticized as plotters against black militants; racists; as militarists and law-and-order advocates; as racist law-and-order advocates; as anti–black militants; as anti–black militants; as the cause of racist violence.

Of the 13 criticisms, 8 are charges of racism—5 coming from reporters.

(It should be noted that three of these editorial opinions equate the conservative advocacy of law and order with racism—a tacit attack on law and order and a rationalization of black lawlessness, as well as an attack on conservatives: 9/27/2 ABC; 9/17/8 NBC; 9/17/9 NBC.)

One can readily deduce that in a news service where all liberals are editorially defined as nonracists and where all conservatives are editorially defined as racists, anti-liberal opinion will be editorially equated to racist-right opinion. And that is generally how anti-liberal opinion *is* selected—on two of the three networks:

On ABC there are four anti-liberal opinions—and three of them come from the racist right—from George Wallace and his running mate. On CBS, there is only one criticism of the liberals—and, again, it is from George Wallace, on the racist right. On both these networks, the selective standard tacitly communicates the idea that a rightist attack on liberals *mean*s a racist attack on nonracists.

NBC deviates from this standard of selection, and must be considered separately. This network conforms to the standardized pattern in that it editorially defines liberals as nonracists; and it aggressively attacks conservatives as racists. But it adds a major element to anti-liberal opinion: it transmits criticisms of liberals which do *not* come from exclusively racist-right sources. NBC gives extensive air time to two articulate black militants: one mocks "liberal guilt," the other savages the liberals who have made money out of poverty programs, leaving the ghetto blacks as poor as ever. (10/22/12, Anti-Liberal.) NBC also invites New Left journalist Jack Newfield and conservative publisher William Rusher to discuss the New Left's newsworthy dislike of liberal policies and liberal big-government (10/15/12). During this exchange, old-time anti-liberal Rusher largely confines himself to a wry "I told you so" and a call for "order"—while New Leftist Newfield conducts a blistering assault on liberal policies, racial and other, in the spirit of a man newly betrayed. Thus the story ends up, primarily, as a vehicle for New Left opinion.

What conclusions about "forcefulness" may we then draw about the total body of opinion aired on the three networks? These:

On ABC and CBS, editorial selection, strongly reinforced by editorial opinion, results in a crude comic strip: All liberals are nonracist good guys and all conservatives are racist bad guys. Granted a monopoly on virtue by the reporters, liberals emerge as morally transcendant—hence as the more "forceful" of the two sides.

On NBC, editorial selection and intervention results in a different political stress: Liberals are portrayed with moral ambiguity, nonracists who are occasionally deluded and corrupt; and conservatives (with the possible exception of Mr. Rusher, whose nonracist position goes unidentified by NBC) are all cast as comic-strip racist bad guys. If NBC's editorial selection results in the enhancement of any position at all, it is that of the New Left, black and white.

Taking the three networks collectively, we may then say that the editorially contrived "forcefulness" disfavors the conservatives. It favors either the liberals or the New Left and it favors the blacks, around whose cause virtually all this opinion revolves.

Statistics notwithstanding, there is no contradiction here of the network bias pattern.

RACE: "THE WHITE MIDDLE CLASS"

The "white middle class" is only one name for this group. It is also known, in network stories, as "the white middle-class majority," "white America," "white racist America," "the middle-class electorate," "the American electorate"—and, on NBC, as "the American people."

It is perfectly clear, from the manner in which this flexible concept is used in network news stories, that it is a symbolic way of referring to "America"—tacitly excepting liberals, leftists and blacks.

By virtue of this tacit exception, the critical opinion on this symbolic group is indistinguishable from the critical opinion on conservatives. If there is any distinction at all, it is that this body of opinion—directed at nobody in particular, and at everybody generally—is more violently antagonistic.

Here, taken from Appendix H, is a fast summary of the opinion, explicit and implicit, which is critical of this symbolic group:

ON ABC: it is criticized as prosperous, self-pitying, mediocre; as materialistic; as unintelligent; as racist and hating the young, the poor and the blacks; as mediocre, hostile to intellectual values; as racist; as intellectually shallow; as devoid of conscience.

ON CBS: it is criticized as racist; as racist; as racist, selfish and mentally limited; as selfish, culturally limited, mentally limited.

ON NBC: it is criticized as responsible for black crime; as authoritarian-racist-militaristic advocates of law enforcement against black criminals; as wealthy advocates of law and order; as violent; as responsible for black crime; as willing to sacrifice blacks' "freedom" for law and order; as racist advocates of law and order; as racist; as racist; as racist; as racist.

Of these 23 criticisms, 18 come from reporters.

Again, as in anti-conservative opinion, reporters equate the middle-class advocacy of law and order with race prejudice, thus tacitly opposing law enforcement and sanctioning black violence. The equations—four of them, all by NBC reporters—are reproduced here:

- 9/17/8 (Anti–White Middle Class): The reporter justifies black violence by equating the middle-class concern for law and order with militaristic and racist-right attitudes.

- 9/18/4 (Anti–White Middle Class): The reporter rationalizes black crime by holding the lawful white middle class responsible for it.

- 10/4/7 (Anti–White Middle Class): The reporter equates the application of law to violent blacks with the willingness of the white middle class "majority" to sacrifice "freedom." The only "freedom" portrayed as being restricted in this story is the "freedom" of blacks to riot.

- 10/22/12 (Anti–White Middle Class): The reporter rationalizes black violence by linking it to middle-class racism and a breakdown of police discipline.

In seven weeks of campaign coverage, this generalized assault on the symbolic "white middle class," with its secondary leitmotif of attacking the law and order position, was the dominant point of view aired on the nationwide newscasts.

What, by contrast, did opinion favorable to "the white middle class" consist of? What virtues of "white America" were portrayed along with its vices? Such favorable opinion was expressed only on

ABC and only within *one* story—by Republican candidate Nixon, and by two of his supporters: All three defended the law-abiding, hard-working, tax-paying middle-class majority. And that is all.

In seven weeks, CBS carried no opinion favorable to "the white middle class."

In seven weeks, NBC carried no opinion favorable to "the white middle class."

It is quite clear that the concept of presenting "equally forceful" affirmative opinion on this symbolic "class" was never considered by the networks. Even when the Republican contender for the Presidency, Mr. Nixon, expressed such opinion as a major theme of his campaign, two of the three networks preferred not to carry it.

RACE: BLACK MILITANTS

Given a consistent editorial position, on three networks, which casts all conservatives as racists, and which casts all "middle-class" whites in the same mold, it is not surprising to discover that pro–black-militant opinion greatly exceeds opinion critical of black militants.

The content of this large mass of favorable opinion can be quickly reviewed in Appendix I. It comes mainly from Black Panthers, Watts militants, Eldridge Cleaver—and reporters. It generally contains protests, demands, threats, expressions of social and economic grievances, expressions of support for black riots and demonstrations; and attacks on Presidential candidates, on police and on "white America." It is largely the voice of black power, heavily reinforced with editorial support.

A significant amount of this opinion glamorizes violent black militants and/or sympathizes with, rationalizes, or threatens violence—riots, arson, political and racial murder. Such opinion can be found in nineteen stories, and I hereby give the references:

ON ABC: 9/16/14, 10/15/5, 10/25/13, 10/28/8, 10/30/11

On CBS: 9/18/3, 9/26/14, 9/27/12, 10/24/12, 10/31/11

On NBC: 9/16/8, 9/17/9, 9/20/5, 9/23/12, 10/3/11, 10/9/10, 10/15/9, 10/21/11, 10/25/8

About 50% of this rationalizing of black violence consists of, or includes, reportorial opinion—on ABC, two out of the five; on CBS, four out of the five; and on NBC, five out of the nine.

The editorial methods for rationalizing violence are so standardized that they can be precisely described. There are five of them:

- Black violence, or advocacy of violence, is conceded, then the blame is transferred to other shoulders, usually those of the "white middle-class majority."

- Black violence, or advocacy of violence, is conceded; then the reporter glamorizes or defends the advocates or practitioners of violence.

- Black violence, or advocacy of violence, is minimized or turned into a joke.

- Black violence, or advocacy of violence, is evaded; and the reporter glamorizes or defends the advocates or practitioners of violence.

- Those who attack black violence are attacked by the reporter.

Here is a rapid survey of this editorial opinion:

ABC

9/16/14 (Pro–Black Militants): The reporter minimizes the significance of burning, looting and rioting in an amusing way, as the work of "amateurs."

10/28/8 (Pro–Black Militants): The reporter, presenting a description of Eldridge Cleaver as Presidential candidate, portrays Cleaver as youthful, as the author of *Soul on Ice,* as a leader with white followers—and omits all reference to his demands for political violence and murder.

CBS

9/18/3 (Pro–Black Militants): The reporter covertly glamorizes Eldridge Cleaver after Cleaver demands that big businessmen, politicians, police and profitmakers be "disposed of" and "shot." The reporter uses euphemistic descriptions of Cleaver's advocacy of murder, calling it "tough talk"; attacks those who refuse to hire Cleaver as "censors"; and reports no criticism of Cleaver's calls for political murder.

9/26/14 (Pro–Black Militants): The reporter rationalizes a violent black-power riot in a Boston school in which twenty people were injured by euphemistically calling it "unrest" and by equating it to an expression of black "pride" and black "identity".

10/24/12 (Pro–Black Militants): The reporter glamorizes a black-power athlete who is threatening to burn cities. He repeatedly calls him a "hero," omits existing black criticism of his conduct, portrays him as the voice of a monolithic black community.

10/31/11 (Pro–Black Militants): The reporter purports to summarize Cleaver's political position, and glamorizes him as a simple integrationist—by omitting any reference to Cleaver's advocacy of murder of whites, police, businessmen, etc.

NBC

9/16/8 (Pro–Black Militants): The reporter equates the

ideological crime committed by Black Panthers to that of all criminal blacks, then blames it on "poverty."

9/17/9 (Pro–Black Militants): The reporter justifies violence by defining as racists those who advocate law and order.

9/20/5 (Pro–Black Militants): The reporter purports to sum up the controversy over the hiring of Eldridge Cleaver at Berkeley. He portrays Cleaver as an "enthusiastic" militant, omitting Cleaver's "enthusiasm" for political murder—thus leaving out the central reason for the controversy.

9/23/12 (Pro–Black Militants): The reporter purports to sum up the controversy over academic freedom at Berkeley involving Eldridge Cleaver, and glamorizes him by omitting all references to his past crimes and advocacy of political murder. His only description of Cleaver is "a noted Black Nationalist."

10/21/11 (Pro-Black Militants): The reporter overtly endorses Black Militants and transmits their threats of violence.

In sum, on all three networks reporters sanction the most extreme, the most violent and the actively criminal elements of the black power movement.

What, by contrast, do we find on the quantitatively weaker side of the controversy—the side that criticizes black militants?

Here the sources of opinion are far more varied, even if the total opinion is quantitatively restricted. Anti–black-militant opinion comes generally, if spottily, from every point of the U.S. sociopolitical spectrum, save the far left: from conservative California Governor Ronald Reagan to liberal New York Mayor John Lindsay, with a heavy component of teachers, union men and blue-collar workers in between.

The criticisms of black militants tend also to be focused on black hostility and violence. They attack: black riots; black demonstrations; black racism; black anti-Semitism; black arson, lootings, muggings; black killing of firemen and police; black harassment and intimidation of teachers; black racist abuse of whites, etc.

Attacks on black violence are found, however, in only 9 stories:

ON ABC: 9/16/3, 9/20/8, 10/31/8

ON CBS: 9/16/1

ON NBC: 9/18/7, 9/19/16, 9/20/5, 10/4/7, 10/9/10

No network gives as much air time to the critics of black violence as it does to its representatives, advocates, and justifiers. CBS is outstanding in its reluctance to air such reproofs, doing so only once—on the first day of the study period—citing candidate Humphrey. The network never carries such a criticism again.

Not one reporter on CBS or NBC is critical of black-power violence during this coverage period. And only one reporter on ABC criticizes such violence—also early in the study period (9/20/8). This is the same reportorial indictment of violence that has already been referred to in the Wallace section. It is the only strong reportorial condemnation of violence in the seven weeks of coverage. It mentions black militants only fleetingly—granting them noble motivations—and objects to violence ultimately because it "might elect George Wallace."

The statistics on black-militant opinion, taken alone, clearly suggest that editorial selectivity has chosen to enhance the black-militant position and render it the more "forceful."

What they do not reveal is that violence is the burning core of the debate, and that network reporters throw their weight almost fully to the violence side. It is ultimately the legitimization of black violence which is the most "forceful" position aired.

When one examines the total body of opinion under the headings of "Liberal," "Conservative," "White Middle Class" and "Black Militants," one sees that it is ultimately the *same* body of opinion, with slightly different stresses. Editorial selective standards and editorial intervention renders the total a crude racist cartoon—with noble blacks pitted against evil conservative white America . . . with noble liberals exempt from the national condemnation . . . and with black violence against "white America" actively condoned and rationalized.

THE LEFT

Considering the explosiveness of the radical movement in America in 1968, there is virtually no opinion on the left wing, its means and its ends.

Pro-left opinion comes largely from a few candidates of old-left parties and two black parties, allowed a ritual split-second each; a few members of left organizations; a few students identified as hecklers; candidate Ed Muskie; and reporters.

Such leftist opinion as exists is fragmentary and consists of a few canned phrases and one-word ideologies: The United States is "imperialistic," what is needed is "socialism" or "a democratic type of Communism," etc. Leftists are not permitted to speak long enough to express any coherent ideas to the public or to allow the public to understand their criticisms, their goals and how they propose to achieve them. A brief inspection of Appendix J will indicate the intense restriction of this coverage.

Apart from this truncated "thought" from the left, the rest is largely from reporters and consists of portraying the left either as the friendly Democrats next door or as a bunch of "restless amusing kids." Thus:

> 10/28/8 (Pro-Left): An ABC reporter sums up the shared goals of all left parties with the concepts of peace and justice—rendering the Communist party indistinguishable from Senator Edward Kennedy's Democratic party.

10/3/8, 10/1/10 (Pro-Left): Another ABC reporter pens a comic sketch of a "Congressional Laugh-In" where the HUAC, investigating violence in Chicago, confronts "top banana" Jerry Rubin . . . and continues his humorous approach two days later when the funny Yippies are being charged with plans to kill policemen and bomb buildings. All this, the reporter assures us, tongue plunged deep in cheek, is "youthful unrest."

10/31/11 (Pro-Left): A CBS reporter allows Eldridge Cleaver to say "oink" about the candidates and portrays him as eager to cooperate with "sympathetic whites"—making this Black Panther leader sound like an old-fashioned integrationist who happens to like to say "oink."

9/25/7 (Pro-Left): Another CBS reporter describes a group of leftists as an "enthusiastic" bunch of students, and fails to mention what ideologies and goals inspire their enthusiasm.

9/19/5 (Pro-Left): An NBC reporter tells us that the radicals are "young people" and says "Americans" should "trust each other."

9/23/6 (Pro-Left): Another NBC reporter thinks it wrong to criticize Communists.

All in all, pro-left editorial opinion portrays the left as harmless, friendly, idealistic, funny, young, "restless" and trustworthy.

What of anti-left opinion? Here there is a distinct difference between the networks.

ABC in two cases airs opinion which attacks the New Left as dangerous. One opinion is from J. Edgar Hoover, who identifies the New Left and the SDS as the sources of the outbreak of political violence in the country. A second is from a HUAC undercover investigator who charges the Yippies with plans to bomb buildings, kill policemen and assassinate candidates. (Although the ABC reporter is amused by it all.)

On NBC no such criminal charges are aired. NBC viewers are not informed of J. Edgar Hoover's warning against the New Left and the SDS; and the Yippies' name and two out of three charges are excised from NBC's story on the HUAC. (10/3/17, Anti-Demonstrators.) On NBC leftists are criticized but for such matters as "bothering the students," and wanting instant success. And conservative William Rusher criticizes the indulgence of "madness" on the left.

As for CBS, no criminal charges are aired either. CBS viewers are not warned of J. Edgar Hoover's charges nor are they informed of the undercover testimony against the Yippies.

In fact, on CBS the New Left as such is not even mentioned.

CBS carries three anti-left opinions during the seven weeks studied. One is the "left half" of a ritualistic criticism by Humphrey of violence by "extremists of the right and of the left." One is a report that George Wallace accuses newsmen of being leftists. And one is an obliquely humorous report that the Prohibition Party candidate doesn't approve of Communists.

Why CBS considers it news that the Prohibitionist candidate does not like Communists but does not consider it news when J. Edgar Hoover warns the country about New Left and SDS present and future violence, only CBS can say.

In summary—the pro-left view is more "forceful" than the anti-left view. An actively agreeable and/or harmless picture of the left is communicated and hard, serious warnings to the country against violent New Leftists by the Federal Bureau of Investigation are suppressed by two networks out of three.

"DEMONSTRATORS"

In addition to opinion on the left, there is a far greater bulk of opinion on a collection of people described variously as: "dissent-

ers," "protesters," "hecklers," "militants," "activists," "demonstrators." In addition, there are somewhat diffuse social groupings such
as: "students," "youths," "minorities," "the poor, the young and
the black," "hippies," "yippies," and "blacks"—"yippies" here used
generically like "hippies."

All of these are collected in Appendix K under the title of
"Demonstrators."

Little or no distinction is made between the network portrait of
the New Left and its beliefs and the network portrait of the "demonstrators" and their beliefs. The two groups are presented by network opinion as ideologically coextensive. Both are said to be
antiwar and for "racial justice"; both are antagonistic to all three
Presidential candidates and to the political-economic system of
the United States.

The chief differences between them in network coverage are
these:

- unlike the left, the "demonstrators" are politically and
ideologically anonymous;

- where the identified left is portrayed as quite harmless
and nonviolent—save for two opinions on ABC—the
politically anonymous "demonstrators" are presented as
the hard-core violent element in United States political
life.

The degree of political and ideological anonymity of the "demonstrators" is quite startling. It is revealed by these simple statistics:

On ABC, out of 13 opinions in favor of . . . "demonstrators" and
21 opinions critical of "demonstrators," *none* identifies them as
members of any political group.

On CBS, out of 8 opinions in favor of "demonstrators" and 18
opinions critical of "demonstrators," *none* identifies them as
members of any political group.

On NBC, out of 15 opinions favorable to the "demonstrators,"
none identifies them as members of any political group (although 2
defenders of the "demonstrators" are identified as an SDS member

and a Cleaver follower); and out of 20 opinions critical of "demonstrators," *none* identifies them as members of any political group.

To sum up: During the seven weeks of coverage, opinion on "demonstrators" appears 95 times on the three networks—and none of these "demonstrators" has any specific political identity. Above all, none are described as "leftists."

The violence of this politically anonymous group of people is a constant theme in both favorable and unfavorable opinion. How is it dealt with? To start with favorable opinion:

On ABC, out of 13 opinions favorable to the "demonstrators," 5 rationalized their violence. All 5 opinions are from reporters.

On CBS, out of 8 opinions favorable to the "demonstrators," 2 rationalized their violence. Both are from reporters.

On NBC, out of 15 opinions favorable to the "demonstrators," 3 rationalized their violence. All 3 are from reporters.

Once again—the editorial methods of rationalization are standardized. They are virtually identical to those named in the black militant section:

- "Demonstrators' " violence or advocacy of violence is conceded, then the reporter justifies it by placing the blame on the shoulders of others—usually the "white middle class."

- "Demonstrators' " violence or advocacy of violence is conceded, then the reporter glamorizes the advocates or practitioners, or presents their grievances as justifications.

- "Demonstrators' " violence is evaded or described euphemistically, then the reporter defends those who engage in these practices.

- "Demonstrators' " violence is actively minimized, and the reporter scoffs at those who take this violence seriously.

- The reporter attacks those who attack the "demonstrators' " violence.

Here is a rapid summary of these editorial rationalizations of the violence of anonymous groups:

ABC

9/26/5: The reporter endorses the "claims" (unidentified) of the "dissenters" whom he defines as "the young, the poor and the black," and warns the audience that if their "claims" are not dealt with "justly" (undefined) by the prejudiced majority, the "young," etc. must inevitably turn to violence. This is a clear-cut threat.

9/30/2: Humphrey denounces the totalitarian and Hitlerian techniques of unnamed groups who threaten massive violence and propose to tear the society down. The reporter names these as "hecklers" and "demonstrators" and says Humphrey is angry at those who "have tried to interrupt his speeches." This euphemistic substitution of "hecklers" for Humphrey's *Hitler jugend* and the suggestion that Humphrey is acting out of pique, ridicules Humphrey and minimizes the Humphrey attack on the violent groups—a covert way of defending them.

10/8/10: A reporter concedes in euphemistic language that "student protesters" break laws, violate people's rights, steal, and threaten people's physical safety. He then justifies the "young" morally because they "speak up" against war and civil injustice. The "yes-they-are-dangerous-but-their-goals-are-noble" formula is the arch rationalization of violence.

10/24/8: The story describes four days of what the reporter euphemistically describes as "student unrest" at

Berkeley over the school's refusal to hire Eldridge
Cleaver. In the course of this "unrest" students engage
in "confrontation" with the police, call them "pigs,"
throw rocks at them, knock out a policeman's front
teeth, and "seriously injure" others. Seventy-six are arrested in this episode of "unrest." The reporter never
calls it a riot, never terms it illegal or violent, never admits antirioter opinion into his story and calls the student
actions a "serious protest." This is a minimization of
and a rationalization of violence from start to finish.

10/24/9: A police officer condemns riot and revolution.
The reporter declares him unsympathetic to "human
problems"—thus suggesting that if one is sympathetic
to "human problems" one will countenance or endorse
riot and revolution.

CBS

9/30/2: The CBS reporter completely suppresses the
Humphrey attack on the totalitarian and Hitlerian conduct of those who threaten violence and propose to tear
down this society—an attack culminating in Humphrey's
statement that no democracy should stand for this.
This story was carried on both ABC (9/30/2, Anti-
"Demonstrators") and NBC (9/30/2, Anti-"Demonstrators"). Instead, the CBS reporter quotes Humphrey as
sanctioning dissent and portrays him as though he were
endorsing those whom he criticized so violently. This
wiping out of an attack constitutes support of those attacked.

10/14/8: The reporter justifies violence by attacking the
American middle class which opposes "violent dissent"
and "student riots." He says they are "white"—suggest-

ing a racist motive—and that they are intellectually "limited." He describes the demand for "an end to violence" as a "Wallace theme"—i.e., a racist theme. This assault on the middle-class opposition to "student" violence and riots is a defense of violence and riots.

NBC

NBC's method of rationalizing this violence is "minimization" of a special kind. It consists of a thrice-repeated pretense that "demonstrators' " violence is not a legitimate national issue.

10/3/12: The reporter is astonished to find voters in Oregon upset by Yippies and blacks. Says the reporter: The Oregonians are disturbed "about things that really don't threaten them." He refrains from mentioning what those "things" are.

10/14/4: The reporter covers an Agnew speech in Virginia in which Agnew denounces Yippies who want to tear down the establishment. The reporter is startled by such an "inappropriate" discussion in Virginia. He can find no reason why Virginians should be concerned over this issue.

10/16/9: The reporter expresses profound surprise at the concern of American citizens in Idaho, Oregon and South Dakota over the conduct of hippies, Yippies and blacks. He insists there are no grounds for their concern. Their distress is a mystery to him.

This is so total a "minimization" of the moral and political significance of the widespread "demonstrators' " violence that it verges on a satire of network practices.

What, by contrast, is the nature of the criticisms of the violent, and anonymous, "demonstrators"?

Such criticisms come from candidates Humphrey, Nixon, Wallace, Agnew and from J. Edgar Hoover, Senator Edward Kennedy, from a few other establishment figures and from a few reporters.

What is most striking in this body of opinion is the extreme moral contrast between the charges of the political leaders and those of network reporters:

On ABC, J. Edgar Hoover speaks of "vicious mobs" in Chicago, Humphrey speaks of totalitarian and Hitlerian techniques, Nixon of "destroyers," Agnew of arson, violence and lawlessness. ABC reporters, however, object to the "demonstrators' " bad manners; criticize them for being "inconsistent, dirty, noisy . . . annoying." In one funny story about "college boys," the reporter amusingly criticizes them for "seizing buildings" and "sacking presidents' offices." One ABC reporter makes a strong criticism of "militants' " violence, warning that it may elect George Wallace: It is the same solitary criticism which we cited twice before, cross-indexed under this heading (9/20/8).

On CBS, J. Edgar Hoover again speaks of "vicious mobs," Senator Edward Kennedy speaks of violence, Humphrey of organized destroyers, Nixon of violence, and Agnew attacks the rationalizers of violence. CBS reporters, however, are silent. One CBS reporter refers obliquely to the problem. He says this: "There is a weird unreality about hunger and deprivation in the middle of enormous wealth, about one of the world's mightiest powers bombing and smashing one of the world's weakest, about a tiny group of (. . .) militants shouting that they will burn the nation down." (10/22/13) In other words, two strong moral condemnations of the country itself as oppressor and smasher of the weak, are packaged along with this criticism of the "militants' " *threats* of violence. Their actual violence is not acknowledged.

On NBC, J. Edgar Hoover, again, speaks of "vicious mobs," Senator Edward Kennedy criticizes violence, Humphrey attacks the hatred of the democratic process, Agnew condemns violence. The NBC reporters, however, have nothing to say on the subject. The sole reporter on NBC to utter a slightly negative word acknowledges "student" violence but amusingly joshes them for *conformity*. To wit:

Students who demanded that they should be given credit for the Cleaver course decided to protest. This is how they did it, taking over the administration buildings. What happened then was in complete conformity with their fellow nonconformists on other campuses. There was a take-over—a sit-in—defiance, violence and arrests. (10/24/11)

And thus ends this survey of opinion on the politically anonymous "demonstrators" and their violence.

What can one say on the issue of "equal forcefulness"?

In terms of total word counts, opinion on "demonstrators" is a paradox. Both on ABC and CBS anti-"demonstrator" opinon substantially outweighs pro-"demonstrator" opinion. Only NBC conforms to the dominant pattern.

These statistics, however, give only partial information. They do not reveal the fact that an internal "debate" of a systematic kind is going on between editorial opinion and "establishment" opinion. On all three networks, the leaders of this country repeatedly charge the "demonstrators" with criminal lawlessness. But reporters on all three networks have either: no criticisms . . . or petty criticisms . . . or cloak the misdeeds with protective euphemisms . . . or actively rationalize their commission . . . or pretend that there is no issue of criminal lawlessness at all.

This is so massive an editorial undercutting of the serious charges as to render the statistics unreliable as guides.

The sheer quantity and severity of the criticism of the "demonstrators' " violence put on the air by the networks cannot be minimized. But it is nonetheless the case that every possible editorial action is taken to undermine this criticism and to render the violent "demonstrators" side of the controversy the more "forceful."

It is essentially unimportant, however, whether opinion on the ideologically anonymous "demonstrators" is "equally forceful" or not. The ultimate problem is that there is no answer to one crucial question:

"Equally forceful" opinion . . . on *whom?*

WHERE ARE THE VIOLENT RADICALS?

According to CBS, on October 7, 1968, the political grouping known as "the left-wing student movement" was one of the "big" American institutions—comparable, said the reporter, to "big government," "big taxes," "the big press," and "the big networks."

The New Left indeed was so "big" according to the CBS reporter that it had intimidated much of the American middle class and accounted in part for the sweep to George Wallace (CBS, 10/7/1, Pro-Left). These Americans, said CBS, didn't like "bigness."

About six days earlier, J. Edgar Hoover of the FBI had also declared the New Left to be "big." But he meant it in a quite different sense. The New Left, he said, was one of America's biggest problems. He declared that the New Left in general and the Students for a Democratic Society in particular were the main forces behind the tremendous outbreak of political violence in America. He reported that the New Left was planning sabotage and destruction for the future. In addition, the FBI charged that "foreign influences" were playing a significant role in the black leftist movement. (ABC, 10/1/11, Anti-Left.)

It wasn't the New Left's numerical "bigness" that was disturbing the Federal Bureau of Investigation in 1968. It was its lawlessness and violence. And, CBS to the contrary, it wasn't the New Left's numerical "bigness" that was disturbing the far "bigger" electorate and generating a "law and order" issue in the 1968 campaign: it was its lawlessness and violence. It was in 1968, as the current Scranton Report on Student Violence reminds us, that terrorist practices began: "Columbia 1968 injected elements of terror and property destruction." (Newsweek, October 5, 1970.)

Given the reported "bigness" of this political movement and its serious lawlessness, one would suppose that the networks would give the radicals "big" coverage. And one would suppose that a great deal of pro and con opinion would be found on the New Left as well as on its violence, and on the violence it was publicly pledging for the future.

Such is not the case.

There is, as we have seen, an extraordinary paucity of pro and

con opinion on the left. What there is portrays the left as an innoc-
uous group—a little bothersome, noisy, given to the use of odd
words like "socialism," "imperialism," and "oink" but harmless
nonetheless. On network TV, the left—save for two jarring intru-
sions by J. Edgar Hoover and the HUAC—is shown as totally nonviolent.

And, as we have also seen, there is a great and mysterious reservoir of politically unidentified "youth," "students," "dissenters,"
"demonstrators," "activists" and "militants" who are not harmless
at all and whose activities often take the form of the systematic violation of the rights of others, of assault and destruction, of rioting
and burning and terrorism.

Who are these politically anonymous violent figures?

And where is the violent New Left?

The second question is answered more simply than the first. Although a large fraction of the country is intensely concerned with
the issue of the violent radicals in 1968, and the subject is constantly aired in the press, almost nobody talks about it on network
television—because network television does not *choose* to present
the violent New Left as an issue of controversy.

In the seven weeks of coverage, there are only three opinions on
the three networks in which a person actually names a specific New
Left group and charges it with violent intentions and/or with violent deeds; all three are from conservative sources:

   • The Hoover opinion naming the New Left and the
   SDS. (ABC, 10/1/11, Anti-Violent Radicals.)

   • The HUAC undercover investigator naming Jerry
   Rubin and the Yippies. (ABC, 10/3/8, Anti-Violent
   Radicals.)

   • Candidate Agnew naming "Yippies." (NBC, 10/14/4,
   Anti-Violent Radicals.) [1]

---

[1] This reference appears initially under anonymous "demonstrators"
because Mr. Agnew's usage was apparently generic—but to give NBC
the benefit of the doubt, I also tally it here.

Nor is there any opinion from any leftist sources which argues openly in favor of a politics of violence although such statements were pouring like cataracts over the campuses. The only quote on the air revealing an advocacy of political violence—the shooting of judges, police, businessmen, profit-makers, etc.—is attributed to Eldridge Cleaver and it is not described by CBS as a leftist position.

This is clearly suppression of information and opinion about the violent left by three network news departments. And it is not opinion on violent radicals alone which was suppressed. It is the radicals themselves who have been obliterated. To an astonishing degree, this "big" American movement was kept under wraps by the networks.

We are left at the very end of this content analysis with: The Mystery of the Missing Radicals.

"Missing" is perhaps a misnomer. One cannot read network transcripts of this 1968 campaign period without an overpowering conviction that radicals in large numbers were being seen and heard on the news programs, incessantly assailing candidates and shouting against the war. And, indeed, this is the conviction of most Americans. Is this widespread belief reflected in the actual words said on the air?

No, it isn't.

The networks did cover the individuals and groups that militantly besieged and assaulted the candidates, and they described them for us. Who were they?

Here, taken from Appendix L, is a complete list of these sources of hostile public opinion as named by the reporters:

Opponents of Nixon and Agnew

ABC described them as: demonstrators; a student; hecklers; students

CBS described them as: grapeworkers; young Democrats; "someone"; students

NBC described them as: "someone"; hecklers; black militant; black militant; university students

Opponents of Humphrey and Muskie

ABC described them as: peace demonstrators; antiwar demonstrators; hecklers; antiwar demonstrators

CBS described them as: costumed demonstrators; young detractors and demonstrators; anti-Vietnam hecklers; "a few unfriendly signs in the crowd"; students

NBC described them as: dissenters and demonstrators; crowds; demonstrators; college students

Opponents of Wallace and LeMay

ABC described them as: protesters; hecklers; hecklers; hecklers; hecklers; hecklers; hecklers; hecklers; a protest group; college students and hecklers; demonstrators; jeerers and fighters

CBS described them as: dissenters; hecklers; hippie-heckler; hecklers; protesters; protesters; people of other persuasions; black people; Nixon supporters; black-power demonstrators and hecklers

NBC described them as: "stop-the-war demonstrators"; anti-Wallaceites; hecklers, mostly Negroes; hecklers; hecklers; protesters; young people; hecklers; hecklers; protesters in hippie garb and hecklers; "someone"; hecklers and demonstrators; hecklers, college students, militant Negroes

Opponents of All Three Candidates

ABC described them as: antiwar student; hecklers

CBS described them as: leaders of demonstrators who battled Chicago police during the Democratic convention; *a leftist*

NBC described them as: a stop-the-war demonstrator

In that total list, there is only one identified radical. CBS (9/25/7) describes *one* student who attacked all three candidates as a "leftist." According to NBC and ABC, those mobs denouncing and assaulting the Presidential candidates for seven weeks contained no radicals or New Leftists at all.

And what of the "antiwar" opinion? It, too, was covered by the networks and those who expressed such opinion were described. Who were they?

Here, taken from Appendix M, are all the sources of public opinion antagonistic to the war, as identified by the reporters:

Antiwar Groups

ABC described them as: peace demonstrators; antiwar student; antiwar demonstrators; antiwar demonstrators; pacifists; hecklers; hecklers; antiwar demonstrators; a would-be marcher; a soldier; actress Vanessa Redgrave; black militants

CBS described them as: leaders of Chicago demonstrators; demonstrators; anti-Vietnam hecklers; *a leftist student;* demonstrators; stop-the-war students; young restless hecklers; an organizer of the Chicago convention disorder

NBC described them as: a Connecticut matron; hecklers; a stop-the-war demonstrator; student; demonstrator; Jerry Rubin, a leader of Chicago antiwar demonstrators; an antiwar protest leader; a soldier; a leader of the 1966 student demonstrations at UCLA and Berkeley; *Thomas Hayden of the Students for a Democratic Society;* President of Yale University; a group of artists

Here—in seven weeks of antiwar protest—we find *two* radicals. Or, to be precise, on CBS the *same* "left" student (9/25/7) who denounces the candidates also denounces the war; and on NBC (10/23/8) Tom Hayden of the SDS denounces the war. Actually, we have found only one new radical.

The almost total absence of individuals and groups editorially identified as New Leftists and radicals in precisely the areas where they operated most intensively in 1968 is a remarkable journalistic phenomenon indeed. It is particularly remarkable since network reporters show no diffidence in identifying Democrats, Republicans, Independent Party members, Black Panthers, McCarthyites, Kennedyites, socialists, UAW members, liberals, or conservatives.

One may conclude from The Mystery of the Missing Radicals that by a vast coincidence no network reporter ever happened to bump into a New Leftist although covering the candidates and antiwar demonstrators for seven weeks—or one may conclude that network reporters simply did not choose to identify New Leftists and radicals, in this context, and deliberately suppressed the information.

The latter is more likely.

Several pieces of concrete evidence exist, drawn from this period of coverage, which reinforce the conclusion that network reporters consider the existence, nature and goals of the New Left to be a manipulable commodity—to be suppressed or mentioned, as deemed politically advisable. To wit:

- On ABC (10/7/5, Anti-Humphrey), a reporter describes a Muskie speech at a college campus which is disrupted by a group of students. Mr. Muskie thereupon invites one of this group to the platform to say his piece. The ABC reporter describes the students poetically as "the disenchanted young," identifies them as "the former supporters of Bobby Kennedy and Eugene McCarthy" and hails Muskie as the "Pied Piper" of this group.

More than two weeks later this very group of "disenchanted young" was retroactively identified as a group of leftists by the ABC reporter. (ABC, 10/25/10, Anti-Conservative.) This belated political identification had only one result: It lent an appearance of balance to a situation in which candidate Muskie invited two Wallace hecklers to speak. By referring to the former group as leftists, the reporter was able to describe Muskie favorably as open to criticism from the right as well as from the left.

• CBS engages in a similar maneuver in relation to this very story, but in reverse. CBS initially relates the tale of how Muskie invited one of a group of "leftists" to the platform. (9/25/7, Anti-Humphrey.)

About nine days later CBS forgets that they were leftists. The reporter recalls that when "stop-the-war" students heckled Muskie, he was willing to listen—but that Muskie is far less courteous to Wallace hecklers. And the CBS reporter asks Muskie why he is more impatient with "Wallace hecklers" than with "young, restless hecklers." Thus the "leftists" change into "stop-the-war" students and then into a touching group known as "young, restless hecklers." (CBS, 10/4/12, Pro-"Demonstrators.")

It is not irrelevant that both stories are making pro-Muskie and anti-Wallace points. The left-wing identification flickered in and out *depending on how useful it was to Muskie.*

• Then there is the case of CBS' wholesale suppression of the major theme and content of a Humphrey speech. (CBS 9/30/2, Pro-"Demonstrators.")

This story has been described before, but I am elaborating on it here: In a Salt Lake City speech, Humphrey delivers a violent attack on the mobs of political protesters rampaging through the country. This speech is covered by ABC and NBC. They do not report that he names leftist groups, but his intentions are overwhelmingly clear and he cites threats by leftist leaders which have been heavily publicized in the press. It is consequently an implicit attack on the violent left, if not an explicit one.

Humphrey charges these groups with using totalitarian and Hitlerian techniques. He reports that they are planning violence and destruction and he quotes their threat that there will be more "Chicago's" in the future. Humphrey declares that no democracy can or should stand for this—that violence is not dissent.

This attack is carried on ABC most fully; on NBC with the very harshest criticisms cut out; and is not carried on CBS at all.

The CBS reporter claims to be covering Humphrey's speech, but fails to communicate its thesis. He lifts out one passage to quote—a Humphrey defense of the right to dissent. It is a serious distortion both of Humphrey's speech and his intent and leaves the impression that Humphrey is supporting the very group which he is denouncing.

This is a willful suppression of Humphrey's attack on what is obviously the violent left.

• NBC was aware of the HUAC undercover investigator's testimony against the Yippies in Chicago. The network carried the story. But where ABC (10/3/8,

Anti-Left) reported that he had charged Jerry Rubin and
the Yippies with planning to bomb buildings, kill policemen and assassinate candidates, NBC suppressed most of
the story, including the plans to kill policemen and bomb
buildings, and all mention of Jerry Rubin and the Yippies was excised from the report. The network said
only:

> During today's hearing by the House Subcommit-
> tee on Unamerican Activities . . . a Chicago
> policeman who worked as an undercover agent
> during the Democratic Convention told the sub-
> committee he overhead one demonstration leader
> suggest that all the Presidential candidates be
> killed. (10/3/17, Anti-Demonstrators.)

On this network Jerry Rubin—who, two years later,
was leading public celebrations at New York colleges
over leftist bombing of buildings ("Boom, Boom,
Boom!")—was turned by NBC into an anonymous
"demonstration leader."

● Finally, as has been said before, there is the suppression by both CBS and NBC of the FBI report on New
Left violence.

These illustrations from three networks, plus the total pattern of
anonymous coverage, suggest that:

> 1) New Leftists are deliberately not identified as
> such when the information is available.

> 2) New Leftists are identified if it serves to make
> a point deemed politically desirable by the
> reporter.

> 3) Charges of totalitarianism against the left-wing
> groups which advocate dictatorship and commit-

ments to assorted world dictators, are suppressed altogether.

4) Charges of lawlessness, violence and crime levelled against radicals and leftists are suppressed.

5) The anonymous "militants," "hecklers," "demonstrators," "dissenters," "hippies, yippies and blacks," "students," and, above all, "youth" are serving as code words for "leftists," "radicals" and "violent radicals."

It seems fairly clear that the mysterious reservoir of politically anonymous violence is mysterious and anonymous only by virtue of such code language. There are no "missing radicals." What is missing is journalistic candor about the left.

In the last analysis, the three overlapping categories—the left, "demonstrators" and violent radicals—must be examined together, for they are an interlocked body of opinion. On three networks, reporters gave support to both the identified and unidentified left and its violence . . . sheltered it by euphemisms, and a set of graduated evasions . . . systematically refused to condemn it . . . and debated the major leaders of the country on its behalf. There is no doubt which side the networks sought to render more "forceful."

CONCLUSIONS

As I have already said, the Fairness Doctrine cannot rationally hold reporters responsible for the "forcefulness" of the opinions of their interviewees in a controversy. It can only ask that reporters take no action to enhance or undercut the potency of either side of the "debate"—however true or false, moral or immoral they may deem it to be.

It is clear that this "debate" discipline is not being used during this period of study. Both by the selective methods and by active editorializing, the reporters of the three networks are molding the evaluative material in their stories to reflect and reinforce their own largely left-liberal political opinions.

These are, curiously, highly restricted in nature, quantity and subtlety. In the coverage of almost every issue, we have uncovered a "party line"—a selective process that tends to stockpile and stress a few crude opinions over and over again:

Humphrey is wise, humanitarian and good . . . Wallace generates violence . . . Nixon is anti-liberal, racist, and bad . . . stop the war . . . stop the bombing . . . liberals are all good people without race prejudice . . . conservatives are all bad people with race prejudice . . . America is a bad country which oppresses blacks . . . blacks are good people who are justified in attacking whites . . . leftists are funny and harmless . . . violent "youth" has noble motivations and moral goals . . .

These primitive little ideological constellations, and the militant restriction of, or evasion of rational qualifications and of alternative views, are the cause of the insistent "cartooning" that emerges in network news. If there is a malady in this coverage over and above extreme bias itself, it is the intellectual crudity and rigidity of these sterotyped selective and exclusionary processes.

But there is yet another malady which deserves examination and that is specifically the bias in favor of the politically violent. If all other forms of bias can be described as "unfair," this bias in particular can be described as dangerous folly.

Clusters of consistent and repetitive editorial opinion which sanction violence have been found in five areas of this study—in anti-Wallace opinion, anti–white-middle-class-majority opinion, anti-conservative opinion, pro–black-militant opinion, and pro-"demonstrators" opinion.

The dominant editorial "lines" in these different categories are of four broadly interlocking types:

- In anti-Wallace opinion, reporters legitimize acts of physical assault on the racist right.

- In anti–white-middle-class and anti-conservative opinion, the reporters undermine the concept of law by equating it to racism.

• In pro–black-militant opinion, the reporters argue that black crime is not the fault of the black who commits it, and should not be subject to law enforcement.

• In pro-"demonstrators" opinion, violence of the un-identified left against individuals, property, and various American institutions is sanctioned on the grounds that the targets are social injustice and war.

All of these editorial attitudes can be subsumed under one state-ment—the statement that serves as the tacit standard of selectivity in much of social coverage:

Violence directed by leftists and blacks against America, her in-stitutions, and the majority of her citizens, is morally legitimate because social evils are its target. The noble ends justify the terroristic means.

This many-faceted endorsement of violence is present in network newscasts in significant amounts: On ABC, reporters sanctioned violence eleven times; on CBS, nine times; and on NBC, seventeen times. In Appendix N a complete list of all references to the stories containing this opinion will be found.

This quiet, steady spewing-out of justifications for violence by allegedly responsible men, under the eyes and ears of allegedly re-sponsible network management, is a pathological phenomenon. Its intellectual source is quite apparent: network attitudes on violence are in part the replica of an attitude that has been prominent for the past few years in the liberal-left world.

When the networks were explicitly charged by Vice President Agnew, one year after the period of this study, with sanctioning the violent and their attacks on American people and American institutions, a cry of anger went out through the country from the liberal world. The very suggestion that network men might be sanctioning New Left violence and America hatred was declared outrageous and unthinkable, McCarthyite, repressive and fascistic.

The reasons for this impassioned refusal by liberals to counte-nance such a charge are somewhat mysterious since liberals had been passionately denouncing other liberals on precisely the same grounds in the public prints for some time. Indeed, long after the Agnew speech, they continued to do so, with mounting intensity.

I cannot give a full history of this internecine struggle, but a bird's-eye view of liberal comment on the violence cult in liberal ranks is necessary to see network violence-advocacy in context:

In 1968, shortly before the period of this study began, the liberal Dr. Edgar Berman, a Humphrey campaign advisor, concluded that many liberal Democrats at the Democratic convention, including TV newsmen, "sided with and even egged on the demonstrations because they . . . would have liked nothing more than chaos at the Convention." (He reported this observation in *The New York Times* Magazine of October 5, 1969.)

Also in 1968, the liberal Norman Mailer observed a "lust for the apocalypse" among educated liberals. And the liberal Daniel Moynihan, quoting Mr. Mailer in the *Saturday Evening Post,* reported that he observed the same phenomenon in the same highly educated liberal groups, noting that they expressed "ill-concealed pleasure" at the thought that "American society is doomed."

In 1969, the year after the period of this study, an article appeared in *The American Scholar* by the liberal Michael Lerner, analyzing the class bigotry of the "good left-liberal." He reported on the "rise, during the '60's of a peculiarly virulent form of black anti-white rhetoric that the white elites tolerated and even in ways encouraged because it was . . . directed to the same lower-middle class and working class groups which they themselves held in such disdain." And he criticized the aberrant tendency of these "elites" to "impute racist motives" to anyone who protested crime, thus, by implication, sanctioning such crime.

Also in 1969 in an interview accorded to *U.S. News and World Report* on November 24, former Vice President Humphrey observed that "there are some people who condone violence . . . sometimes they are called liberals." And Mr. Humphrey, who had himself justified black riots in 1968, declared that he did not believe "the cause of Liberalism" would be advanced by making "excuses for outright violence and destruction," and chastised those who did.

In 1970, when the black militants and New Leftists were actually shooting judges, killing policemen and bombing buildings, as announced in 1968, there was a virtual epidemic of castigations of liberals by liberals:

On January 16, 1970, the liberal *New York Times* burst forth in editorial indignation over Leonard Bernstein's now famous party for the "para-military" Black Panthers. Wrote the *Times* in part: "Emergence of the Black Panthers as the romanticized darlings of the politico-cultural jet set is an affront to the majority of black Americans." This was followed some months later by the liberal Tom Wolfe's now classic *Radical Chic*—a scathing analysis of the cult of liberal intellectuals for black violence.

On March 11, 1970, the famous Moynihan memo to President Nixon was leaked to *The New York Times*—precipitating an indignant hue and cry in the liberal-left world. In it, liberal sociologist Daniel Moynihan warned President Nixon of the "semi-violent protest" of "the middle-class mob" which had forced President Johnson's resignation. He identified that "mob" as consisting of "college professors, millionaires, flower children and Radcliffe girls" . . . and of men like Yale Chaplain William Sloan Coffin, who "openly espouse violence . . ." Mr. Moynihan condemned the cultural leaders who, he said, had rejected the basic values of American society, and were taking with them much of the middle class, particularly the young. He warned the President of the chaos that would be further generated by this proviolence "middle-class mob," and wrote sardonically: "it is their pleasure to cause trouble, to be against, and they are hell-bent for a good time."

And on April 12, 1970, in *The New York Times* Magazine, liberal Irving Howe criticized TV newsmen for their assiduous attention to SDS activities and attacked an array of famous liberal intellectuals for joining the new cult of violence-glorification. He charged them with capitulating to the irrationalities of the New Left: " . . . it's not as if everything leading up to the present debacle on the New Left—the elitism, the authoritarianism, the contempt for democracy, the worship of charismatic dictatorship, the mystique of violence—hadn't already been visible to all three years ago when such intellectuals began offering the New Left an aura of intellectual respectability. What the young radicals needed from the intellectuals was sober criticism; what they got too often was a surrender of critical faculties."

The climax of this castigation of liberal by liberal was reached in the summer of 1970. The liberal AFL-CIO president George Meany warned that the Democratic Party had fallen into the hands of violent New Leftists and was losing the labor vote. And, in August, 1970, liberal political analysts Richard Scammon and Ben J. Wattenberg published *The Real Majority,* a book that traumatized the liberal Democratic world. The authors warned the liberal Democrats that they had made the profound blunder of equating firmness against crime and rioting with racism, bigotry and fascism. They warned Democrats that they would cease to be a politically viable party unless they ceased sneering at the American majority and recognized the "non-negotiable demands" of this majority for lawfulness and order.

At which point, history records, many liberal Democrats—particularly those whose political careers were at stake—defected en masse from the fashionable proviolence position to an aggressive antiviolence position. As columnist Stewart Alsop put it in *Newsweek,* December 14, 1970, the liberal Democrats "scuttled towards the center to save their skins." The scuttling was led by former Democratic Presidential candidate Hubert Humphrey. In a speech in St. Louis in August, Mr. Humphrey voiced the new liberal law-and-order position. He proclaimed that "liberals must stop using the words 'well-meaning' about those who see violence and law-breaking as the way to influence public policy"—and he asked liberal Democrats to renounce the notion that "law and order" was a code term for repression.

This much is sufficient to place the violence-addiction of network newsmen in context. It makes it clear that it is not an accident that we see such concerted support of violence on the air during the period of this study, and that it is not a malady unique to this particular body of reporters. The cult of violence is clearly a part of the liberal cultural of this period. Almost inevitably it emerged in the attitudes of three liberal news agencies.

There is, unfortunately, something less than perfect candor on this phenomenon among educated liberals who will admit liberals' espousal of violence to each other—but to no one else. During the 1970 elections—which may go down in history as the Scammon and Wattenberg elections—liberal Democratic politicians and reporters joined hands to deny flatly to the nation the Republican charge that liberal Democrats had unremittingly sanctioned violence. The grandest denial of all was voiced on network television by a solemn Ed Muskie . . . who had himself justified black riots during the campaign of 1968 . . . who had idealized college radicals as bemused "teenagers" . . . who was not quoted once during the campaign by network TV as attacking the violent left . . . and who was praised for his "statesman-like" performance by the very network reporters who had found his attitudes so sympathetic in 1968.

Nonetheless, history cannot be rewritten. The liberal cult of violence is on record, on film, as well as in scholarly analyses and journalistic castigations of this cult. As Irving Howe says, many in this group did surrender their "critical faculties" to the most irrational, violent element of the New Left.

On network TV, during the period of this study, they surrendered them most lavishly.

"Nonpartisan . . . ?"

Editorializing, as we have seen, is a significant element in the generation of network bias. Exactly how significant is it?

To the degree that the reporters are the sole, or major, communicators of any particular opinion or set of opinions, it is all-significant. There is no question, for example, that most of the sanctioning of violence and most attacks on "the white middle class" emerge from reportorial mouths.

But most editorializing is not on this subject at all, and most of it does not have this monopolistic status. It is scattered about in the stories, showing up in all issues, in varying amounts. In Appendix O a total breakdown can be found, by network, of the precise amounts of "for" and "against" opinion on all issues coming from editorial as opposed to other sources.

The fastest way to get a perspective on the total role played by editorializing is to know the percentages of reporter opinion in relation to the total body of opinion analyzed—a body of opinion coming from about *half* the stories aired during the study period:

ABC

The total number of words of opinion from all sources was:	32,219
Of this total, the number of words of opinion from reporters was:	15,470
The percentage of reportorial opinion was:	48%[1]

CBS

The total number of words of opinion from all sources was:	19,340
Of this total, the number of words of opinion from reporters was:	5,945
The percentage of reportorial opinion was:	31%

NBC

The total number of words of opinion from all sources was:	25,825
Of this total, the number of words of opinion from reporters was:	4,699
The percentage of reportorial opinion was:	18%

It is obvious that there is a striking difference in the editorial participation at the three networks. The significance of this difference will be examined in the next chapter. Here, we are concerned only with the fact that, however varied the quantity per network, editorial opinion is an important element in the generation of the bias we see on the air.

It is consequently worth understanding, in some detail, of what precisely this editorial opinion consists, where it is to be found, and

---

[1] At the period of this study, ABC had an unusually large number of commentators. This network has since reduced the number to two.

how it is communicated. It is particularly worth understanding since the press, in general, and the networks in particular, have surrounded the issue with a tissue of professional mysteries and myths.

At the networks, the most important myth is the one that proclaims that editorial opinion is only to be found in two forms: "commentaries" and "editorials." All other journalistic forms are said to be neutral and "objective," and these allegedly neutral forms have a variety of different names: "news," "news analysis," "news interpretation," "news backgrounders," etc.

So strong is the myth that these "analyses" and "interpretive" forms are not carriers of opinion, that NBC's News Vice President Reuven Frank could say, unselfconsciously, in *The Viewer,* published by The National Audience Board, in its issue of April 1970:

> There is more news analysis on NBC Television than there used to be on NBC Radio. There are more news analysts: Huntley, Brinkley, Newman, Chancellor, McGee, Scherer, Hangen, Utley, Kiker, Dickerson, Frederick, Kaplow. That's for openers.

In fact, there is no difference in any of these forms from the point of view of freedom from editorializing. These supposedly neutral forms are frequently indistinguishable from each other. Political opinion by reporters is to be found in all of them and there is absolutely no distinction between the *kind* of political opinion that shows up in all of them. Indeed, there is often far stronger opinion in an allegedly factual news story, than there is in a commentary. There is often a harder one-sided position taken in a news story than in an even-handed editorial. And where news stories frequently contain overt opinion, commentaries frequently contain covert opinion.

Much to-do has been made about the uniqueness of commentary, in particular. There has been much solemn talk of the necessity of distinguishing it visually from the "impartial" news reporting by posting signs, etc., to "let the viewer know" he is hearing commentary, not news. According to the results of this study, it makes no difference whatever if the networks do or do not post signs—or send up warning flares—when commentary takes place. The striking fact is that during the period of this study, ABC has a *great many* commentators, CBS only *one* commentator, and NBC has *no* commentators, yet the findings reveal an extreme and similar bias in all three networks.

Since the principal question to which this study addresses itself is: what kind of political opinion is to be found in these broadcasts? —no distinction whatever is made between these alleged differentiae. In this study, political opinion is called political opinion. When the source is a network reporter, it is called: editorial opinion.[1] And it comes in only two forms—overt and covert.

Overt editorial opinion needs no explanation: it is a straightforward expression of opinion by a reporter who is not attempting to disguise the fact that what he is expressing is opinion—and that it comes from him.

Covert opinion is disguised opinion. There are only two types. In the first, the reporter does not disguise that what he is saying is opinion, he disguises its source—so that it does not appear to be coming from *him*. In the second, he is obviously the one interpreting, but he communicates his opinion in a circuitous, devious, implicit, or coded fashion, so that it doesn't appear to be opinion— but fact.

Most of the time, overt and covert opinion are intermixed. It is impossible for a reporter to weave a tissue of implication for any length of time without becoming totally unintelligible—and it is impossible for him to speak openly for any length of time without

---

[1] Before leaving NBC, Chet Huntley conceded publicly that the assorted terminology in use at the networks was senseless. *Variety* on March 25, 1970, reports that Mr. Huntley recommended that newsmen should avoid "all those confusing words which are frequently applied to our trade: editorializing, slanting, analyzing, commenting, observing, opinionating, and so on and so on." He suggested the substitution of a single word: "judgment." "Judgment," of course, means: opinion.

arousing the wrath of viewers. Consequently, editorializing reporters shuttle back and forth between the explicit and the implicit—often leaving the viewer stunned with the confused conviction that he has just heard opinion, but is not quite sure what it is—and, above all, *whose* it is.

Like any game, however, the mysteries dissipate once one knows the rules. And there are "rules" in network editorializing. They are standardized, save for an occasional individual specialty. They are used singly or in combinations at all three networks. And in the course of this study, I isolated 33 of them. Although in principle each of these 33 techniques can be used to support either side of a controversy, in practice the vast majority of them are used in support of Democratic, liberal or left positions.

I hereby list them—with illustrations and references to my own research files, which contain detailed analyses of every editorial opinion found during the study period.

ATTRIBUTION TO AN EXTERNAL SOURCE

The most important category of covert editorializing takes place by means of attributing the reporter's own ideas to an external source, so that he appears to be "reporting" impersonally on other people's opinions. There are two outstanding techniques of this type:

Mind-Reading

This is the single most consistently used technique of expressing covert political opinions. The newsman pretends to be reporting authoritatively on the views of various human beings, ranging from individuals all the way to aggregates of multimillions. Characteristically he "reports" on the inner feelings, the buried emotions, the concealed thoughts and goals and the unconscious psychological motivations of: single persons; small groups; crowds ranging from ten thousand to a half-million people; entire socio-economic classes; inhabitants of great geographical areas, states and nations; the whole voting population of the United States; and whole races. And invariably the reporter draws vast political generalizations from this "reporting."

This technique, absurd on the face of it, is carried to ludicrous heights when the reporter is not merely content to inform us what 600,000 people thought at a Nixon rally or what all blacks in Delaware feel or what emotions "the white middle-class majority" is experiencing, but engages in "multiple mind-reading." Here the newsman "reports," for example, on what *he* believes *Humphrey* believes that all *Democrats* believe about *Humphrey*. (ABC 10/21/5, Pro-Humphrey.) Or what *he* believes *White House officials* believe *the North Vietnamese* believe about *Johnson* and *Nixon*. (ABC 10/16/1, Anti-Nixon.)

In fact all this is nothing but a claim to telepathy—a claim made incessantly on all three networks by virtually all reporters. It is a cynical device. No network reporter can read single minds, let alone unconscious motivations, let alone the unconscious motivations of unknown millions. This is pure editorial opinion projected into other minds—and falsely "reported" as hard fact.

It is significant that all "mind-reading" *invariably* results in opinion supportive of Democratic or liberal or left causes. No "mind-reading" is *ever* supportive of Republican or conservative or white middle-class causes, and is usually opposed to them.

Anonymous

Occasionally the reporters hide behind "anonymous" sources of opinion. Scattered throughout news stories are such phrases as "critics feel, . . ." "observers point out, . . ." "experts believe, . . ." "it is widely thought . . ."; along with "Nixon aides believe, . . ." "the Humphrey people think, . . ." "the police feel, . . ." and "the North Vietnamese say . . ." These sources are totally uncheckable and must be taken on blind faith.

The transmission of anonymous opinion by vague "observers" and "critics" is a remarkable luxury in which to indulge, in a 22-

minute newscast into which the major events of the universe must be stuffed each day. It suggests that the reporter has a tenacious desire to transmit those particular opinions.

Not coincidentally, "anonymous" sources *invariably* support liberal or Democratic or left causes; *never* the other side. In all cases of "anonymous opinion" in this study, the reporter is flatly credited with it as his own.

OMISSION

If projection or "mind-reading" is the most important single device of the network reporter for presenting his own political views on the air, *omission* (or *exclusion*) is his most important single device for keeping political views he dislikes *off* the air. There are four characteristic types of *omission:*

Evasion or Suppression

This is the grossest form of omission and the most widely used. While allegedly covering both sides of a controversial issue, the reporter evades or suppresses crucially relevant material—material which is readily available—so that his story actually presents only *one side* of the controversy.

The most startling use of this technique on all three networks was made in the coverage of the Presidential campaign. Network reporters presented story after story on this campaign, reporting on the battle between Democrats and Republicans, and on the political shift in the country away from the Democrats—*without including any anti-Democratic opinion from Republican or conservative citizens to account for it!* All anti-Humphrey and pro-Nixon statements can be scoured in vain for such public opinion.

Perspective

This technique is exclusionary policy at its purest. Here the network newsman reports on a controversy or a political clash without even pretending to cover both sides. He simply reports on one side, reflecting that side's attitudes, language, and emotions exclusively.

Thus, in one story of a student riot at Berkeley, all language, all emotions, all attitudes, all values, all purposes reported on, were those of the rioters. The sole perspective transmitted was theirs. One would not have known that anyone else existed, either at the university, in the city, in the state or in the country, who had a different perspective on this situation. (See ABC 10/24/8, Pro-"Demonstrators.")

The most striking campaign example of this technique was a long "news analysis" conducted by three reporters about the campaign—the entire discussion conducted from beginning to end from a Democratic perspective. One could not know from the analysis that a drastically different Republican perspective existed on the very issues they were discussing. (See ABC 9/27/2, Anti-Nixon.)

Euphemisms

This selective technique is so crude that it has been widely recognized and commented on in the country, and has already been thoroughly illustrated in this study. It consists of using evasive terminology when discussing illegal, violent or criminal activities—always to the advantage of practitioners of political violence. Violent mob outbreaks are called "restlessness"; violent disruptions of people's rights of free speech are called "protest"; violent assaults on persons are called "heckling"; violent provocations of the police are called "confrontations" or "demonstrations"; violent assaults on property are called "liberating buildings"; thefts of property are called "commandeering"; acts of arson are described as "fire dances"; radicals shrieking abuse at candidates and threatening to destroy society are called "youth."

By omitting the correct legal and moral nomenclature, the network reporter omits the critical opinion of organized society itself on such actions and tacitly communicates his sympathy for them.

Last Word

This technique in writing conclusions to stories is commonplace. After reporting on conflicting opinions on a controversial issue, the reporter climaxes the story with a quotation or a paraphrase or an endorsement of *one side*—omitting all recapitulation of the other side.

Thus, after reporting on the conflicting opinion of the black militants and the New York Teachers Union in the New York school strike of 1968, a reporter "summed up" with the black-militant position only—effectively endorsing it. (NBC 10/21/11, Pro–Black Militants.)

GLAMORIZATION

Yet another body of techniques can be grouped under the title of "glamorization." By using them, the reporter glamorizes or morally idealizes an individual, group or cause. The greatest beneficiaries of this technique in the study period were: candidate Edmund Muskie, the violent student "demonstrators," and the violent black militants. There are six distinct types of "glamorization." Some of the illustrations of these techniques have already been previewed in the analyses of editorial justifications of violence:

Praise

> *Example:* A reporter praises the character and courage of Vice Presidential candidate Muskie before and after Muskie praises radicals as "teenagers" with "honest doubts about the validity of our system." The reporter thus morally endorses both Muskie and this beneficent interpretation of the radicals. (NBC 9/19/15, Pro-Left.)

Suppression of Negatives

> *Example:* A reporter's sole description of Eldridge Cleaver, in a story about a controversy over Cleaver, is the courteous title: "a noted black nationalist." The reporter suppresses all reference to this "noted Nationalist's" criminal record as a rapist, his pending murder trial, his advocacy of murder as a political policy. (NBC 9/23/12, Pro–Black Militants.)

A variant of this technique might be called "what negatives?" It is an NBC specialty. The reporter travels around the country and repeatedly pretends not to know why Americans are so agitated over the militants. (NBC, 10/3/12, 10/14/4, 10/16/9, Pro-"Demonstrators.")

Naming and Glamorizing Negatives

> *Example:* The reporter presents Eldridge Cleaver calling for "black armies" to drive "white dogs" out, and calls him an "enthusiastic" fighter for Negro rights. (NBC 9/20/5, Pro–Black Militants.)

> *Example:* A reporter describes a violent black-power riot in which many are injured, and justifies it as an expression of "black pride" and "black identity." (CBS 9/26/14, Pro–Black Militants.)

Naming and Ignoring Negatives

> *Example:* A reporter states that students committed acts of violence but criticizes them for "conformity"— as if he were not aware of the violence. (NBC, 10/24/11, Anti-"Demonstrators.")

> *Example:* A reporter covers a black militant threatening to create "flaming cities" and repeatedly calls him a

"hero" as if he has not heard the threat. (CBS, 10/24/12, Pro–Black Militants.)

Enlarging Significance

Example: The reporter portrays a splinter minority of "student activists" as intellectually dominant at a university, intimating that the majority of the students accept their goals. He thus inflates the significance of the splinter group. (NBC 9/23/12, Pro-"Demonstrators.")

Example: The reporter describes the minority left-wing student movement as "big" and compares it to "big government," "big taxes," "the big press," and "the big networks," thus inflating its significance. (CBS 10/7/1, Pro-Left.)

Attacking Opponents as Immoral

Example: The reporter attacks those who condemn black political violence as racists, authoritarians and militarists. (NBC 9/17/8, Anti-White Middle Class.)

Example: The reporter attacks those who oppose student riots, violent dissent and class warfare as intellectually limited racists. (CBS 10/14/8, Pro-"Demonstrators.")

DEGLAMORIZATION

There is a negative parallel to "glamorization," and that is "deglamorization." Here, the reporter disapproves or undercuts the moral character of an individual, group or cause.

There are seven distinct modes of communicating editorial disapproval—all of them in frequent use at all three networks.

The most dramatic victim of these techniques during the seven-week campaign period was Richard Nixon.

Direct Attack

Direct attack from reporters is relatively rare, but it exists. The most unbridled editorial attacks on Nixon are to be found on ABC, 10/21/5, 10/25/7, 10/30/6, 11/4/4 (Anti-Nixon); CBS, 9/17/3, 10/24/6, (Anti-Nixon).

Indirect Attack

The reporter attacks not the individual but his associates and, if a candidate, his supporters.

> *Example:* The reporter portrays Nixon campaign aides as dehumanized squares. (CBS 10/28/15, Anti-Nixon.)

> *Example:* The reporter portrays Nixon as supported by shallow and closed-minded people. (ABC 10/21/5, Anti-Nixon.)

Double-Standard Attack

Network men attack an individual by standards that are not applied to anyone else. Nixon was the principal victim of this practice:

> *Example:* Nixon is attacked for being "unyoung, unhandsome, and unsexy" (CBS 9/17/9, Anti-Nixon), although neither of the other middle-aged candidates was criticized by this or any other network on such grounds.

> *Example:* Nixon is criticized for giving the same speech over and over again (NBC 10/29/5, Anti-Nixon), although all candidates are reported as giving the same speech over and over again (NBC 10/18/9, Anti-Nixon). Humphrey is never criticized for this.

> *Example:* The reporter condemns Nixon for failing to

give complex solutions to national problems at his public rallies (NBC 10/18/9, Anti-Nixon), but the network never attacks Humphrey for this same "failure."

Example: The reporter condemns Nixon for "scorn and ridicule" of Humphrey, but NBC never condemns Humphrey for "scorn and ridicule" of Nixon. (See NBC 10/16/7, Anti-Nixon, for the attack and examples of Humphrey's ridicule of Nixon which go uncriticized.)

Example: One ABC man suggests Nixon is a liar because Nixon exults over a crowd of 600,000 when ABC says it is 400,000 (ABC 9/30/5,6A, Anti-Nixon); while another ABC man warmly empathizes with Humphrey for exulting over a crowd of 10,000 and does not question the estimates of size (ABC 10/3/5, Pro-Humphrey).

Example: The reporter attacks Nixon for "formula" campaigning in key states, in big cities, with motorcades at high noon through crowded thoroughfares—when this is and always has been the "formula" of all candidates. No other candidate is attacked for this. Since the alternative to the "formula" is to campaign in minor states, in small towns, in unpopulated areas, down rural roads on foot, when no one is there, this particular attack has its humor. (CBS 9/20/4, Anti-Nixon.)

Humor, Sarcasm, Satire and Irony

Network reporters use all of these forms to undercut an opinion, idea, doctrine, group or cause, to render it unimportant, silly, laughable or ridiculous.

Example: A reporter minimizes looting, burning and rioting and mocks those who take such "amateur" crimes seriously. (ABC 9/16/14, Pro–Black Militants.)

Example: A reporter informs the country that Humphrey was standing near a men's room when he received an important call about the war from the President, a gratuitous absurdity. (CBS 10/16/4, Anti-Humphrey.)

Example: A reporter mocks a Congressional hearing about alleged Yippie violence and jokes about the events at the hearing, communicating his view that such an investigation is laughable. (NBC 10/1/10, Pro-Left.)

Argument

This technique of disapproval is used with a certain frequency. The newsman is allegedly reporting on a controversial issue or situation but in fact serves as the voice of one side—by "debating" with the other side. This "debating" technique varies in types— some are more overt than others. In certain cases the reporter structures his entire story like a running debate allowing one side to speak—then challenging the speaker's statements, character, value or integrity; allowing that side to speak again, then challenging again, etc.

The two most dramatic illustrations of this reportorial infighting with the subject of a story can be found in NBC 10/11/5, (Anti-Nixon), CBS 9/17/3, (Anti-Nixon). In both of these stories the reporter is locked in combat with candidate Nixon.

Guilt by Association

This technique of disapproval is an ancient one and much in vogue at the networks. It consists of constantly linking a political group with unsavory or immoral practices.

The primary objects of such linking during the seven-week period were: Nixon, the Republicans, the conservatives, the right, the police, the middle class and the U.S. majority—all of which were continuously linked to "racism." (See all opinion files, Anti-Nixon, Anti-Conservative, Anti–Middle Class.)

Code

An attack on an individual or group is too controversial to be delivered openly—so it is delivered symbolically. Some of the linking to "racism" described above was done by means of code references to "law and order," "justice," "Strom Thurmond," etc. (ABC 9/27/2, CBS 10/3/7, Anti-Nixon.)

Similarly, Nixon was frequently linked to a hard-core anti-liberal, anti-Communist past by means of code references to "the old Nixon," the man who goes after his enemies "with a club or a meat axe," the man who "impugns the patriotism" of his opponents, the man from whom one shouldn't "buy a used car," etc. (ABC 10/25/7, 10/30/6; CBS 9/19/21, 9/26/3, 10/24/6; NBC 9/23/6, 9/27/5, Anti-Nixon.)

FAKE NEUTRALITY

There is yet another category of editorializing which may be described as "Fake Neutrality." It consists of a calculated effort to make the reporter appear neutral when in fact he is taking sides. There are six such techniques:

False Compliment

The reporter pays a limited compliment to the character or mind of a political figure—and then surrounds it with one or both of the following:

     a) A thorough and extensive contradiction of the compliment, thus wiping it out.

     b) Extensive praise of his opponent.

In this technique, the compliment is hypocritical: It is a camouflage for an attack. It is essentially a device to make the reporter seem "objective"—one who sees both the pros and cons, the virtues and flaws. It serves as a peg on which to hang its opposite—an attack on the person and/or praise of an opponent.

Virtually all of the rare compliments bestowed on Richard Nixon by reporters were of this "false" type. They were almost invariably annulled—embedded in attacks on him and/or praise of Humphrey. For a reference to Nixon's "thoughtful" and sometimes "profound" speeches buried in a violent attack, see ABC 11/4/4 (Anti-Nixon). For a reference to the "intelligence" of Nixon campaign associates, buried in criticism of them as computerized squares, see CBS 10/28/15 (Anti-Nixon).

Mrs. Nixon was the object of a particularly tortuous use of the "false compliment" technique, on ABC, in which praise of her was imbedded in a massive attack on her mind and character, along with equally massive praise of Mrs. Humphrey. (ABC 10/10/9, Anti-Nixon.)

False Criticism

This is the precise reverse of the false compliment technique. The reporter issues a mild reprimand to a political figure—then follows it with such substantial praise as to wipe out the criticism, and/or a severe attack on his opponent. Mr. Humphrey was the beneficiary of such treatment on several occasions. For an illustration see CBS 10/9/13, (Anti-Nixon).

False Series

This technique was evoked on CBS alone and appears to be the invention of a particular reporter. It is a violation of a basic rule of logical categorizing, taught to children on the well-known children's show "Sesame Street" by means of a little refrain: "One of these things is not like the other." The reporter creates an ostensibly logical series in which "one of the things is not like the other." To cite one example: The reporter indicates with great precision that he intends to present a series of criticisms of *all three* Presidential candidates on certain grounds. He explains the grounds. He then cites an illustration of Mr. Wallace's errors in this matter. He follows by an illustration of Mr. Nixon's errors in this matter. But when it's time to get to Mr. Humphrey's errors in this matter, the reporter . . . changes the subject. (CBS 10/2/18, Anti-Nixon.)

False Prototype

The reporter here presents the opinion of one individual, asserting that he stands for a huge political group in the U.S. The reporter lets the "false prototype" speak, standing aside, and saying nothing, acting as the embodiment of neutrality.

Actually, by endowing the individual with the status of a spokesman for millions, the reporter is endorsing the significance of these opinions. The most dramatic usage of this device was on NBC which offered two Black Militants from Watts as representatives of black thought, and allowed both men to make the longest statements aired during the campaign period. (NBC 10/23/9, Anti-Middle Class.)

Half-Debate

The reporter claims to be presenting the arguments on both sides in a controversy—but in fact does not. Instead he presents the reasoning of one side very strongly—and omits the reasoning on the other side altogether. Two striking uses of this technique can be mentioned.

> *Example:* The reporter is "summing up" the argument within the administration over a bombing halt—and leaves out the arguments of Johnson-Rusk-Rostow and the generals. (CBS, 9/25/22, Anti–U.S. Policy on the Bombing Halt.)

> *Example:* The reporter is "summing up" the argument between the pro-Reagan and the pro-Cleaver forces re Cleaver's being hired to teach at Berkeley. He leaves out all references to Cleaver's past criminal record as a rapist, his current advocacy of mass murder as a political method and the fact that he is, at the time of the story, awaiting trial for murder. These, of course, were the grounds for the opposition's argument. (NBC 9/20/5, Anti-Conservative.)

Double Talk

The reporter, affecting neutrality, literally contradicts himself—then elaborates on half of the contradiction.

> *Example:* A reporter states that he does not intend to quote Rap Brown's attack on the United States as a uniquely violent country—but does so in different words, elaborating extensively on Brown's opinion. (NBC 9/18/1, Anti–Middle Class.)

> *Example*: A reporter states explicitly that Nixon's panel shows are not rigged, then spends the rest of his story covertly indicating that they are rigged. (ABC 9/25/13, Anti-Nixon.)

OUTRIGHT FALSIFICATION

Yet another category of covert editorializing is that of outright falsification. The type discovered was:

Distortion

The reporter summarizes a quotation, a speech or an issue with gross inaccuracy—resulting in the reinforcement or support of one side of a controversial issue.

The most serious example of distortion occurred on CBS in which a section of a Humphrey speech was quoted out of context, leaving the impression that Humphrey supported violent radicals when he had attacked them strongly as totalitarians and compared them to Hitler's youth. (CBS 9/30/2, Pro-"Demonstrators.")

EDITORIALIZED STRUCTURE

There is another group of three editorializing techniques—all of which are accomplished by means of structure and organization—and which consist of burying or inflating material in accordance with reportorial sympathies:

"The Poison Sandwich"

The reporter buries opinion favorable to a candidate between a negative introduction and a negative conclusion—sandwiching it in between, so to speak. This undercuts the favorable opinion, and, if skillfully done, virtually causes it to go unnoticed.

In network coverage, a striking example of this technique can be found on ABC (9/20/2, Anti-Nixon) where the reporter sandwiches Nixon's triumphant reception in Philadelphia between a report on a catastrophe that never occurred and speculation about a failure that may not occur.

"The Sugar Sandwich"

This is the reverse technique—of sandwiching a negative opinion in between a favorable introduction and conclusion. This device has already been mentioned in the study. It was used by *U.S. News & World Report* to bury Carswell's past history of racism.

For an illustration, see CBS (10/10/8, Pro-Humphrey) where the suggestion that Humphrey is a manipulating politician is sandwiched in between sentiment and poesy.

Inflation of Detail

The reporter inflates and elaborates on a negative detail, giving the impression that a candidate is widely disliked where this is not necessarily the case.

A striking example of this is to be found on ABC (10/22/6, Anti-Nixon) where extensive discussion of a small piece of trash thrown at Nixon takes up *half* of a story on his Ohio campaign tour—a tour declared successful by CBS and NBC.

This same technique is incessantly used against Wallace, who as the campaign progresses is hardly visible, so intent are the networks on recording flying tin cans, rocks and apple cores.

MISCELLANEOUS TECHNIQUES

There is, finally, a miscellaneous collection of editorializing techniques, which are usually used in association with others. There are four of them:

Overgeneralization

The reporter makes a sweeping and groundless generalization about hundreds of thousands of millions of people—supported by no polls or studies. (This is usually but not always associated with mind-reading.)

> *Example*: A reporter states that the "majority" of Americans are willing to "pay any price" in freedom to preserve law and order. (NBC 10/4/7, Anti–Middle Class.)

Unproved Theory

The reporter states an unproved theory or a controversial hypothesis in the social sciences as if it were proven scientific fact —to support one side of a controversy.

> *Example*: The reporter states as a fact that law-abiding, middle-class white citizens are responsible for the actions of individual black criminals—when this is a highly disputed doctrine in the social sciences, not to mention the law. (NBC 9/18/4, Anti–Middle Class.)

Leading Question

The reporter asks a question of an interviewee which contains an opinion on a controversial issue.

> *Example*: A reporter states that Humphrey is a "drag" on George McGovern's "kite," in an attempt to get Senator McGovern to criticize Humphrey. McGovern declines. (NBC 10/1/4, Anti-Humphrey.)

> *Example*: A reporter states that all Americans are a "subconsciously" violent people, in an attempt to get Ramsey Clark to confirm it. Clark declines. (NBC 9/18/1, Anti–Middle Class.)

One-Word Editorial

The reporter uses one word or a phrase to communicate a rapid endorsement or criticism of an individual, group or position.

> *Example*: Before George Ball's violent attack on Nixon as "tricky, cynical, shallow and irresponsible," the reporter describes Ball's attack as "pithy." (NBC 9/27/5, Anti-Nixon.)

This list is not all encompassing. There are unquestionably other editorializing techniques in existence—and in use at the networks. But these are the ones that were used with sufficient frequency as to consider them the basic editorializing devices.

Of all these techniques, "mind-reading" and the omission-evasion-suppression category are the most frequent and potent. By the means of one, the reporter expresses his views. By means of the other, he keeps opposing views off the air. A revolution in network reporting could occur overnight if these two techniques alone were abandoned.

It would be an error to conclude from this that network news reporters have maliciously invented these devices to delude an unwary public. They have invented none of them. These are standard slanting techniques in use in the press, and they have probably been in existence in partisan communication since the beginning of time. Indeed, there are probably hundreds of other means of slanting and distorting communication beyond those I have named.

It would also be an error to conclude that these techniques have any intrinsic tie to liberal or left-oriented content. They do not. They are as useful to a partisan or evasive journalist working for the John Birch *American Opinion* or for the conservative *U.S.*

News & World Report as they are to network liberals—and, indeed, partisan and evasive journalists of the right employ these very methods.

Nonetheless, this is a study of the network news product—not of the full spectrum of the press—and the network product in particular is skewed, editorially, to the liberal-left. Whatever this editorial opinion is called; whether it is identified or not; whether it is overt, covert, or a mixture of the two; whether it is 18% of total opinion as at NBC, 31% as at CBS, or 48% as at ABC: it is present on the air in significant quantities.

It is a serious contributor to the total bias picture.

"The Parallel
Principle"

What now are we to make of the striking contrast between the amounts of editorial opinion to be found at the three networks? A range of 18% to 48% is enormous. This great diversity is clearly a function of different network policies and practices—the practices not necessarily reflecting the policies. What is most significant about this diversity in the role of editorial opinion is that it results in no meaningful difference in the bias patterns on all three networks.

What makes this identity of bias possible? Why does NBC, with only 18% editorial opinion and 82% opinion from other sources, end up with the same general bias as ABC whose reporters opine 48% of the time—almost as much as all other sources combined?

To understand how this can occur, one must know the relationship between editorial opinion and the opinion of all other sources on the air.

In Appendix O, the reader will find four tables giving the total number of words of reporter opinion on the candidates and the issues, and the total number of words of opinion from other sources on the candidates and the issues. These tables will allow him to make detailed comparisons of opinion totals and bias ratios.

Here, I will simply present the conclusions to be reached from such a comparison. It is this: most of the time there is no difference whatever between the political slant of the reporters on a subject, and the political slant of the others whom we hear voicing their opinions on the air.

It is important here to remember who those "others" are. They are a nationwide collection of: Presidential and Vice Presidential candidates of the Republican, Democratic and Independent Parties; politicians of all parties; individual members of the public and spokesmen for organized national groups; and a worldwide collection of foreign statesmen and foreign groups. Those I symbolically refer to as "others" stand, in fact, for the nation—and the world. Nonetheless, the selective process, on the three networks, is such that, most of the time, the entire nation and the entire world ends up predominantly reflecting the political slant of the reporters!

To what degree do they reflect this slant? Here are the essential facts to be culled from the comparison of the four tables in Appendix O.

There are three networks and 13 issues—consequently, there are 39 situations in which the bias of reporters and the bias of "others" could come out on the same political side. How do they come out?

> • In *two* of these situations, ABC (Pro-Viet Cong) and CBS (Anti-Middle Class) presented *editorial opinion only*.

> • In *three* of these situations, CBS (Anti-Liberals), and ABC and NBC (Anti-Violent Radicals) presented the *opinions of "others" only*.

> • In *nine* of these situations, ABC (The Left; White Middle Class); ABC and NBC (Liberals); CBS (Wallace, Humphrey); and ABC, CBS and NBC ("Demon-

strators"): *the bias of "others" contradicted the bias of the reporters.*

• And in *twenty-five* of these situations, *the bias of "others" is the same as the bias of the reporters.*

To wit:

Parallel Bias

	THE BIAS OF REPORTERS	THE BIAS OF "OTHERS"
Nixon ABC CBS NBC	Against Nixon	Against Nixon
Humphrey ABC NBC	For Humphrey Against Humphrey	For Humphrey Against Humphrey
Wallace ABC NBC	Against Wallace	Against Wallace
U.S. Vietnam Policy ABC CBS NBC	Against U.S. VN Policy	Against U.S. VN Policy
U.S. Bombing Halt Policy ABC CBS NBC	Against U.S. BH Policy	Against U.S. BH Policy
Black Militants ABC CBS NBC	For Black Militants	For Black Militants
White Middle Class NBC	Against White Middle Class	Against White Middle Class

	THE BIAS OF REPORTERS	THE BIAS OF "OTHERS"
Conservatives ABC ⎤ CBS ⎦— NBC	Against Conservatives	Against Conservatives
Left CBS ⎤— NBC ⎦	For Left	For Left

Parallel Silence

	REPORTERS	OTHERS
Viet Cong NBC ⎤— CBS ⎦	Silent	Silent
Violent Radicals CBS	Silent	Silent

Thus, of the 39 situations in which parallelism is possible, it occurred 25 times—or in 64% of the cases. And in another 5% of the cases, opinion on a subject is restricted to reporters alone.

To state it differently—in 69% of these situations, reporters are either failing to present opinions other than their own, or are so selecting the opinion of "others" that the bias or mutism of those "others" parallels their own.

It is perfectly clear that during the period of this study—the Presidential campaign of 1968—the reporters are loading the decks in favor of their own political sympathies and their own political evasions—in a massive fashion.

These parallels obviously do not represent an accidental occurrence or a curious coincidence that developed during the seven weeks of this study. In the face of any pattern of selectivity that reinforces editorial opinion, and that repeats itself 25 times, on three networks, with roughly equal frequency—7 times at ABC, 8 times at CBS and 10 times at NBC—one can state with certainty that this is an active and institutionalized principle of network selectivity.

I will refer to it, henceforth, as "the Parallel Principle"—namely: *Bias in the selection or exclusion of the opinions of "others" reflects, or runs parallel to editorial bias.*

On the face of it, this fully explains the mysterious identity of the overall bias on all three networks, although the actual quantities of editorial opinion are so widely divergent.

What, however, are we to make of the exceptions to "The Parallel Principle"? What information can we glean from these?

A close inspection of the 12 exceptions (omitting the 2 editorial monopolies) indicates, above all, their spotty and sporadic nature. Seven of them occur in the smallest bodies of opinion: opinion on "violent radicals," the "left," and on "liberals," which have already been identified as politically illusory and heavily distorted areas. The eighth, on Wallace, a large body of opinion, appears to be random. Why, on CBS, the "others" end up with a pro-Wallace bias, I do not know. It represents neither the bias of CBS, nor the bias of the electorate. It appears to mean nothing.

Only 4 exceptions to "The Parallel Principle" are so politically startling as to require special explanation.

Why do the "others" on CBS come out with an anti-Humphrey bias, when CBS is editorially working hard to elect the Democratic candidate?

And why, above all, do *all three networks* give "others" an anti-"demonstrators" bias—when they are steadily supporting the "demonstrators" editorially? This is a massive violation of "The Parallel Principle"—the only reversal of this principle that occurs in three networks simultaneously, as opposed to the uniform phalanx of 25 parallels in triplicate.

These questions do require explanations—and answers are available.

To begin with Democratic Presidential candidate Humphrey: In one respect, opinion on Humphrey is unique in this study. Here, and here alone, the networks' editorial biases do not resemble each other like peas in a pod as they do on all other major issues.

Where candidate Humphrey is concerned, the networks are split. The internal rift in the Democratic Party world taking place at this time is reflected in network coverage—with reporters dividing into "establishment" pro-Humphrey supporters and New Left anti-Humphrey critics. Thus ABC's editorial opinion is slanted for Humphrey, and so is the opinion of the nation, as the nation is seen on ABC. NBC's editorial bias, on the other hand, is against Humphrey, and so is the nation's, as the nation is seen on NBC. This is, of course, a superb illustration of the ultimate meaning of "The Parallel Principle," namely that editorial bias creates reality in the network's own image.

Only at CBS does the nation not come out on the same side as the reporters. At CBS, total editorial opinion is slanted for Humphrey, but CBS' "others" are slanted against Humphrey.

There is a reason for this, but it cannot be deduced from the statistics or the opinion content. It pertains to individuals. In this study, I have systematically refrained from identifying specific reporters, because my interest is solely in the bias patterns. But at CBS a unique situation prevails: 80% of the pro-Humphrey opinion comes from *one* reporter, stationed primarily in *one* city, who ran a Humphrey campaign of his own on the air. His colleagues, collecting the opinions of "others" across the country did not share his partisan zeal for the old Democratic guard—and the nation, as it appeared on CBS, tended to reflect *their* selective processes.

It is quite clear that internal Democratic Party discord alone caused this violation of "The Parallel Principle" on a major campaign issue—just as it caused the refreshing diversity within and between the networks. Needless to say, when the choice was between Humphrey and Nixon, this diversity vanished and all three networks in chorus favored Humphrey over Nixon. It is exclusively left-of-center diversity.

The other outstanding violation of "The Parallel Principle" is opinion on "demonstrators," the politically anonymous "activists," "militants," "students" and "youth," etc. who took time out from generating campus "unrest" to "heckle" the candidates and express dissent on the war.

Here on all three networks the opinion of the "others" who are allowed to speak stands in active contradiction to editorial bias. What is more, these "others" carry a strongly *conservative* bias— namely, the advocacy of a law-and-order position and the denunciation of violence.

It is so extraordinary to see a massive conservative bias in the opinion of "others," let alone such a bias on all three networks, that it is worth inspecting this phenomenon even more closely.

On ABC the total number of words of opinion on "demonstrators," including editorial opinion, is quantitatively balanced: 1441 anti, 1401 pro. *But with editorial opinion removed, the bias swings drastically to the conservative or anti-"demonstrator" side: 1024 anti, to 196 pro.* Thus we see that the law-and-order "others" and the reporters have been actively pitted against each other with the reporters holding up most of the pro-"demonstrators" side.

NBC's totals, including editorial opinion, are biased in *favor* of the "demonstrators," 1705 to 1473. *When editorial opinion is removed, the bias reverses itself sharply, shifting to the conservative or anti-"demonstrator" side—1449 to 1076.* Once again, the reportorial opinion had been actively pitted against the conservative "others" but had dominated.

On CBS, by contrast, *the totals on "demonstrators" are consistently biased to the conservative or anti-"demonstrator" side of the issue—both with editorial opinion and without.* Total pro-"demonstrator" opinion, including editorial opinion, is 609; with editorial opinion eliminated, it drops to 240. Total anti-"demonstrator" opinion, including editorial, is 1304; with editorial opinion removed it is 1285. The reporters here, too, were pitted against the law-and-order "others" and had been holding up the pro-"demonstrator" side, but had not dominated.

In this area of coverage, the networks were doing one thing that was absolutely uniform: as I said in Chapter III, all three actually ran a debate. On one side, "establishment figures," many of them candidates, condemned the "demonstrators" and their violence. On the other side, a heavy concentration of reporters defended them.

The networks handled the outcome of the debate in slightly different ways. CBS let the "law-and-order" voices win over the editorial voices. ABC almost matched the law-and-order voices with editorial voices. And NBC editorially out-talked the law-and-order voices. But on all three networks, the basic opinion coverage—the voice of "others"—was pro-"law-and-order."

Why this much generosity suddenly to conservative opinion when editorial opinion was almost consistently on the other side? Two reasons suggest themselves strongly:

1) Many of the "law-and-order" voices were those of candidates. To suppress their views on a major campaign issue was not possible and indeed would have been legally hazardous. Faced with the obligation to run a great deal of "law-and-order" opinion, the three networks did the next best thing: they fought it editorially—with NBC insisting on winning the fight.

2) More importantly, perhaps, it was just a few months after the Chicago riots. The nation had administered a massive reprimand to the networks for supporting violent "demonstrators." And at the time covered by this study, the FCC, an executive commission and two Senate commissions, were investigating charges against the networks on just this subject. It is highly likely that the networks did not wish to court disaster on this very issue by engaging in their usual methods of selectivity—namely, of bolstering up editorial opinion with the similar opinion of "others" and thus minimizing the anti-"demonstrator" position.

Certainly one cannot ascribe the sudden generosity to opposition opinion to a genuine concern for coverage of the "law-and-order" position. The consistent sanctioning of violence, the consistent equation of the "law-and-order" position to racism, "The Mystery of the Missing Radicals," the virtual burial of the issue of radical violence, and the suppression by CBS and NBC of the FBI report on New Left violence forbid such an interpretation.

Nor can this be construed as some kind of sudden impulse to "fairness." Why would the three networks simultaneously succumb to the temptation to be "fair" on one and the same issue in a campaign period when they had so successfully withstood that temptation on all other major issues?

Clearly something most unusual moved the networks to turn over so much air time to the political enemy, and zeal for "fairness" was no part of it. The most plausible hypothesis is: a severe post-Chicago attack of political nerves.

And so much for the exceptions to "The Parallel Principle."

It is enormously revealing that the sporadic, minor exceptions to this principle come almost invariably from areas infested with evasion techniques—and that the two major exceptions to the principle are both functions of highly abnormal political situations: a split within the liberal world, and a subject on which the networks are being investigated by both the executive and legislative branches of government.

The very aberrancy that surrounds these exceptions is itself a testimonial to "The Parallel Principle"—and to the grip it holds over network selectivity. It is clear that only one thing causes any significant divergence from this systematized portrayal of the nation in the image of reporters' biases: political fear.

We can now fully answer the questions we set out to answer in this chapter: How do all networks end up with roughly the same bias pattern, when the editorial roles played by their reporters are so diverse? Why does it not make a jot of political difference that ABC's reporters opine 48% of the time, CBS's 31% of the time, and NBC's only 18% of the time?

The answer is: it does not matter *who* is voicing the opinions—it matters only *what* opinions are being voiced. So long as reporters can choose whose opinions are to be aired, and so long as they are determined to choose them to reinforce their own partisan biases, these reporters can speak or be silent as they please. The results, in bias, will be much the same.

There is a widespread illusion in the United States that if network reporters would stop injecting their own opinions into stories and just let "others" speak, the results would automatically be objective or nonpartisan.

It is a benevolent illusion shared by some newsmen themselves. When James Hagerty was News Chief of ABC some years ago, he claimed that ABC News was seeking to be fair and objective. "We are reporters," he said. "We get interpretations from *other* people and present them. If any one on this network is expressing his own opinions—well, if I catch him, I won't permit it." (*TV Guide,* April 11, 1964.)

As we have seen, "others" are no protection from bias. Indeed, they are the very fountainhead of bias because their views are chosen by reporters, because their views appear in the greatest quantity—and because few viewers are fully aware that when they see men voicing opinions spontaneously before the camera, that these men may simultaneously be reporters' puppets.

In the last analysis, everyone who speaks in a story is the reporter's puppet—with the reporter pulling the strings. Or, more precisely: aiming the camera . . . cutting the film . . . asking the leading questions . . . excerpting the statements . . . editing the final dialogue . . . and writing the final integrative report which weaves a web of fluent words over the cuts, the breaks and the seams . . .

Fortune editor Max Ways declares journalism, by virtue of precisely this type of selectivity and dramatic casting, to be an art form—and this is not metaphoric.

"Others" are to the reporter what characters are to a playwright. They are one of the primary means to his ends. These ends can be a passionate desire to present his best and fairest understanding of a complex truth. They can also be to favor his friends and harm his foes and push a crude party line.

Where we see the repeated use of "The Parallel Principle," we are seeing "party-line" journalism.

Mr. Agnew and "The Silent Majority"

On November 13, 1969, Vice President Spiro Agnew delivered a speech in Des Moines, Iowa. In it, he charged the three networks with being infiltrated with political bias.

The Vice President's major charges, some of which apply retroactively to the period of this study, and all of which pertain to the issues analyzed by the study, can be summarized as follows:

1) Network newsmen reflect the views of a closed, like-minded "provincial" Eastern "establishment."

2) Regarding the Vietnam War: many network reporters are biased against the policies of the United States government—as evidenced by their own opinion and the opinion they select for transmission.

3) Many network reporters are hostile to Richard

Nixon—and some, during the campaign period, were biased against him to the point of slander.

4) Many network reporters were biased during the convention period against Hubert Humphrey and on behalf of the antiwar demonstrators and rioters.

5) Many network reporters are biased in favor of violent protesters and demonstrators, black and white—giving opportunity of expression to these and not to the nonviolent.

6) The networks are giving "more than equal time" to "that minority of Americans who specialize in attacking the United States, its institutions, its citizens."

It is apparent that the findings of this study generally support Mr. Agnew's charges where they apply to the period of the study, and that they support Mr. Agnew's other charges, in principle.

The response to Mr. Agnew's speech was complex and came from many sources. The most important was the explosive response from the broad American public, known as "The Silent Majority."

What were that "Silent Majority's" attitudes to network news and to Mr. Agnew's charges? And how did the media report on them? Both questions can be answered simultaneously by reviewing both the public's reactions—as revealed in mail surveys and polls—and the media's interpretations of them.

It is highly illuminating to follow the reports in strict chronological succession, and, for context, to start more than a year *before* the Agnew speech . . . with the public's indictment of the networks' coverage of the antiwar riots at the Chicago convention of 1968.

At the time of the Chicago riots, a clear majority of the public found TV news coverage biased in favor of the radical rioters, and against the police. Poll results ranged from 54% to 70%—indicating a massive outpouring of condemnation of the networks. From that time on, mail protests to the networks were voluminous, with the public letter-writing unceasingly charging network TV news with demonstrating sympathy for the violent radicals.

More than one year later—about two months before Mr. Agnew's speech—a Louis Harris poll was taken to check on these attitudes to TV news. As reported in *Time* Magazine on September 5, 1969, Mr. Harris' findings indicated that this anger had not yet abated in the public; and that a substantial number of the angry were the highly educated:

- "By a ratio of nearly 3 to 1 viewers believe that the TV camera can lie, *a view that runs strongest among professional people, the college-educated, and the young.*"

- "When asked to give examples of unfair television coverage, one out of three mentioned the Democratic Convention in Chicago and 21% cited race riots."

- Nearly half of those surveyed say television news was "too full of violence."

It was against this backdrop of simmering public antagonism that Mr. Agnew delivered his indictment of network bias on November 13, 1969. On November 20, 1969, a week after Mr. Agnew's speech, *The New York Times* reported that the mail was running 24 to 1 in support of Mr. Agnew's speech against networks. The mail count shows that 38,736 supported Mr. Agnew's charges and 1,692 disagreed. The mail and telephone responses as tallied by the networks and their affiliated stations across the country confirmed these results: Mr. Agnew's speech had triggered a national explosion.

Immediately, the press started to interpret the response in terms antagonistic to the public. On NET in New York on November 24, 1969, Norman Isaacs, President of the American Society of Newspaper Editors, declared that a substantial percentage of those who were charging the networks with bias were anti-Semites:

The sad and frightening thing to me is the sick mail

. . . [it] is vicious and venomous. And it's my first experience with a volume of mail of this kind that refers flatly to the Jew-owned and Jew-dominated medium of communication and the open demand for censorship by government.

Four days later, on November 28, 1969, under the title "The Voices of the Silent Majority," James Reston in *The New York Times* developed the charge of anti-Semitism and added racism and anti-Communism to it—a curious constellation of evils:

> One doubts that [Mr. Nixon] intended to arouse the old back lash extremists on the right, but with the help of the Vice President he has apparently done so. For the crusade against the "Eastern snobs" has not only aroused support for his Vietnam policy but revived the always latent anti–New York feelings in the country, and this in turn has produced some ugly anti-Negro and anti-Semitic and anti-Communist reactions . . .

Mr. Reston added: "This is not a major theme of the letters coming into this office, but it is clearly an element in the controversy." And he chose to devote a good part of the remainder of his column to this "nonmajor" theme.

About ten days later, the voice of the public was heard again. On December 1, 1969, Lou Harris released the results of another nationwide poll—with the following findings, reported in his column in *The New York Post:*

> • By 67 to 14%, most Americans gave Agnew credit for "having the courage to speak out against radicals, blacks and students where others don't dare."

> • Agnew was supported by 62% of those who had voted for Nixon, by 46% of those who had voted for Wallace, and by 27% of those who had voted for Humphrey.

> • On an average Agnew was supported by 40% of the public, as opposed to 42% who opposed him.

In other words, Mr. Agnew's bias charges were supported by approximately one-half the country, including 62% of the Nixon vote, meaning once again, a substantial segment of the most highly educated people in the country.

And once again came a wave of media attacks on the public—with *Time* Magazine, on December 19, 1969, reintroducing the theme of anti-Semitism. In the lead story of that issue, *Time* said:

> Several newspapers report a greater volume of critical mail than at any time since the McCarthy period. Many of the letters are unexpectedly heavy with vitriol . . . a significant number reflecting a disturbing increase in overt anti-Semitism.
>
> NBC said last week that it had received more than 500 anti-Jewish letters; the *New York Times* reported a dozen such letters . . .[1]

And again came the voice of the public: On January 19, 1970, *Newsweek* Magazine reported on the Gallup Poll's findings as follows:

> • The country was "almost evenly divided" in its views of TV coverage.
>
> • 42% thought that TV news tended "to favor one side" of the political and social issues—many believed it to be the liberal side.
>
> • *Distrust of TV "increased with the amount of education the respondents had received."*
>
> • *53% of those with college training considered television news slanted.*

For the third time the message had been beamed to the press that a substantial majority of the educated citizens of America were part of that "Silent Majority." And for the third time, the press

---

[1]The Reston column, it appears, was based on only twelve letters.

chose to ignore that message. Again, it launched a counterattack on that public:

On March 16, 1970, Gloria Steinem in *New York* Magazine reintroduced the interpretation of racism and anti-Semitism: "As for Agnew, writers and television analysts who criticize him get some flavor of his support from their mail. Pete Hamill, Tom Wicker, Walter Cronkite and even one Agnew column I wrote for the supposedly 'Eastern liberal' readership of this magazine have elicited record numbers of letters with words like 'kike,' 'homo,' 'Jew bastard,' 'nigger lover,' and 'Commie' in them . . . if Agnew wants to know who some of his most loyal supporters are, he should read our mail."

This contrapuntal "dialogue" between the voice of the public and the voice of the liberal-left press tells us this: that long before —and long after—information was available about the highly educated nature of many of Agnew's supporters—that they included 53% of all college graduates—the New York liberal-left press, as well as representatives of CBS and NBC, were actively pushing the concept that those in the public who charged network bias were McCarthyite–anti-Semitic–racist–Neanderthals.

I have seen none of the protest mail about network bias received by those who have so insistently publicized this "fascist" stereotype. But I have read every word of the protest mail about network bias that arrived at *TV Guide* in response to a *TV Guide* interview, "There *Is* a Network News Bias"—an interview which will be discussed in the next chapter. The interviewee supported and developed on Mr. Agnew's charges. These letters, which I have on file, overwhelmingly support Agnew, and they absolutely violate the "fascist" stereotype. On the contrary, they support the Harris findings of 1969 and the Gallup findings of 1970 to the effect that awareness of bias grows stronger in the highly educated: Only one is in less than perfectly literate English. The writers demonstrate respectable to excellent use of the language. A substantial proportion appear to be professionals. Not one expresses racist attitudes. Not one expresses anti-Semitic attitudes. Not one expresses ugly threats.

What these letters do express is *suffering*. One *TV Guide* editor comments of these letters: "Their outstanding characteristic seems to be a tremendous sense of being alone in the conclusions they've drawn as if no one else sees what they see."

It is mail from human beings who are repeatedly being asked to doubt the evidence of their senses.

There is no reason to suspect that *TV Guide,* a national publication with thirty million readers, has not received a legitimate cross section of the views of those Americans who charge the networks with liberal-left bias.

It is true that there are racists and anti-Semites in the United States. And some were doubtless writing letters. It is nonetheless quite obvious that the media were selectively focusing on such mail and were automatically generating the "mindless racist" stereotype to account for the public's bias charges. *They were "discovering" in the mail identically the same "mindless racist" stereotype we find in network editorial opinion on "the white middle class majority," "white America," and "the American public."*

This stereotype appears to have axiomatic status for many in the liberal-left world. Before Mr. Agnew ever became the Vice President—during the 1968 campaign period—Nathan Perlmutter, Associate Director of the American Jewish Committee, declared in *The New York Times* Magazine of October 6, 1968, that "liberal intellectuals," once the leaders of middle-class whites, were now "scorning them as 'white racists,' 'bigots' and miscellaneous euphemisms for 'honky'." He charged that the "white racist" stereotype was itself racist, and warned that an inevitable anger over such abuse was building in the white middle class, which might manifest itself at the polls.

Long after Mr. Agnew's speech—also in *The New York Times* Magazine, September 13, 1970—socialist Michael Harrington declared that the "chic stereotype" of the American worker as a "reactionary (or neo-fascist) slob" was false. And Mr. Harrington, who also was confronting an electoral period, warned, "If the middle class reformers persist in their barely concealed contempt for working people they may help drive the union men to the right."

It is obvious that this same "chic" honky-fascist stereotype was deeply imbedded in network news coverage—and was then used by the "liberal intellectuals" and "reformers" to interpret the indignant responses to that very news coverage.

This conceptual circularity had a crippling effect on "liberal intellectuals'" understanding of the nationwide reaction to Mr. Agnew's speech. In fact, they perceived nothing but their own stereotyped thought.

On January 9, 1970, a Harris poll appeared in *Life* Magazine. It offered a striking contrast to the media's "honky-fascist" view of "the public." It portrayed a complex and changing picture of American society in its racist and nonracist strains. To cite just a few statistics on the subject of benevolent racial attitudes alone, which are shared by blacks and by whites: 73% of all Americans say that blacks need to find their own identity as a people. 75% of whites and 75% of blacks do not believe that black militants represent what Negroes want from this country. 59% of whites accept black people as neighbors. 58% of whites and 65% of blacks share a common Horatio Alger value system. 90% favor expanded job training for disadvantaged groups.

And Bayard Hooper who wrote the Harris Report, says: "Despite the racist turmoil of the last five years, there seems to be a solid and growing sympathy for the goal of racial equality."

It is perfectly obvious that the liberals' racist-Neanderthal caricature does not accurately reflect the variegated body that is "white America." If "the public's" response to network coverage and to the Agnew bias speech is *not* the venomous outpouring of an undifferentiated honky-fascist horde, what is it?

Kenneth Crawford, in *Newsweek* (January 26, 1970), offers a more rational alternative:

> In appealing for the support of a "silent majority" and repudiating "effete snobs" of the Northeastern intellectual-academic-journalistic complex, [Vice President Agnew] pressed an emotional release button of surprising potential . . . It develops that millions of middle-

class people, blue-collar to upper-suburban, feel that
they have been patronized too long by a self-celebrated
cultural elite. They may have got this notion from journalists who keep calling them know-nothings . . .

And a *Wall Street Journal* editorial (reprinted with permission)
on January 12, 1970, makes a similar point:

[Mr. Agnew's] popularity among the masses . . . is
mirrored by apoplectic convulsions among the elite. No
doubt the elite generally views the Vice President the
way a friend of ours does, as rallying "the rednecks"
against "the thinking people." . . . The phraseology is
unconsciously revealing. The heart of the Agnew phenomenon is precisely that a class has sprung up in this
nation that considers itself uniquely qualified ("the
thinking people"), and is quite willing to dismiss the
ordinary American with utter contempt ("the rednecks").
Mr. Agnew has merely supplied a focus for the inevitable reaction to this arrogance.

This type of analysis is strongly supported by the findings of this
study. If one reads them, one does not need to resort to prefabri-
cated stereotypes to understand the anger of half of America over
network bias.

It is reasonable to suppose that much of this anger is coming
from:

• Those whose intelligence has been repeatedly insulted
by network newsmen.

• Those whose character and moral status have been repeatedly insulted by network newsmen.

• Those who have been insulted as a class by network
newsmen.

• Those who have been insulted as a race by network
newsmen.

- Those who have been insulted as voters by network newsmen.

- Those whose Presidential candidates were dealt with unfairly by network newsmen.

- Those whose political opinion was scarcely allowed a foothold on the airwaves by network newsmen.

- Those who are outraged by the repeated sanctioning of violence by network newsmen.

- Those who cannot tolerate the antagonistic stereotypes directed at the majority of the country by network newsmen.

In fact, on the basis of the findings of this study, it would be a miracle if a substantial portion of the nation were not indignant at network newsmen on grounds quite irrelevant to the race problem.

The voice of the "Silent Majority" is still being heard. One year after the Agnew speech on October 12, 1970, *Broadcast* Magazine published the details of the speech public-opinion analyst Louis Harris delivered before the International Radio and Television Society. Mr. Harris reported:

> Consistently for the past nine months a majority of 57% of Americans are prepared to go along with the criticism leveled against television . . . by the Vice President . . .

And one month later, a Gallup poll conducted by *Newsweek* Magazine revealed that the charges of bias were still strongest in the most highly educated groups—with college graduates agreeing with Agnew by a ratio of 3 to 2.

The belief, in the "Silent Majority," that network news is biased has held firm for several years. As of this time of writing, it can be said, at a minimum, that the problem is unresolved.

Minority Charges of Bias

The networks have generally allowed the protests of half the country to be classed as "racist" and "anti-Semitic." They have also made known the fact that they are being attacked by the minorities: that they are called "racists" by blacks and are charged with "censorship" by radicals.

This is widely offered by the networks as evidence that they are really "neutral"—a loose supposition being that the attacks by blacks "cancel out" the attacks by whites and that the attacks by the left "cancel out" attacks by conservatives. This supposition does not hold up under even the most superficial investigation.

The findings of this study make it abundantly clear why blacks and radicals would be extremely hostile to the networks and why this does not cancel out the bias charges of the more conservative half of the country. The black protest against the networks and the radical protest against the networks are of drastically different types and must be explained separately.

BLACK CHARGES

There is nothing startling about the widespread black view that network television is racist. Network news does not report on black Americans. It reports most often on a stereotype called "the black" or "the Negro." Definitionally, a stereotype about a racial group is racist thinking. In 1968 that stereotype is a criminal black, a thug-"revolutionary" hybrid, who steals and kills and shrieks for enormous sums of money, demands power and threatens to burn American cities and kill white Americans.

Virtually nothing but this stereotype is covered by the networks. As the reader of this study can see by turning back to the summaries of opinion on black militants, the overwhelming bulk of such opinion both pro and con links blacks to crime, violence, looting, murder and arson and presents the most extreme black power advocates and separatists as the voice of the blacks. Where the complex, multi-class, morally, intellectually and politically differentiated black community should be, there is a void.

On June 1, 1968, four months before the period of this study began, *TV Guide* writer Neil Hickey published a revealing report of the failure of Detroit's local TV stations and network affiliates to cover life in the black community. He interviewed a variety of black citizens; the managing editor of a black publication, religious leaders, sociologists and urban officials, and over and over again his black informants charged TV with being racist and made the following points:

- That normal black existence is never covered.

- That the television cameras only show up when a black man steals or rapes or kills—or to film rioting, looting and violence.

- That TV creates its own black "leaders" to feed the newsmen the line they want.

Richard Marks, the secretary-director of the city's Commission on Community Relations, thus described Detroit TV's three basic stereotype-Negro news stories: (1) the 101-year-old ex-slave interview; (2) the interview with odd colorful ghetto characters; (3) the riot, arson and looting stories.

On network TV during the campaign of 1968, the black stereotype was not even that diversified. And the identical racist charges that Detroit blacks made about local coverage can be made about network national coverage.

"Normal" black existence—a vision which would stress the human values shared by blacks and whites alike—is totally missing. Not once was there an opinion from a black citizen who revealed that he repudiated parasitism, that he shared the Protestant "work ethic," that he valued individual responsibility and personal effort.

And yet at least one network had unusual insight into what Lou Harris calls the "Horatio Alger" values of an overwhelming majority of the black community. Nathan Perlmutter, in the middle of the campaign, reported in *The New York Times* (October 6, 1968) that CBS-TV had commissioned the Opinion Research Group to do a survey on black attitudes and that some of the results had been startling. When asked why Negroes had not made more progress, the black respondents violated liberal mythology:

> Only 45%, a figure stunningly less than would be expected in view of the liberal rhetoric, blame discrimination. What should be even more disconcerting to liberals who mistakenly view the black community as monolithic, is that fully 22% of the black interviewees said that Negroes had not worked hard enough. Another 18% answered "both."

This information—that 40% of the New York black community thought that insufficient effort had been exerted by many Negroes to achieve educational and professional goals—clearly suggests that some blacks are more enterprising and responsible than others. This was apparently so "disconcerting" to the "liberals" at CBS that this network did not choose to be guided by this information in its selective processes. No blacks with such high and self-demanding standards ever got near a CBS camera or that of any other network.

What was shatteringly missing from black coverage was the essence of "normalcy" in the United States: a vision of black
achievement. Not once during this period did we hear opinions
from black scholars, doctors, engineers, poets, businessmen, magazine editors—from the black middle class with its many dignified,
sophisticated, intellectual and able people. Not once did we hear
the opinions of law-abiding, honorable and noncriminal black workers. And only once, on NBC, despite the three networks' intensive
coverage of black militants, did we hear the ideology of black-militant *intellectuals*. The only black of major achievement covered
during the period of this study was a Negro general, Frederick Ellison Davis, briefly interviewed by NBC on the occasion of his pro-
motion (NBC 9/17/18).

Because the "normal" range of black existence was excised from
the screen, what was missing above all was a vision of black diversity—of individuals with different personalities, different minds,
different moral qualities, different levels of knowledge, different
levels of aspiration and achievement. This view of blacks as real
human beings who range, like whites, from illiterate, mindless
thugs to men of tremendous intellectual, spiritual and social distinction, is totally absent from network news coverage. By creating
a black stereotype and a criminal stereotype at that, the networks
were reinforcing the essence of race prejudice—a negative, indeed
degraded, view of blacks.

And this is not the worst of it. Because of the selective pattern,
and the obsessional focus on black criminality, we did not hear a
word in seven weeks from the "normal" black community *which
steadfastly repudiates black criminals and asks for protection from
these criminals.*

In his famous memo to President Nixon, published in *The New
York Times,* March 1, 1970, Daniel Moynihan paints a picture of
the urgency of the problem of black crime for the black community. He writes:

> It is the existence of this lower class, with its high
> rates of crime, dependency, and general disorderliness,

that causes nearby whites (that is to say working whites, the liberals are all in the suburbs) to fear Negroes and to seek by various ways to avoid and constrain them.

It is this group that black extremists use to threaten white society with the prospect of mass arson and pillage. *It is also this group that terrorizes and plunders the stable elements of the Negro community—trapped by white prejudice in the slums, and forced to live cheek by jowl with a murderous slum population.* (italics mine)

During the entire campaign period, network TV refrained from giving any significant air time to the view that American blacks are the chief victims of black crime. It was, unfortunately, a law-and-order viewpoint, hence unacceptable. Network newsmen did not appear to know that by their maudlin attitude to black criminals, they were betraying the noncriminal blacks who were the victims of these criminals. They also did not appear to know that this was the crudest and most time-honored expression of racism.

In October, 1969, Max Ways, a member of *Fortune*'s board of editors, wrote:

From the end of the post-Civil War Reconstruction period to the mid-fifties, American journalism was virtually silent on the subject of how black Americans lived. Lynchings were reported and deplored, as were race riots and the more sensational crimes committed by blacks against whites. *But crimes by blacks against blacks were regularly ignored as a matter of explicit news policy on most newspapers. This was symptomatic of an implicit journalistic assumption that blacks were not a significant part of the American scene.* Journalism bears a considerable share of the responsibility for white society's disengagement from the Negro and his problems. (italics mine)

Network TV continued in 1968 to hold this assumption of the "insignificance" of crimes by blacks against blacks. Murdered blacks, raped blacks, robbed blacks, blacks whose homes were destroyed by roving arsonists did not arouse network newsmen's pity. They were too busy airing unproved sociological alibis for the murderers, the rapists, the thieves and the arsonists.

Indeed, network editorial opinion insistently argued that "law and order" was an expression of "racism"—thus tacitly equating crime with blacks and reinforcing the criminal stereotype.

This was not the view of most American Negroes who are themselves opposed to violence and crime and who resent network TV's incapacity to make moral differentiations—its incapacity to perceive the distinction between an honorable black and a black thug. As Whitney Young put it (*Time,* April 4, 1969): "Whites seem to be able to distinguish their own crackpots from the rest, but when it is a riot of blacks, it is all just blacks."

Vincent Baker, parliamentarian for the New York Branch of NAACP, writes in *National Review* (August 25, 1970):

> For the great majority of Negroes in our big cities, law and order is not a code phrase for white racism. It is a crying necessity, for we live under unbelievable terror by day and night. We hold no brief for crime or criminals. We are their chief victims. Help from our fellow Americans would be welcome.

And he adds, ironically: "We even believe that *non*-criminals have civil rights."

Such statements could have been aired in profusion on network television during the 1968 campaign by black citizens—totally destroying the criminal stereotype—but there was not one in seven weeks.

Network news betrayed most Negroes in yet another way: by stereotyping them all as followers of black militants who were calling for "separatism" and demanding funds to set up "black nations." The networks explicitly described such separatists as "black leaders" without qualification: and NBC indeed declared that these attitudes were representative of contemporary "black thought."

This was not true, and it was not a favor to most black Americans, who do not want "separatism" and do not support the threats and blackmailing demands for the financing of a separate Negro nation. And it is not the old and tired Uncle Toms who repudiate this, as is being suggested. In 1968—the year of the campaign—Lou Harris reported that "92% of black students, including the most militant, still favor integration." (*Time,* April 4, 1969.)

Howard K. Smith on April 30, 1969, referred to this poll and said on the airwaves: "A Lou Harris poll says that 92% of Negroes want integration but the few who want separatism dominate—supported by the liberals."

Whitney Young was more specific about who was building up the separatists. He pointed his finger at the press. He was quoted by *Time* (April 4, 1969) as saying: "Some leaders are followed by 7 Negroes and 70 screaming reporters."

This morbid quest of the press for "black leaders"—to the point that publicity-seeking frauds in the black community have now gone into the "leader" business—is, of course, a racist phenomenon in itself. It rests on the tacit premise that all blacks are as one and that a single voice can speak for them—a notion held only by people who perceive blacks as a mob of faceless black sheep and assume there must be a bellwether.

To postulate further that all blacks are revolutionary and that violent fanatics are their "voices" is a still further step away from complex reality. It is, in fact, the expression of a symbolic deduction:

> Whites oppress blacks.
> Blacks feel rage.
> ∴. Any enraged black speaks for all.

As a symbol it has a certain validity. Carl Rowan, a black journalist, speaking at the American Newspaper Publishers Convention in New York on April 21, 1970, said that Stokely Carmichael, Bobby Seale and Eldridge Cleaver differ from the ordinary black citizen in "degree": "Their well of bitterness runs a bit deeper than does that of the average black. Their cup of hope is considerably emptier than is that of the average black. Their rage has produced some irrationalities that lead them to believe their own rhetoric of violence and sometimes engage in acts of self-destruction. But I guarantee you that in every ghetto of this city, every black man believes some of what Stokely Carmichael has to say."

But differences of degree are important, and Mr. Rowan describes this coverage as unrepresentative. "I will agree with you that Stokely Carmichael is not representative of the mass of American blacks in that they all want to go out and blow something up . . . I think [the men in broadcasting and the press] see Stokely Carmichael as a symptom of a bigger sickness with which they believe the nation has got to deal."

At best, network TV is portraying a "symptom" or, more precisely, it is putting symbolic psychodrama on the air with Stokely Carmichael—or in 1968 Eldridge Cleaver—playing the Enraged Black Id. It may be fascinating drama but it is dangerously faulty journalism. To portray Eldridge Cleaver, a real human being with the record of a criminal psychopath who screams compulsively about murdering real people, about exploding real buildings, and setting real cities on fire, as a "leader" of all American blacks, is factually false. And to fail to portray the black majority as opposed to such crime and violence, as significantly less embittered, as significantly more hopeful, is to compound this factual falsity.

Last year, a Lou Harris poll was published in *Time* Magazine on April 6, 1970. It documented the complex mixture of bitterness and hope described by Mr. Rowan, and it revealed the magnitude of the difference in degree between the majority of the blacks and the most fanatic militants:

> In view of the long and unyielding list of grievances, it is noteworthy that the majority still rely on orthodox methods of working within the system. When asked to assess the effectiveness of four different types of black leadership, a majority of blacks make the distinction that although militants may build up black pride, they are not necessarily the most effective. At the top of the list are "elected black officials," cited by 71% as "very effective." They are followed by "civil rights leaders,

such as the N.A.A.C.P.," viewed as "very effective" by 67%, although by only 56% of the under-21 group. Behind them are "black ministers and religious leaders," given a "very effective" rating by 56%. At the bottom of the list—despite "pride" expressed in the Panthers in another context—are "leaders of black militant groups." They are given a "very effective" mark by only 29%, though an additional 29% say that they are "somewhat effective."

A chart appears with this story, "Whom Do Blacks Respect?" *At the top of the list,* with the most massive percentages, are those individuals and groups who work to solve problems within the system: the NAACP; SCLC; Cleveland Mayor Carl Stokes; Fayette, Mississippi Mayor Charles Evers; NAACP Director Roy Wilkins; the National Urban League; Justice Thurgood Marshall.[1] *At the bottom of the list* are: Eldridge Cleaver, Stokely Carmichael, the Black Panthers, Bobby Seale, Elijah Muhammed.

The Harris poll also tells us that 84% of all blacks are opposed

---

[1] Such moderate black leaders were virtually nonexistent in the news coverage of the period studied—a characteristic omission which these leaders have bitterly protested. In the October 1968 issue of *Crisis,* the organ of the NAACP, Clarence Mitchell, director of the NAACP Washington Bureau, charges the networks with "biased and vindictive" coverage of the Democratic convention and with active prejudice against the moderate Civil Rights leaders and their achievements. He writes: "For this writer, there was high drama and great fulfillment of the American dream . . . Almost all of the colored persons from the South could boast of impressive records in the fight for civil rights. Yet, somehow, all of this was played down by NBC and CBS. These networks chose, instead, to feature . . . Negroes who were attacking the Johnson-Humphrey team. One colored delegate who attempted to burn his admission card was given preferred treatment. It is ironic that, in a political convention that nominated the most dedicated of fighters for civil rights and was attended by more Negro delegates than any other, there would be so much emphasis on discord and division in the news media-account . . . It appeared that the surest way to be on camera was to try to disrupt the convention while wearing either hippy or African attire."

to the use of political violence—59% opposed to it save in a
hypothetical situation "when all else has failed"; and 25% believing
that violence should be avoided at all cost."

Finally, the report reveals a strong element of hope:

> All of the bitterness and frustration notwithstanding,
> blacks in America express strong confidence that life is
> improving for them and will improve further in the days
> ahead. Sixty-four percent feel that things are "getting
> better than they were four to five years ago." Why? Sev-
> enty-seven percent say that "more blacks being admit-
> ted to college" has given them a great deal of hope;
> 70% cite "new kinds of jobs opening up for blacks" as
> a major cause of optimism; 63% see "great hope" in
> what they believe is the "rising racial pride among black
> people"; and 63% observe the same in the "increase in
> black-owned businesses."

It is clear that network selectivity, at the time of this study, is
rigorously excluding such a vision of moderation and optimism
from its coverage. Specifically, it is excluding the black middle
class. Harvard Professor James Q. Wilson, former Director of The
Joint Center for Urban Studies of MIT and Harvard, writing in
New York Magazine (April 27, 1970) describes this group as "the
upwardly mobile and the newly created middle class" who has
made "striking economic progress" in past years, whose youngest
group (up to age 24) now earns 99% of white income and has
virtual economic parity with whites; the group that has been moving out of the ghettos at a breakneck pace between 1964 and 1969
in the fastest-growing population movement in the country.

If this is the group being excluded by network coverage, what selective pattern then is producing the thug-"revolutionary" stereotype? The answer is very simple: the networks are electing to cover
only the lowest class of blacks in the inner cities, along with their
alleged spokesmen.

These are the blacks whom Professor Wilson describes as "the
most deprived, the least mobile, and the most pathological"; "who

increasingly live in certain neighborhoods, where, free from the constraints of a stable working class population, and envious of the progress of others who have 'made it,' they prey on one another or escape into the empty world of drugs."

These blacks are the ones that Daniel Moynihan describes as the class "with the high rate of crime, dependency . . . *the group that black extremists use to threaten white society with the prospect of mass arson and pillage.*" (italics mine)

It is actually this alliance of violent black demagogues and the pathological-criminal element in the black world that network TV has elected to portray to America as "the black." It is from this alliance that the thug-"revolutionary" comes.

By some irrational definition of "news," a surge of striking economic and social progress on the part of the blacks after a long and blighted history is not included in network coverage of this period! Only the state of the "pathological" is defined as "news."

If one translates this morbid sociological-selective pattern into a psychological-selective pattern, one gets a disturbing result: Network selectivity tends to *exclude* black effort, black struggle, black courage, black resiliency, black strength, black growth, black progress, black hope, black benevolence and, above all, black intelligence—all the qualities of humanity as opposed to bestiality. Network selectivity excludes every element that might teach those who do not yet know it that blacks are men.

Network selectivity has principally allowed into its camera range parasitism, dependency, hostility, spite, malice and mindlessness. It is *this* which network men describe as "black pride"! And even more grotesquely, it is precisely this dangerous violence of the pathological thugs which network men are covertly sanctioning and glamorizing.

The tragic irony is that even the most extreme black demagogues are afflicted by this antihuman vision: the Black Panthers' most impassioned cry of protest against network coverage is that they are not portrayed as thinking beings, with philosophies, plans and programs.

The fact is that while affecting to be deeply concerned with "the black," network news coverage has given white Americans no insights into black dignity or achievement, and few insights into the magnitude of black pain. By their selective process, reporters have worked *against* generating empathy for blacks. To respond empathetically to a man's pain, one must, at a minimum, perceive a man.

"The black" on network TV, in 1968, is as intense a selective distortion as is the fascist-honky "white American"—against whom he is used as a terrifying threat. They are two malevolent caricatures—both artificially divorced from the full context of the American race problem.

It is not at all surprising that black resentment of the networks runs deep, even though the networks used the black stereotype as a bludgeon with which to beat "the white middle class." There are no contradictions between the charges of angry middle-class blacks that network coverage is racist, and the charges of angry middle-class whites that the networks are involved in a covert coalition with criminals and violent militants. Both charges are true.

The tragic fact is that the white charges and the black charges are harmonious—and that few blacks and few whites realize it. On April 4, 1969, *Time* Magazine, in an essay on "The Future of Black Leadership," wrote:

> If literally fulfilled, Black nationalism might be disastrous . . . separatism might incite rampage and also tragically alienate the Negro middle class, *which has more in common with the white middle class than with the black poor.* (italics mine)

If the networks had not been so busy pretending, in 1968, that there was no striving, growing, achieving, hopeful black middle class, and that all blacks were ready to see the nation ablaze, they might have forged a bridge of *value unity* between middle-class whites and blacks.

They did not choose to do it.

The damage they did by pitting false black and false white sterotypes against each other is incalculable.

On October 6, 1968 in the middle of the campaign period, an article appeared in *The New York Times* Magazine under the headline "We Don't Help Blacks by Hurting Whites." It was written by Nathan Perlmutter, who analyzed with great lucidity the liberal pitting of black stereotype against white stereotype, and its boomerang effect against the black community.

Mr. Perlmutter wrote: "The racial stereotype is newly astir and, ironically, liberals, intellectual ones at that, are its broadcasters." There were two variants of the racial stereotype, he said—the black stereotype and the "white racist" stereotype. He discussed each in turn.

The "liberal intellectual's" black stereotype, he said, was a statistics-based view which overlooked "the individual and the preciousness of his right to be judged on his own merits." And he warned that the result of such statistical packaging would be "viewing Negroes qua Negroes as responsible for muggings, knifings, dope addiction and hustling, all of which beset our cities." The "liberal intellectuals," Mr. Perlmutter said, were unwittingly forging a criminal stereotype.

In addition, he warned that they were building up the extremist black groups: "White liberals . . . mistake the resonancy of factions for the voices of the majority. In so doing, they strengthen the vocal and often extremist minorities while weakening the softer-spoken moderate majority."

And, finally, he charged "liberal intellectuals" with violating the moral principle that the end does not justify the means and declared they were sanctioning violence by the extremist groups: ". . . liberal temporizing has validated political thuggery on the grounds that its declared end was presumably related to racial justice."

As for the stereotype of "white racism," Mr. Perlmutter pointed out that such a stereotype was itself racist:

> To the extent that it lends itself to viewing the white man as an abstraction, essentially malevolent, and so defined by his pigmentation, it is itself dangerous racism. No longer are whites good guys or bad guys; we are neither radicals nor liberals, neither conservatives nor

reactionaries; no matter that this white man freedom-
rode the buses in Mississippi and that it was the other
fellow who burned the cross. Instead, we are all cast as
dub-ins for Ralph Ellison's "Invisible Man," playing
the anguished role in white-face. Racist tit for racist
tat . . .

He observed that "liberal stereotypy" was boomeranging—that
the steady insulting of all Americans as "white racist" was accom-
plishing the very antithesis of that which it is designed to bring
about: "The liberals' litany, white racism, is actually deflecting the
nation's attention from the horrors of slum life, is putting off our
confrontation with our responsibilities to Black America and engaging us instead in an emotional, perhaps yet political, resistance
to the Negro community's needs."

Mr. Perlmutter in this article was describing the racist pattern of
thinking of "liberal intellectuals" in general. But in doing so, he
was obviously describing the two racist stereotypes in use at the
networks—stereotypes pursued in defiance of facts, in defiance of
common sense, and where covert support of "political thuggery"
took place, in defiance of elementary decency.

The 1968 electoral events proved Mr. Perlmutter right. The
"liberal intellectuals' " racist distortions did boomerang. A known
racist candidate was able to conduct a nationwide campaign which
required the full strength and fortunes of the liberal unions to
block. Mr. Wallace at one point told the newsmen: "You made
me." He understood it. They didn't.

No matter how complex the American racial problem is, no matter how deep its roots and agonizing its manifestations, a profoundly salutary effect could be achieved by letting "white" America and
"black" America know how each has been falsely pitted against the
other by the television networks of this country.

It is lamentable that the networks are using the black attack on
their racism to "prove" that white charges of pro–black-militant
bias are wrong. This is merely a continuance of the automatic pitting of one race against the other.

It is in no sense a demonstration of their "neutrality."

RADICAL CHARGES

New Leftists have an ambivalent relationship with the networks. They summon them to their demonstrations and riots, often scheduling these at hours convenient for coverage and expect to see cooperative newsmen show up. As Yippie Abbie Hoffman puts it: "The media is the message. Use it! No fund raising, no full-page ads in *The New York Times,* no press releases. Just do your thing; the press eats it up." (*Saturday Review,* July 11, 1970, and copyright 1970 Saturday Review, Inc.)

However, in situations where they do not want publicity, the same New Leftists will ostentatiously denounce the "pig networks" and refuse to allow newsmen into their meetings. On the whole, they distrust the networks as capitalist institutions, and charges of anti-left bias are frequent.

In October, 1968—at the time of the period covered by this study—New Left Columbia student James S. Kunen (later to be the author of *The Strawberry Statement*) declared, typically, in an article in the *Atlantic Monthly*: "You can *say* whatever you want but you won't be heard because the media control that . . ."

After the Agnew speech in Des Moines, a good many New Left voices declared that his charges of biased coverage were justified. More recently, in March, 1970, in *Ramparts,* writer Frank Bardacke asserted: "Spiro Agnew is right about the press."

And assorted observers, such as FCC Commissioner Nicholas Johnson, Yale Professor Charles A. Reich, and MIT sociology Professor Herbert J. Gans, have charged the networks with "censoring" or giving short shrift to the views of the New Left, the SDS, et al.

Such charges that the networks "censor" the left are eagerly used by the networks as a "refutation" of those who charge pro-left bias, and as further evidence of their "neutrality." Again, this defense does not hold up under analysis. The incredible distortion in the coverage of the radical movement revealed in this study actually makes both sets of charges intelligible and noncontradictory.

It is quite true—despite massive evidence of sympathy for the principal left positions, during this period, the networks *do* "censor" the New Left. Or, more precisely, they do subject the New Left to an exclusionary selective process.

As I have already shown, the networks in the period analyzed —a period of intense New Left activity—virtually do not cover the New Left at all. Given the network support of major New Left positions, the nature of the obliteration of the New Left from the screen deserves serious attention:

1) Actual references to members of the New Left, even in areas which are the political stamping grounds of New Left activity are, as we have seen, almost non-existent. It may seem likely that certain individuals or groups are New Leftists because of the nature of their views or actions on behalf of a known radical cause. But the networks do not *say* they are New Leftists. Real people are almost never identified as leftists or radicals in network news.

To all intents and purposes, network news behaves as if the New Left scarcely exists. The networks in effect are "censoring" the New Left's identity.

2) Serious political or ideological analyses by New Leftists and radicals are almost never allowed into network news.

Only once in seven weeks is a brief theoretical analysis of the social situation by an identified New Leftist allowed on the air: NBC invited Jack Newfield to exchange a few views with conservative publisher William Rusher—on the legitimate news ground of an apparent rapprochement between a small strain of the left world and the right. But it was the only attempt to cover New Left thought, and at that it was an atypical issue.

One might say validly that this total suppression of

ideology is not uniquely a New Left problem. Network TV is almost unbelievably incapable of incorporating *ideas* into its coverage at all, save for a few endlessly reiterated liberal bromides. But in 1968 the ideas of the New Left in particular constituted cultural news of the first magnitude, both in the best and in the worst sense.

In the best sense, an emerging intellectual rebellion was taking place against the corporate-welfare state, which had frozen into a thousand oppressive incongruities after almost a half-century of "liberal" philosophy. Such rebellious intellectuals as Tom Hayden and Paul Goodman—to cite but two—had, and still have, profoundly serious, interesting and challenging things to say about what is wrong with American society in a period when the more conventional sources of thought seem to have gone bankrupt. And, whether one agrees with their causal explanations and proposed solutions or not, their analysis of American symptomatology is often penetrating and brilliant. But no such ideas were transmitted by network news during the seven weeks studied.

Even on the specific issue of the New Left's opposition to the Vietnam war, the networks, while favoring it quantitatively, betrayed it qualitatively. One heard slogans and chants and shouts of hostility—but not *thoughts. Not one reasoned explanation of the New Left's most serious historic, economic and political grounds for opposing the war was aired by network news during the crucial period of this study.*

To omit reporting on this body of new thought—thus intensifying the despair and anger of the very best of the New Left—was a drastic miscalculation by the networks. It is due entirely to their ineptitude and anti-intellectuality, not to their definition of news. When nudism became a new aesthetic trend in the arts they were able to report on it as a cultural development of interest. It is *ideas* they do not know how to take seriously, to report on and to popularize in an interesting way.

This is particularly tragic because there is very little else which is of importance in what might be called the most rational segment of the New Left. Ideas worthy of consideration and discussion are its sole manifestation. Instead, there is a total blackout of legitimate New Left thought, and the cry of "censorship" is all too understandable.

3) If the few admirable aspects of the New Left explosion were excluded from coverage so were the nonadmirable aspects. And here the omission is far less explicable because the news, although still in the realm of ideas, was provocative, and often shocking. Even in the simplest domain of all—the constant expression of "grievances" associated with acts of violence—we barely got to hear what individual New Leftists were so "aggrieved" about.

The same thing can be said of 1968 coverage that Herbert J. Gans said in *The New York Times* Magazine on January 11, 1970: "What usually appears on film is only the most dramatic portion of a fire fight, a riot or a demonstration. This may make the event look more alarming than it really is and it may also leave out important aspects. For example, a group of radicals disrupted a medical convention in order to present their views, but the film showed only the disruption and not the views they expressed."

But even more important, there was an absolute ban on reporting on the most organized ideologies of the New Left. Never once during these seven weeks is the public told that New Left intellectuals (as opposed to slogan-eering followers) are dominantly students of Marxist, Maoist and Marcusian doctrines—doctrines which advocate authoritarian repression of opposing opinion, political violence, and ultimately, class murder and dictatorship.

The emergence of a hard-core totalitarian group in the very heart of U.S. academia—the institution which is a major determinant of American culture—is news of the first cultural magnitude. It would seem imperative for the networks—who claim to be concerned with "the public interest"—to alert the nation to such a development and to present contrasting opinion on it.

But the networks chose not to cover this ominous phenomenon. They chose not to introduce the public to the young Marxists, Maoists and Marcusians; to identify their groups; to portray their devotion to brute force as a means of "solving" political problems; to put their opinions on the air and subject them to the impact of critical opposing opinion.

The totalitarian commitments of the major New Left intellectual leaders behind whom thousands of heedless youngsters were rallying went unacknowledged.

Perhaps the most noteworthy aspect of the new totalitarian movement in America was that strain of it generated by philosopher Herbert Marcuse—the "father" of the American New Left. What exactly was Professor

Marcuse teaching these young Americans to generate a
homegrown totalitarianism? The networks saw no reason to seek out Professor Marcuse's opinion or to
present opinion on his ideas.

On March 10, 1968, Cornell Professor Andrew Hacker
wrote in *The New York Times* Book Review—a publication available to network newsmen—the following
description of Professor Marcuse's ideas: Marcuse, he
said, considered the purpose of philosophy to be the
"intellectual subversion" of the establishment. The "po-
lemics and placards" of the campus "revolutionaries,"
said Hacker, "have all carried paraphrases of the Marcusian litany." And he said, startlingly: *"Marcuse's
security stems chiefly from the fact that most of our professional patriots have neither the training nor the intel-
lect to understand the implications of his analysis. . . ."*
(italics mine)

It seems that network newsmen are not more intellectually competent in this matter than American Legion-
naires. They did not appear to understand the implications of the professor's analysis, either, or of his role in
inspiring destructive and terroristic outbursts in American colleges.

Yet this kind of opinion was also available to the networks. It was available in the movement itself—in its
books and its press. And it was available in the regular
press. Well before the study period, on May 5, 1968,
The New York Times published an interview with a
Buffalo University graduate student who explained Professor Marcuse's role in New Left violence. Said the
graduate student:

Do you know why the demonstrations and protest movements succeeded? Because we didn't
play by the rules of the game. Our movement
wasn't organized democratically. We kicked the
Dow people off the campus though they had every
right to be there. It was our unrepressed intolerance and thorough antipermissiveness that brought
our actions success. But who gave us the intellectual courage to be intolerant and unpermissive?
I think Herbert Marcuse more than anyone. He is
the New Left's "Professor."

No such illuminating views ever appeared on network
TV during the period studied.

Network newsmen covering campus outbreaks at this
time did general stories on the "activists" versus the
"nonactivists," allegedly explaining what made both
tick. But this philosophical-totalitarian dimension of the
New Left's motivation somehow eluded them.

If such coverage was too abstract for the network newsmen, they could not even seem to grasp the significance
of the crude, concrete New Left plans for violence and
murder and destruction of the society when the New
Left was (and still is) shrieking these plans from the
housetops.

During the campaign period of 1968 the SDS and the
Black Panthers were in full cry—the Panthers announcing their intention to kill policemen and judges; the SDS
announcing its intention to destroy the universities;
both announcing their intentions to engage in guerrilla
warfare for the purpose of destroying the system. Nonetheless, these views and plans, openly stated, widely
publicized, were not reported by network news.

In fact only once on network TV during the campaign
period studied was any radical reported to hold such
opinions and, significantly, it was not a white radical, it
was a black: Eldridge Cleaver. Even then Eldridge
Cleaver's Marxist commitments were not named by
CBS. His advocacy of the mass shooting of the capitalist bourgeoisie was simply presented as "Cleaver" opinion—not as a mass murder project rationalized by
Communist theory and practice.

*To all intents and purposes, networks news behaved as
if the totalitarian intellectual superstructure of the New
Left and its formal commitment to violent warfare
against this society did not exist.*

4) In addition to censoring the identity and the ideologies of the New Left, the general style of New Left
political behavior was also excluded from network coverage.

The "politics of obscenity"—i.e., the dirty speech movement—which includes verbal obscenity and other
unique forms of protest, was not mentioned. Save for a
few coy references to "bad manners" and "noisiness"
no opinion on the phenomenon pro or con was to be
heard on this subject on network television.

On October 5, 1969, a revealing burst of retroactive
controversy over TV's Chicago campaign coverage took
place in the pages of *The New York Times* Magazine.
Times columnist Tom Wicker, in an article called "The
Place Where All America was Radicalized," retroactively described the "kids" as "youthful but not all
bearded . . . neat . . . orderly . . . polite . . . and clean-
cut," suggested that they were "the young and the brave

and the pure in heart," and described them as America's own "rebellious children."

In response, Dr. Edgar F. Berman, a member of Humphrey's campaign staff in the 1968 campaign, described this as the "hard press and TV line," and charges Wicker with evading reality and reporting only what he saw on TV:

> I saw more of it than I care to remember, and the "kids" were mostly an ugly, violent, undisciplined mob . . .
>
> Wicker . . . is too genteel to repeat the chants of "up against the wall, motherf——" or "LBJ eats s——," which were reverberated through bullhorns all night long by these polite young people in the park. Yes, America saw "its own rebellious children" as the camera was directed, but the TV watchers didn't see the neat young middle-class ladies, their Levis down, squatting to fill plastic bags to be thrown at police or just squashed in hotel lobbies. Nor did they see their male counterparts lined up to fill bags with urine for the same purpose. I saw this—but not on TV.

A month later, on November 4, 1969, a similarly revealing bulletin appeared in *National Review,* signed by William F. Buckley, Jr.:

> Shortly after the convention at Chicago, *Time* Magazine commissioned our old friend and colleague, Garry Wills, to write an essay on the Politics of Obscenity. He produced as brilliant an essay on a disturbing contemporary phenomenon as I—or the editors of *Time*—have ever seen. But after prolonged agonizing, *Time* decided against general publication of the article. Because it con-

> tains graphic descriptions of some of the obsceni-
> ties performed and spoken at Chicago and, not
> without reason, the editors reasoned that the stuff
> was too strong for the general stomach. The piece
> was returned, and we now have title to it.
>
> We went through some of the same soul-search-
> ing. Should we publish it in *National Review* Mag-
> azine? No, we decided: for the same reasons *Time*
> decided. . . . We have under the circumstances de-
> cided that we will send the essay in mimeographed
> form to any reader who asks for it.

These same consciously chosen "political techniques,"
these same ritual obscenities, this same reliance on uri-
nation and defecation as expressions of "protest" were
in use during the campaign period, shortly after the
conventions. Not one reference was made, however restricted, as in these two examples from *The Times* and
National Review, by any network, to this "revolutionary" technique.

*To all intents and purposes, network news behaved
as if these practices were not standard techniques of
new Left "confrontation politics."*

Thus we see that the networks (1) suppressed "the New Left's
identity," (2) suppressed its key ideological content, and (3) suppressed its standard modes of "protest." But when one suppresses
these three elements of an ideological movement—the people, the
philosophy and the behavior—one has suppressed that movement
out of existence, leaving only a few concrete positions.

If advocates of New Left ideology were suppressed, the critics of
the New Left were suppressed too.

In 1968 during the period studied, antagonism to the New Left
was portrayed by the networks as the special property of the racist

right as personified by George Wallace and Curtis LeMay, and of
the FBI. This was a severe distortion of the nature of the opposition to the New Left.

As I have already said, the antiwar movement in the country
was itself strongly opposed to the radicals. In the *American Political Science Review* of December 1969, it is reported that a clear
majority of the Americans who were against the Vietnam War in
1968 were opposed to the "protesters"—and 23% of them were
extremely "hostile."

Socialist Michael Harrington, citing this study, says today that
"some of the peace sentiment in America developed in spite of
rather than because of the activists (particularly in my opinion in
spite of those who flaunted Vietcong flags)." (*The New York
Times* Magazine, September 13, 1970)

But in 1968 during the seven weeks studied, no network man
ever bumped into any of these opponents of the war who disliked
the violent radicals.

Again: many civilized liberals and socialists—not just George
Wallace—were opposed to the totalitarian New Left. Men like Sidney Hook and Irving Howe, men like George Kennan, Arnold
Beichman, Walter Laqueur and Norman Podhoretz, men like John
Roche and Irving Kristol, expressed their condemnation of the violent New Left during that period. They were appalled both by the
violence and by its source—what Podhoretz has since described, in
Commentary, November 1970, as the "barbaric hostility to freedom of thought which by the late 60's had become one of the hall-
marks of the radical ethos."

But in 1968 during the seven weeks studied, network TV exclusively pushed the line that only racists and reactionaries were opposed to the New Left. No network man ever discovered a liberal
or socialist critic of the new totalitarianism.

Again: by mid-1970 more than 80% of the liberals on university
and college faculties had become convinced that "campus demonstrations by militant students were a threat to academic freedom";
76% thought disruptive students should be expelled; and 46.8%
thought that the far left groups were the source of the trouble.

These are the findings of a study by The Carnegie Commission on Higher Education (*The New York Times,* April 23, 1970).

But in 1968 during the seven weeks studied, no network man ever discovered a single strongly condemnatory professor on the disrupted campuses he covered.

To all intents and purposes, the networks behaved as if the violent totalitarianism of the New Left was not an issue of controversy among civilized people of all political persuasions from coast to coast.

The charges by the New Left of being "censored" and "suppressed"—i.e., of being subjected to exclusionary selectivity—are thoroughly validated.

But this is only part of the complex story. In other issues where the reporters do not choose to relay certain material to the public they simply omit it and that is that. In this issue the networks engaged in a curious ploy. They didn't cover the New Left as such, but as we have seen, they covered a great many anonymous groups instead. And on the airwaves there is a great proliferation of Tom Wicker's "rebellious children" diversely described as: "restless youth," "Kennedy and McCarthy followers," "students," "nonconformists," "hecklers," "dissenters," "protesters," "demonstrators," "teenagers," and "the disenchanted young"—all invariably calling for the noblest of goals: "peace" and "justice." And these are, strangely, the violent ones. Their violence is rarely named as such: it is thickly encrusted with euphemisms. And it is repeatedly ascribed to the highest social idealism.

The networks did not *cover* the New Left—they *buried* it under an avalanche of euphemisms and sentimental idealizations of "the kids." *Instead of New Left coverage, they created a special white stereotype called "youth."* It is a misleading stereotype. It glamorizes the New Left by vastly inflating the significance and size of the group which shares its attitudes; and, conversely, it smears American "youth" by equating it to the violent and totalitarian New Left.

On June 2, 1969, Kenneth Crawford reports in *Newsweek* Magazine on an Elmo Roper study of political attitudes on campuses. He says:

> Various "in-depth" studies of campus attitudes are beginning to correct the impression that college students are the vanguard of a revolutionary generation bent upon ripping up society and letting the pieces fall where they may. The latest of these, a study by Elmo Roper, financed but not interfered with by Standard Oil of New Jersey and employing the pollsters' usual techniques, shows that the noisy militants one reads so much about in the newspapers and sees so much of on television constitute a less-than-10 per cent minority and that a majority consider American institutions "basically sound."

In 1971, Lou Harris still finds the same results: 92% of the students are strongly opposed to violence, and are willing to work for change "within the system." Mr. Harris, too, believes that network television has smeared the American students.

Ironically, this erroneous magnification of the New Left did not placate the New Leftists. They were aware that they were the object of incomprehension and evasion. They disliked being sentimentally camouflaged as "restless" adolescents; they did not perceive their position as a case of exaggerated teenage fervor. Millions of Americans have also made it clear—albeit for different reasons—that they are angered by this sentimentalized portrayal and magnification of the New Left.

There is nothing contradictory whatever about the "glamorization" and "white wash" charges of the "right" (57% of the nation), and the radicals' charges that they are being censored. Both are protesting the same phenomenon—the networks' evasion of the radicals' identity, philosophy, methods and goals.

They do not "cancel each other out."

If contradiction there be, it lies within the political purposes of the men at the networks—purposes which led them systematically to support major New Left positions, and to sanction New Left violence, while pretending equally systematically that the New Left did not quite exist, save as part of a large body of "young idealists."

This pattern of support-plus-evasion-and-glamorization is so commonplace in modern political history that it can be readily identified. Historically, in the Western nations, the liberals or "social democrats" have always followed the ideological leadership of the revolutionary left, while tending to evade the left's policies of tyranny, violence and murder and/or justifying them in the name of the left's "idealism." This is the essence of the liberal's "anti-anti-Communist" position—a position which tacitly prohibits criticism of the old left, and enshrines evasion and glamorization on principle. It is precisely the pattern we see in network coverage of the New Left.

The objects of this glamorizing evasion by liberals have never appreciated it, although they have consciously and consistently exploited it. The Communists, historically, have never trusted their self-blinded bourgeois fellow-travellers, even as they used them assiduously. They have considered them, correctly, to be politically unreliable allies who would betray them when their own short-range bourgeois interests were at stake. And this, today, is precisely the attitude of New Leftists (black and white) towards the liberals: they exploit them systematically and they distrust them.

Only those who lack historical context will find the politically ambivalent relationship between network liberals and New Leftists mysterious. It is this ambivalence, in the last analysis, that generates both charges of pro-leftism and of anti-leftism against the networks. It is not surprising that liberal newsmen should provoke anger in both the bourgeois majority and the revolutionary minority. As representatives of a group which affects a prorevolutionary "stance" while clinging to bourgeois elite vested interests, they actually betray both the bourgeois majority and the revolutionary left. They are inevitably despised by both sides.

The apparent contradiction in the public's bias charges is actually a direct response to the political contradiction within the liberal position itself. The contradiction may be called "radical chic"—to use the term of writer Tom Wolfe when he describes the prorevolutionary posturing of the liberal bourgeois elite. It may be called "limousine liberalism," to use the language of conservatives, describing the same revolutionary play-acting of the liberal rich. It may be called "altruist liberal hypocrisy," to use the language of the New Left. Or it may be called "the treason of the social democrats," to use the language of the Old Left. It doesn't matter much what the liberal contradiction is called—so long as one understands that it is not a contradiction in the bourgeois majority and leftist minority from whom the dual charges of bias emerge . . . and so long as one understands that it is not evidence of network "neutrality."

Do The Networks Know
What They Are Doing?

To what degree are network newsmen aware of bias in their own newscasts? And is it deliberate? There is no single answer to this question—and above all there is no collective answer that applies to all individuals.

It is fairly apparent that awareness ranges from abysmal confusion to a high degree of understanding. There is unquestionably genuine confusion on this issue at all three networks. The evidence of such confusion takes several different forms.

One is sheer illiteracy on the epistemological issues involved in the nature of bias and in news coverage itself. The gibberish which emerged from the mouths of Walter Cronkite and former CBS news president Fred Friendly when they were seeking to analyze "objectivity" and "fairness" (see Chapter I) illustrates this point painfully well.

Similarly, only a severe defect in understanding that value judgments underlie acts of selectivity could lead ABC's former news president James Hagerty to say: "We're trying to be objective . . . we are reporters! We get interpretations from *other* people and present them. If anyone on this network is expressing his own opinion—well, if I catch him I won't permit it." And only a refusal to acknowledge the phenomenon of selectivity at all can explain the astonishing claim of CBS news president Richard Salant, published in *TV Guide* on April 11, 1964: "We believe in objective coverage. Our reporters do not cover stories from *their* point of view. They are presenting them from *nobody's* point of view."

The concept of news itself is a source of massive confusion at the networks, where—in a political crisis—management invariably pretends that "News," like a platonic archetype, has an immutable, independent existence and that neither human choices nor human evaluations nor human acts of selectivity or exclusion have anything to do with the phenomenon.

Thus NBC president Julian Goodman, in a speech to broadcasters made on June 23, 1970, said: "There are many viewers—and some public officials—who feel that television, if it were handled properly, could make bad news good, and who charge that, through some kind of ill will, television insists on making good news bad. *The fact is, of course, that any responsible television news organization does not make the news at all. It reports the news.*" (italics mine)

Mr. Goodman had not consulted with his star reporter, David Brinkley, who says: "News is what *I* say it is. It is something worth knowing by my standards."

Again: Mr. Goodman told the broadcasters, "Television is not a political instrument or a social theory—it is [a] means of communication. . . ." He had not, apparently, attended the International Radio and Television Society luncheon on February 4, 1970, just a few months before, where his other star reporter, Chet Huntley, had defined news as "social and political criticism."

Another manifestation of confusion lies in insufficient education. A good many partisan ideas are being beamed over the airwaves by men who suppose that they are repeating scientifically established truths. Thus reporters announce—as if it is fact—that "poverty causes crime" and are, apparently, quite unaware that they are proselytizing for an unproved theory.

On August 23, 1969, a review appeared in a sophisticated New York magazine, *The New Yorker,* on two sociological books: *On Understanding Poverty,* edited by Daniel P. Moynihan and *On Fighting Poverty,* edited by James L. Sundquist. Both are anthologies—the products of a year-long sociology seminar sponsored by The American Academy of Arts and Sciences. Wrote the astonished reviewer chosen by *The New Yorker* for this assignment: "These two volumes . . . teach us that we are only beginning to find out how little we know about poverty. *In the first volume, we learn that all our concepts of poverty are merely theories, and that none commands the assent of every sociologist."* (Italics mine)

It is certain that it would come as an equal shock to many network reporters to discover that their overworked bromide, "Poverty causes crime," is a hypothesis, not a truth—and a dubious one at that, since a causal principle which doesn't operate in most cases isn't much of a causal principle. Similarly, the notion that "society is guilty" of people's crimes is a hypothesis, not a truth. It is challenged by every philosophical, theological, moral, psychological and legal school which advocates volition, free will and moral responsibility. But reporters spew it over the airwaves as though it were a test-tube fact.

The arch value of these two theories is *political.* If "poverty causes crime" and if "society is guilty" of a man's crime, then, of course, we must tax "society" and make it pay for his regeneration, etc., etc. All of which furthers the redistribution of wealth much favored by certain political groups.

Men who repeat such pop-sociological bromides as factual truths may well be extremely confused by a charge that they are injecting politically loaded opinion into the coverage of social problems. Their actual sin is not bias so much as it is that they are ill-educated and intellectually pretentious. They have not read the books they are pretending to have read. Some, indeed, are not even aware of the existence of these books. They belong to the group defined by George W. Ball as "the illiterate intellectuals." Men of this type are slanting their stories—but they literally do not know that they are doing so.

In addition to the confused and the ignorant, there are those who are quite simply party liners. Many of these are guilty of little more than the pathetic crime of being parrots—of rushing to cover stories the way they have seen others cover them, of rushing to interview certain people because others have interviewed them, of expressing certain opinions because others have expressed them.

There are enough of these second-hand brains at the networks to have caused CBS' Bill Leonard to list this for *TV Guide,* September 27, 1969, as one of his chief problems as a news executive: "Most reporting is lousy. It is lousy because people are lazy . . . because they approach things in rote fashion."

These are doubtless the kind of men referred to by Whitney Young when he said that "many leaders are followed by 7 Negroes and 70 screaming reporters." The first two or three men who build up a unknown character as "leader" and who give him nationwide significance may be quite clearheaded about what they are doing— but how many of the others in the screaming pack genuinely know what they are doing, is unknown.

Indeed, it is ABC commentator Howard K. Smith's conviction that most of the party-line journalism at the networks is of this mindless, imitative sort—the incestuous parroting of an "in" group. In *TV Guide,* February 28, 1970, he denounces network "conformism." Liberal newsmen, he says, have a set of automatic reactions: "They react the way political cartoonists do—with oversimplification. Oversimplify. Be sure to please your fellows, because that's what's 'good.' They're conventional, they're conformists. They're pleasing Walter Lippman, they're pleasing the *Washington Post,* they're pleasing the editors of *The New York Times,* and they're pleasing one another."

And whom are these overlords pleasing? According to Theodore H. White, author of *The Making of the President, 1968*: "The moral heights of New York are held by journals like *The Village Voice* and *The New York Review of Books.* They are so pure, and shriek with such passion that, in fashionable New York, they are the pulpit-voice of The Church of Good Liberals." *(Newsweek,* September 8, 1969)

The picture of ignorance, confusion and parroting is further complicated by the existence of men of varying degrees of genuine insight into their own and each other's bias. This insight covers a remarkable range of issues and one cannot arrive at a solid assessment of network awareness without knowing what they are.

Here is a detailed survey of the kind of understanding newsmen have displayed in the past few years—*before* the indictment of network bias by Vice President Agnew.

Many understood that selectivity was the cause of bias.

On April 11, 1964, a group of prominent broadcast newsmen stated for publication in *TV Guide* that selectivity was the essence of their work; and that it was impossible to cover news or produce public affairs programming of any kind without injecting their point of view.[1]

It was in this context that David Brinkley, of NBC, said: "News is what *I* say it is. It's something worth knowing by my standards."

In addition:

John Secondari, of ABC, said: "It's absolutely impossible to write a broadcast or put together pictures without having a point of view."

Gerald Green, of NBC, said: "It's impossible not to have a point of view. Once you start selecting facts and choosing what and whom to put on the air, a point of view is implicit."

Don Hewitt, of CBS, said: "Of course . . . news documentaries do take a point of view . . . it has to be understood that personality has to come through."

And Quincy Howe, a former president of the Association of Radio-TV News Analysts, said: "All news presented on radio and TV editorializes. The newscaster editorializes in what he emphasizes and what he plays down, in what he omits and what he includes."

---

[1]"Why Speech on Television is Not Really Free" by Edith Efron.

At this same time, many of the men on network staffs agreed that the point of view that prevailed could be defined as "moderate liberalism."

NBC's news chief at that period, William McAndrew, said: "The prevailing opinion of the network, I would say, is moderate. We have the political spectrum interpreted by moderates."

CBS' Don Hewitt said: "The networks are in the hands of groups which see the issues the same way—as moderate liberals."

Many were aware that the prevailing network bias was distorting American realities.

In 1968, after the nationwide protest over TV's alleged role in furthering the race riots, several prominent network newsmen declared in *TV Guide,* July 20, 1968,[1] that network coverage was falsifying the picture of the nation:

Chet Huntley, of NBC, said: "Our attention has been turned to the cities. That's where the problems are. But it is distorted. It doesn't reflect the rest of the country. We're ignoring the rest of America."

NBC Producer Bob Rogers said: "The responsible man, the productive man, the man without a chip on his shoulder, is 'the forgotten man.' You hardly ever see him on TV . . . The imbalance in coverage is causing Americans to mistrust each other."

Howard K. Smith of ABC said: "TV news isn't telling people the way life is. We're giving the public a wholly negative picture on a medium so vivid that it damages morale with a bombardment of despair."

NBC Producer Lou Hazam said: "I know this [distortion] has hurt people. It has hurt and frightened *me.* I often wonder, myself, is *everything* I love dying?"

Many were aware that network reporters were using news stories as vehicles of personal expression.

In 1968, after the nationwide protest over network TV's reporting of the antiwar riot in Chicago at the Democratic convention,

---

[1] "The Program That Explored *Real* America" by Edith Efron.

awareness grew among political reporters that they were interpreting political news through the selective filter of their own values. Many indeed went so far as to argue, after the election, that this was psychologically inevitable:

David Brinkley, speaking on NET (December 22, 1968), said: "If I were objective, or if you were objective, or if anyone was, we would have to be put away somewhere in an institution because we'd be some sort of vegetable. Objectivity is impossible to a human being."

Frank Reynolds, of ABC, said: "I think your program has to reflect what your basic feelings are. I'll plead guilty to that."

Bill Moyers, one of ABC's commentators during the campaign period, said: "Of all the myths of journalism, objectivity is the greatest."

Many were aware that many Americans felt the networks were favoring the radicals.

In *TV Guide,* September 27, 1969, this recognition was voiced by men at all networks.[1]

CBS News Chief Bill Leonard said: "The right and the middle complain that we put on irresponsible people from the left."

ABC producer Steve Fleischman said: "People feel we've given too much play to the radicals."

NBC News President Reuven Frank said: "The general view of the public is that we have too many radicals in network news departments."

And NBC producer Shad Northshield avowed: "Bias is on everybody's mind. We've claimed we don't have it. And the viewers say: 'Yes, you do.' I was stunned by the public reaction to Chicago. We all were. I was stunned, astonished, *hurt.* It is the key thing that opened my eyes to the cleavage between newsmen and the majority."

Many felt there were legitimate grounds for the bias charges of the majority.

---

[1]"The Silent Majority Comes Into Focus" by Edith Efron.

Again, in the same *TV Guide* article, newsmen conceded that network coverage had been improperly focused on the protesting minorities, to the exclusion of the interests, values and views of the majority groups in the nation.

CBS' Phil Lewis said: "We're beginning to realize we've ignored the majority. America doesn't end at the Hudson!"

NBC's Shad Northshield said: "In TV news departments we appear to know a lot about the black minority. It's the silent majority we must explore. We haven't done it. We didn't know it was *there!*"

CBS newsman Joseph Benti said: "We spend so much time on angry blacks, angry youth. But what about that vast forgotten army out there? How many hard-working law-abiding whites are mad as hell because *their* story isn't being told?"

CBS's Desmond Smith: "The left and SDS have been getting a great deal of play. Americans are getting to feel they're not getting the whole story."

Some were aware that this bias was caused by uniform democratic-liberal thinking.

In the same *TV Guide* story, Fred Freed of NBC said:

> This generation of newsmen is a product of the New Deal. Those beliefs of the New Deal are the beliefs that news has grown on. This is true of the networks, of *Newsweek,* of *The New York Times,* of all media.
>
> Men of like mind are in the news. It is provincial.
>
> The blue and white collar people who are in revolt now do have cause for complaint against us. We've ignored their point of view. It's bad. It's bad to pretend that they don't exist.
>
> We did this because we tend to be upper-middle-class liberals. We think the poor are "better" than the middle class. We romanticize them. The best thing that happened to me was a month I spent working in the Detroit slums after the riots. I stopped romanticizing the poor.

I've come to understand that it's really the same with
all classes. You've got to sit down with the cop, with the
little storekeeper, and get their views. They're human
beings like everyone else. Their attitudes emerge logically from their interests and values. They should be
covered that way.

*And some men in management conceded that there were reporters
who slanted their stories.*

Again, in the same story, CBS's Bill Leonard declared that keeping bias out of reporters' stories was one of his most difficult problems as an executive of CBS News: "The worst problem of all is
the reporter who doesn't ask the next question—the cheap, lousy
reporter who will quote an attack but doesn't go to the other side
because the answer might kill his story . . . and these producers
who develop and edit a broadcast from the point of view of the
way *they* want it to turn out—with their own prejudices showing.
That happens quite often . . . if we could get rid of those people,
we'd be a lot closer to our goal of objectivity."

*It was two months after these statements were made that Vice
President Agnew made his speech in Des Moines charging network
bias.*

What insights did reporters have *after* the Agnew indictment?
Very few.

One week after Mr. Agnew's Des Moines speech, on November
20, 1969, a letter appeared in *The New York Times* from David
Jayne. It said:

As a reporter and later a producer for one of the
three networks for more than eight years now, I believe
Vice President Agnew's comments on television news
are in the main accurate, fair and long-overdue.

Television news is controlled by a few powerful men
who do think alike on most major issues. This control is

not manifested, as Mr. Agnew may have implied, in a conspiratorial concerted attempt to present or distort the news according to these men's bias.

But the end product, what's seen and heard on the air, especially in live programming, too often results from these biases. The reason, I suggest, is not conscious prejudice, but the common implicit assumptions influencing the major commentators and producers. As the Vice President said, they do live in the provincial and parochial confines of Washington and New York City. They do read the same newspapers, bound on one flank by the *Times* and on the other by the *Washington Post,* with perhaps some turning to *Newsweek* and the *New Republic.* Their constant interaction does reinforce their common viewpoint.

There is an establishment point of view shared by the television news elite.

Several days later on CBS (November 25, 1969), Howard K. Smith of ABC, while expressing concern over the appearance of intimidation, said:

. . . let us admit what we knew before Mr. Agnew said it: there is a problem.

The tradition, deeply ingrained, of American journalism is negative. We are attracted mostly to what goes wrong in a nation where we must be doing something that is right. The emigration figures of people trying to get out of this country are very few. The immigration figures of people trying to get in are high. They must know something we are not adequately reporting.

I am in no degree mystified that the public is irritated by daily reports of little but trouble, nor that politicians may exploit that irritation. I know of no specific solution that can be quickly stated—just exercising self-discipline, try harder to be fair . . .

On January 10, 1970, Terry H. Lee, TV Division Head of Storer Broadcasting, which owns CBS outlets in Detroit, Cleveland and Atlanta, as well as ABC affiliate in Milwaukee and NBC affiliate in Toledo, charged that editorial opinion was infiltrating the network newscasts that the networks were offering to the public. This station-group threatened to flash a disclaimer on the screen ("The views being expressed here are not necessarily those of the management of this station.") when network newsmen voiced what these stations felt to be editorial opinion in newscasts.

There may have been other such statements. If so, I have been unable to find them despite intensive research.

To the best of my knowledge, nothing else was publicly conceded in a major forum of opinion by anyone associated with the networks until February 28, 1970—five months after the Agnew speech. On that date, an article appeared in *TV Guide* based entirely on an interview with ABC commentator Howard K. Smith.[1] It is the most extensive analysis of network bias ever made by a network newsman. Here is a summary of Mr. Smith's major points:

Network bias, said Mr. Smith, is massive. The bias, he said, begins with the political composition of the staff, which is virtually all liberal. Liberals, by definition, have "a strong leftward bias": "Our tradition since FDR, has been leftward."

According to Mr. Smith, a series of positive and negative patterns of selectivity are determining much of the coverage. Here are the illustrations he cited of this negative selectivity:

"*Race:* During the Johnson Administration, six million people were raised above the poverty level . . . And there is a substantial and successful Negro middle class. But the newsmen are not interested in the Negro who succeeds—they're interested in the one who fails and makes a loud noise. They have ignored the developments in the South. The South has an increasing number of integrated schools. A large part of the South has *accepted* integration. We've

---

[1]"There *is* a Network News Bias," by Edith Efron.

had a President's Cabinet with a Negro in it, a Supreme Court with a Negro on it—but more important, we have 500 Negroes elected to local offices in the deep South! This is a tremendous achievement. But that achievement isn't what we see on the screen.

"*Conservatives:* If Agnew says something, it's bad, regardless of what he says. If Ronald Reagan says something, it's bad, regardless of what he says. Well, I'm unwilling to condemn an idea because a particular man said it. Most of my colleagues do just that.

"*The Middle Class:* Newsmen are *proud* of the fact that the middle class is antagonistic to them. They're proud of being out of contact with the middle class. Joseph Kraft did a column in which he said: Let's face it, we reporters have very little to do with middle America. They're not our kind of people . . . Well, I resent that. I'm *from* middle America!

"*The Vietnam War:* The networks have never given a complete picture of the war. For example: that terrible siege of Khe Sanh went on for five weeks before newsmen revealed that the South Vietnamese were fighting at our sides, and that they had higher casualties. And the Viet Cong's casualties were 100 times ours. But we never told *that*. We just showed pictures day after day of Americans getting the hell kicked out of them. That was enough to break America apart. That's also what it did.

"*The Presidency:* The negative attitude which destroyed Lyndon Johnson is now waiting to be applied to Richard Nixon. Johnson was actually politically assassinated. And some are trying to assassinate Nixon politically. They hate Richard Nixon irrationally."

Here are illustrations Mr. Smith cited of positive selectivity:

"*Russia:* Some have gone overboard in a wish to believe that our opponent has exclusively peaceful aims, and that there is no need for armaments and national security. The danger of Russian agression is unreal to many of them, although some have begun to rethink since the invasion of Czechoslovakia. But there is a kind of basic bias in the left-wing soul that gives the Russians the benefit of the doubt.

"*Ho Chi Minh:* Many have described Ho Chi Minh as a nationalist leader comparable to George Washington. But his advent to power in Hanoi, in 1954, was marked by the murder of 50,000 of his people. His consistent method was terror. He was not his country's George Washington—he was more his country's Hitler or Stalin . . . I heard an eminent TV commentator say: 'It's an awful thing when you can trust Ho Chi Minh more than you can trust your President.' At the time he said that, Ho Chi Minh was lying! He was presiding over atrocities! And yet an American TV commentator could say that!

"*The Viet Cong:* The Viet Cong massacred 3000 Vietnamese at Hue alone—a massacre that dwarfs all allegations about My Lai. This was never reported on.

"*Doves:* Mr. Fulbright maneuvered the Gulf of Tonkin Resolution through—with a clause stating that Congress may revoke it. Ever since, he's been saying: 'This is a terribly immoral thing.' I asked him: 'If it's that bad, aren't *you* morally obligated to revoke it?' He runs away! And yet Mr. Fulbright—who incidentally has voted against *every* civil-rights act—is not criticized for his want of character. He is beloved by reporters, by everyone of my group, which is left-of-center. It's one of the mysteries of my time!

"*Black Militants:* A few Negroes—scavengers on the edge of society—have discovered they're riding a good thing with violence and talk of violence. They can get on TV and become nationally famous.

"*The New Left:* The New Left challenges America. They're rewriting the history of the Cold War. Some carry around the Viet Cong flag. Some shout for Mao—people who'd be assassinated in China! They've become *irrational!* But they're not portrayed as irrational. Reporters describe them as 'our children.' Well, they're not *my* children. *My* children don't throw bags of excrement at policemen . . . If right-wing students had done what left-wing students have done, everyone, including the reporters, would have called in the police and beaten their heads in. But we have a left-wing bias now, that has 30 years of momentum behind it."

The "emphasis" in network coverage, said Mr. Smith, is "anti-

American." It tends to omit the good about America and focus on the *bad*. And it is also biased in *favor* of attackers-of-America by tending to *omit* the bad about them and focusing on the good. This, Mr. Smith finally said, is a reflection of the New Left line. "The New Left," he concluded, "has acquired a grave power over the liberal mind."

This is the interview to which I referred in Chapter V. It is generally confirmed by the findings of this study. It provoked an avalanche of mail from American citizens thanking Mr. Smith for having the "courage" to tell the truth.

After the Agnew speech, there is only one more concession from a network newsman that I am able to find, and it was made shortly after Mr. Smith's analysis.

On March 4, 1970, Walter Cronkite of CBS, interviewed on WTOP-TV in Washington, D.C., conceded what he had never conceded before: that the networks had been wrong in Chicago, two years earlier. Reported *Variety:*

> Cronkite said that the one area of criticism of network coverage of the 1968 Chicago Democratic Convention that he thinks is valid was the fact that "we hadn't shown provocation in the streets of Chicago."

In 1968 this would have been major news. By 1970 it was minutiae.

After the Vice President's indictment of network bias, only Howard K. Smith, of all the major figures on the air, had the moral capacity to concede the validity of the Vice President's general criticisms—criticisms known to be true by many of his colleagues because they had made these criticisms themselves.

For this, Clarence Streit, editor of *Freedom & Union,* hailed him in an extraordinary editorial entitled "Personal Tribute to a Brave Man" (May 1970). Mr. Streit, a former *New York Times* correspondent, writes: "Only a veteran newsman can appreciate fully the courage this took . . . I would rate it very high and rare . . .

When the emotions of one's clan have reached the sizzling point, non-conformity takes special courage. Howard Smith's on this still echoing occasion was the more outstanding because it was so lonely . . ." (Copyright, *Freedom & Union*, 1970.)

Why did it take such "courage" for Howard Smith in a free country with the majority of the people, as well as the government, on his side to speak his mind? And why was he alone? Is Mr. Smith really the only man in the networks who perceived a bias so gross it was evident to 57% of the country? And if he is not—as he is not—why are the others silent?

The answer, as Mr. Streit names it, is that "clan" emotions have reached a "sizzling" point. It is a delicate way to describe psychological intimidation.

Psychological intimidation by blindly conformist thinkers is nothing but authoritarianism. Authoritarianism in the "liberal intellectual" community has become fierce in recent years—and the headquarters of ferocity is the communications world.

In *The Making of the President, 1968*, Theodore White describes "a new avant-garde" which "dominates the heights of national communication" and which "has come to despise its own country and its traditions." In a letter to Stewart Alsop, which Alsop reports on in *Newsweek* on September 8, 1969, Mr. White expands upon this thesis. He says: "In the new intolerance, the United States government is the master of all evil, the chief world agent of repression; the 'establishment' is as corrupt as the Romanov dynasties; and the spokesmen of the new intolerance are infected with a morality so stark that any deviation from their morality is heresy, any difference of opinion villany."

Mr. Alsop quoted this and said: "Mr. White's punishment was swift and merciless—his book which received very enthusiastic reviews in other cities was savagely attacked by almost every New York reviewer. . . . White, a passionate and life-long liberal, was described as 'anti-peace,' 'anti-intellectual,' 'against students,' and 'against blacks'—a choice collection of demonstrable untruths."

We have in the past few years seen a series of other "swift and merciless punishments" of the same kind. Such men as Dean Rusk, Walt Whitman Rostow, Sidney Hook, S. I. Hayakawa, et al., have been virtually excommunicated from the "liberal intellectual" world for supporting the war and condemning violent radicals. And reports are now coming from the universities of the "reign of terror" by leftists on the faculty against those who disagree with them. John Roche, Brandeis professor of history and former National ADA chairman, writing in *The New York Times* Magazine on October 18, 1970, compares liberal academics these days to "Holy Rollers" and to an "Anabaptist Sect"; he reports on "intimidation" in the intellectual community; and he compares faculty meetings to "lynch mobs."

This is why certain men are silent in the networks. They have seen what happens to liberals who deviate significantly from the entrenched line. They heard the invective that hit Chet Huntley and Howard K. Smith for supporting the war in Vietnam. They saw the professional punishment meted out. According to *New York Times* TV critic Jack Gould, "Mr. Smith was practically in TV's coventry for his commentary . . ." (March 10, 1970). They saw both men repudiated by colleagues who had been close friends for 20 years. And when Howard Smith refused to genuflect before pathological black extremists, they heard the newsman who had been foremost in TV's battle for civil rights described by a prominent CBS Murrow-legatee as a "Southerner who had reverted to type." Finally, after his bias analysis had been published, they saw Mr. Smith subjected to abuse by ABC and CBS men who sneered at him in print in *Newsweek,* March 9, 1970, as "Howard K. Agnew," who attacked him for "using a meat ax, Agnew style," for being on the side of the "far right," etc.

They also saw Mr. Smith's fellow commentator, Frank Reynolds, who was responsible for the most virulent personal attacks on candidate Nixon that were aired during the campaign period, win an Emmy . . .

This meting out of liberal "justice" could have been predicted. Mr. Smith, who, indeed, was filled with dread before the publication of his bias analysis, in anticipation of attack by his colleagues, predicted his own destiny to me. Any newsman at the networks who thinks as Mr. Smith does can predict it as easily. Those who know that this authoritarian strain has infiltrated into the networks are silent in order not to suffer such attacks.

And here—although there may be other types of reactions at the networks—I can stop using types of awareness because the variety given is sufficient.

If one reviews all these reactions—gibberish, confusion, inadequate education, varied levels of understanding to full comprehension (whether publicly expressed or not)—one will see that no single generalization will do to describe the state of awareness of the networks on the subject of their biased newscasts. Some men do know what is happening in network news coverage and approve of it. Some know and disapprove of it. Some don't know. Some "sort of" know. Some don't want to know. Some are afraid to know.

It is perfectly clear, however, that whatever the diversity of understanding, whatever the internal conflicts and fears, whatever the genuine confusion, one other element exists: active dishonesty.

On the top official level of the networks, the failure in honesty is gross—particularly in response to Vice President Agnew's bias charges.

At that time the heads of the three networks flatly denied the validity of these charges in statements redolent with professional exaltation and righteous indignation. And the single most striking thing about these statements is that all three of the networks engaged in blatant evasion of the bias admissions made by a group of their most prominent men *just two months before.*

If genuine confusion were their only state, and if honesty were their goal, every single network president and network news president would have conceded publicly that virtually all of Mr. Agnew's charges had already been proffered, in principle or concretely, by some of their own most trusted staff; that, as NBC's Shad Northshield had put it: "Bias is on everybody's mind"; and that the networks were struggling with these very issues behind the scenes.

But not one of the network officials said anything of the sort.

They issued flat and pompous assertions of their impeccable fairness; they attacked Mr. Agnew as "repressive" and as embodying a "McCarthyist" trend: They pretended that their own reporters had not admitted what they had admitted in a publication read by 30,000,000 people.[1]

Perhaps the most dramatic illustration of cynicism was manifested by ABC. On December 10, 1969, ABC rushed a release to the press entitled: "ABC News Coverage of Major Issues Judged Balanced and Fair in Survey Conducted by Team from University of Minnesota Journalism School." The release announced that this university team had conducted a study of ABC's coverage, and had ascertained that ABC's coverage of controversial political issues was neutral.

On December 12, a second release followed. This time, the headline read: "Minnesota Journalism Professor Explains How ABC News Content Analysis Study Was Done." The entire story follows:

Page One:

A team of seven researchers, supervised by Dr. Irving E. Fang of the University of Minnesota School of Journalism and Mass Communications, worked for eight days to complete a survey of all regularly-scheduled ABC hard news television programs aired between January 1, 1969 and November 27, 1969.

Announced recently by Elmer W. Lower, President of ABC News, the survey showed that ABC News television newscasts had achieved a high standard of fairness and balance. Mr. Lower termed fairness and bal-

---

[1] At the time of their appearance, these network admissions were treated as news by an estimated 300 publications, including *Editor and Publisher* and *The Village Voice,* and were repeatedly discussed on television talk shows, including "The Tonight Show." After the Agnew speech, however, the liberal press, as well as the network spokesmen, "forgot" what had been admitted. The only unimpaired memories were to be found in the Republican and conservative press.

ance "personal and professional credos" of the journalists who work for him.

Dr. Fang who worked with ABC News staff researchers, described the methodology of the survey this way:

"After the content analysis scheme was laid out, the
actual study took eight days. This included examining
each script and log, counting, rechecking, summarizing,
and writing the final report."

"ABC News writers and researchers formed the research group. After an initial briefing, with an item-by-
item dissection of several newscasts, each researcher
was assigned all newscasts for one month. The project
director (Dr. Fang) worked side-by-side with each researcher, in turn, to be sure that decisions were reached
in harmony with the group. All members worked in
close quarters, so that the frequent questions raised by
one researcher or another about the disposition of a
particular news item could be heard by everyone. At
several brief meetings, key decisions were reviewed, to
be sure that everyone was thinking together and that everyone personally felt the group decisions were the right
ones."

Dr. Fang and his ABC News research team had a
total of 95 hours and three minutes to study. The key
news areas, which they broke down into categories for
more detailed analysis, comprised about two-thirds of
the total news time. The survey studied the five-night-a-
week "ABC Evening News with Frank Reynolds and
Howard K. Smith" and the twice-a-week "ABC Week-
end News."

Page Two:

Areas where fairness and balance of ABC newscasts
were weighed were coverage of the Nixon Administration, the Vietnam war, the Vietnam issue in the United
States, the Mideast, other international political news,

the Chicago 8 trial, crime and trials generally, the Kennedy-Kopechne case, the Fortas case, the ABM controversy, military spending, space and the Haynsworth nomination to the Supreme Court.

Dr. Fang, who holds degrees in English, journalism and speech, worked for wire services, newspapers and in television beginning in 1951. *Until September, 1969, he was the assistant manager of the ABC News Political unit,* the group which provides voting information, analysis and projections for ABC on election nights.

Mr. Lower said of the study results, "I think they prove that we have been true to our policy of fairness and balance. Our reporting has been fair and impartial—the kind of journalism which is the obligation of newsmen protected by the free guarantee we enjoy under the First Amendment."

Mr. Lower revealed that the survey and analysis of news program content would continue at ABC News.

———

NOTE: A release dated December 10 concerning results of this survey was headlined, "ABC News Coverage of Major Issues Judged Balanced and Fair in Survey Conducted by Team from University of Minnesota Journalism School." *The only member of the survey team from the University of Minnesota Journalism School was Dr. Fang, and the survey was not a study conducted by the school.*

(Italics mine)

In other words:

1) *ABC news writers and members of the ABC news department conducted this study of their own product under the guidance of a man who had been an employee of ABC news throughout most of the period studied.*

2) *ABC announced to the press that this was a study by a "team of researchers" from the University of Minnesota Journalism School.*

3) *In the second release one does not learn until paragraph 3 that the "team of seven researchers" mentioned in the lead were "ABC news staff researchers"; and one does not find out until paragraph 5 that the "team" included ABC news writers.*

4) *One does not learn until the bottom of page 2 that this was not a University of Minnesota Journalism School study at all.*

5) *Nowhere on the second release does it say that an error was made.*

One might suppose this to be an incredible error by an irresponsible "underling," who, ordered to correct it, compounded it. Unfortunately, one cannot draw that conclusion.

On December 10, the day of the *first* release, Elmer Lower, president of ABC News, delivered an address at the Columbia University School of Law. In it he said:

"Shortly before Thanksgiving, I determined to commission a . . . complex survey of our news content . . . this was to be a content analysis. To do the job properly, a team of seven ABC news researchers was put to work."

This unexplained reference to "ABC news researchers" was made in his introductory comments, and was never again referred to. He continued:

"The concept and methodology of the study were devised by Professor Irving E. Fang of the School of Journalism and Mass Communication of the University of Minnesota . . . " and Mr. Lower proceeded to present a detailed report on the findings of this study which he had "commissioned."

At no time during the rest of his extensive exposition did Mr. Lower mention to the Columbia Law School audience that ABC "news writers" were part of the team evaluating their own work. After the first glancing reference, the ABC group was referred to simply as "the researchers."

And Mr. Lower never explained what the "criteria" of the study were—simply that the test was "that everyone personally felt the group decisions were the right ones." In other words, the *feelings* of a group of employees of ABC News were the final arbiters of the study.

After relaying the "neutral" findings to the Law School audience, Mr. Lower had the audacity to say: "Why, with such balance as I have reported here, do we suffer the slings and arrows of bias charges? I expect it is because many of our critics suffer from severe cases of selective perception . . ."

The astonishing press releases were of a piece with the ABC News president's speech.

Several months later on February 28, 1970, Howard K. Smith's bias analysis appeared—creating a shock wave throughout the broadcasting world. Mr. Smith is ABC-TV's most prominent commentator. One might have supposed that a third release would have followed in which Mr. Lower withdrew the study he had "commissioned"—or announced that he had fired Howard K. Smith as an infernal liar. Mr. Lower did neither. Mr. Lower did nothing. ABC played possum.

Nor did any other network news president, equally compromised by Mr. Smith's charges, acknowledge their existence—either to refute them or concede them. CBS and NBC also played possum.

On the staff level, too, as we have seen, a similar collapse of candor took place. The very men who had admitted to various types of bias over a period of months and years before the Agnew speech, kept absolutely silent after the Agnew speech. They tacitly consented to official network statements—statements which they necessarily believed to be untrue. These particular men granted no interviews to the press, and did not challenge the statements of their vociferously defensive colleagues, even when again, they necessarily believed them to be untrue. And they sanctioned a press and TV campaign of attack against the Vice President of the United States knowing that they themselves had made many of his charges and knew them to be valid. They, too, played possum.

Newsweek magazine suggests, tacitly, that an "anti-squeal" premise dominates network life as it dominates gangster life. Loyalty to the gang transcends loyalty to professional ethics, truth, the public and the law. According to *Newsweek,* network newsmen were "shocked" by the fact that Howard K. Smith, in granting the rectitude of Mr. Agnew's position, had "turned against his colleagues."

There is, finally, a dishonesty that I have already intimated— the dishonesty of those individuals who know perfectly well that they and others have been slanting their stories, in some cases violently; who are fully aware that they and others have campaigned on the airwaves for and against candidates, groups, issues, etc.; and who, in denying bias, are quite simply telling lies. That such outright liars exist is obvious from the opinion itself. There are degrees of attack and even of hysterical vituperation, that cannot be "unconscious."[1]

The ultimate and most unpleasant question that one must answer is this:

Despite even extreme confusion over an admittedly complex issue, can *any* network newsman be speaking candidly when he claims to be unaware of liberal bias at the networks?

I think not.

The reason for which I say this is primitively simple: There isn't a man on the network staffs who is not aware that the overwhelming majority, if not 100%, of the network reporters are liberals. And

---

[1] This analysis of network dishonesty is written in terms of the major conflict in the country—namely, the conflict between the more conservative majority and the liberal networks. There is a parallel condemnation of network dishonesty in the minority New Left world, however. The New Left press frequently reports on anonymous network newsmen whose views are allegedly similar to those of the far left, although kept secret. Depending on the disposition of the writer, such network newsmen are either denounced as "sell-outs" to the Establishment, or are commiserated with as helpless wage-slaves, condemned to ideological duplicity by "repressive capitalism."

it is precisely with the *staff*—the individuals whose judgments will culminate in news stories—that the selective processes start. *The liberal composition of network staffs renders it impossible for network news departments to be anything but liberal news agencies— with the full regalia of characteristic liberal biases.*

This is so painfully obvious a fact—that it is obvious to most network newsmen, for all their talk of "professionalism."

It is so painfully obvious a fact that when Vice President Agnew charged network newsmen with belonging to a "provincial" ideological world quite alien to the rest of America and with talking only to each other, the network response verged on idiocy.

On CBS' "60 Minutes" a remarkable performance was delivered by Walter Cronkite in which he indignantly listed the American birthplaces of the major newsmen; and network men granted interviews to *Time* and *Newsweek* in which they indignantly explained that they had not spoken to each other for months or years. But the newsmen had not been charged with having been born in Lodz or Omsk or with being in constant telephonic communication. They had been charged with *thinking* alike.

The magnitude of this evasion reveals the utter vulnerability of the networks on this issue. They could not even afford to admit that they *understood* the charge.

Jeffrey Hart in *National Review* (December 30, 1969) commented at the time: ". . . none of the media spokesmen hazarded anything resembling rebuttal. None stepped forward to say something like: 'Why, the Vice President is simply mistaken; we do present various points of view; although Mr. Brinkley, for example, is a liberal Democrat, Mr. Vanocur is an admirer of Governor Reagan; and if admittedly Charles Collingwood is pretty liberal, we also have Marvin Kalb who adores Nixon. Our staff is not only able, it is various.' But, of course, no such reply was possible."

It was not possible.[1] And it is not irrelevant that, in all three

---

[1] Network defenders did point out that ABC's Howard K. Smith and NBC's Chet Huntley supported the war, in contrast to their colleagues. This "defense" subsided rapidly, however, when this proved to be the

networks, a series of smokescreen-myths exist, in institutionalized form, on this very subject. No one who has ever dealt with network newsmen has failed to encounter this implacable mythology. And to understand the ultimate weapon of the news departments on the bias issue—ironclad evasion—one must know these myths.

There are three of these myths—all interlocking. Together they constitute the means by which a group of liberals can engage in liberal selective and exclusionary practices, and pretend to others and to themselves that this is not what is happening.

The first is *"The Myth of the Nonexistent Liberal."*

This myth is recited at the slightest provocation in an attempt to conceal the all-liberal composition of network staffs. It consists of saying, with a straight face, that the speaker does not know what a liberal is, does not know how to identify a liberal, and does not know whether he himself is a liberal. (The speakers, however, have no comparable difficulty in identifying liberals or conservatives on the air.)

Thus, without cracking a smile, ABC News Vice President Elmer Lower told his audience at the Columbia School of Law how he had no idea whatever of the political composition of his own staff. He said: "We don't buy the argument that most of the people who work for us are necessarily liberal. . . . While a man may take the liberal side on one issue, he may take a more conservative side on another issue."

Similarly, Chet Huntley, in his farewell article in *TV Guide,* August 1, 1970, said: "I do not know whether I am a liberal or a conservative."

Similarly, Wally Westfeldt, producer of the Huntley-Brinkley show, denied to *Newsweek,* right after the Agnew speech, that network newsmen were "liberals" while simultaneously expressing uncertainty about what a "liberal" was. He told *Newsweek* on November 24, 1969: "If being a liberal means that I am trying to find

---

sole exception anyone could dredge up to the rule of network conformity on major issues. As the arch-exception to the rule, it had been repeatedly covered as "news" by the press.

where society has gone wrong and show where it has gone wrong, and find where it is functioning, and show where it is functioning, then, yes, I'm a liberal."

Similarly, Walter Cronkite of CBS, according to *Variety*, November 4, 1970, revealed perplexity over the nature of liberalism. Although he conceded that he was a "true liberal", he defined this position as having no content at all: A liberal, said Mr. Cronkite, was one who "is not bound by doctrines or committed to a point of view in advance."

Similarly, on January 16, 1970, Eric Sevareid held forth in remarkable confusion over the meaning of liberalism with *TV Guide* reporter Neil Hickey. The exchange illustrates the evasive mechanism so brilliantly I reproduce it here:

> HICKEY: There is a conviction around the country that newsmen in general both in TV and in print tend to be liberal and therefore are more friendly to the notion of dissent and change.
>
> SEVAREID: Yes, Agnew feels that obviously; Frank Shakespeare has made whole speeches about it. I'm not quite so persuaded . . .
>
> HICKEY: But whether we like it or not, most TV newsmen tend to be liberal, don't they?
>
> SEVAREID: I don't know. I've never seen a head count of this kind [in the country]. How do you divide up these ideologies? . . .
>
> HICKEY: It's the network people that Agnew and Nixon are complaining about. Isn't it an observable fact that most of them are liberal?
>
> SEVAREID: Well, you're using that word carelessly, it seems to me. I don't know what that means, the word liberal, except a kind of open-mindedness, a basic humanitarian view of life and concern for people. It does

not mean a whole set of positions about these bills in Congress or a dogmatic view in which you lump all this kind of action. That isn't what it is to me . . .

HICKEY: Isn't there, though, a kind of unspoken unanimity among what Agnew thinks of as the Eastern Establishment intellectual journalists that the Yippies and the hippies and the protesters are expressing something of real value in their dissent, that they're closer to the truth than some others?

SEVAREID: Oh, I'm not entirely persuaded of this. You're trying very hard to get me to say, yes, this whole thing is overly balanced with people of a particular political persuasion. But I don't know, I have great doubts about this . . .

HICKEY: But that's what a lot of people say; they think they detect a large portion of bias.

SEVAREID: A lot of people say a lot of things . . .

HICKEY: But intellectuals, wherever you find them, do tend to be liberal.

SEVAREID: Well, again, I don't know what you mean by this. They tend to be humanitarian in basic instincts and are concerned for oppressed people. They don't like injustices. Now why is that to be a liberal? And is a conservative the other way? I don't know . . .

Just a few weeks before on November 21, 1969, *Time* Magazine had said this of Mr. Sevareid: "Thoughtful, deliberate Eric Sevareid probably comes closest to the liberal intellectualism that is anathema to Agnew."

And three days later, *Newsweek* had published an off-the-record interview with an unidentified CBS newsman. Wrote *Newsweek:* "Like others who invoked the shade of Joseph McCarthy, a veteran CBS Washington commentator admitted deep alarm. 'My feeling,' he said, 'is that the White House is out to get all of us, all the liberals in the media. They've taken on television first because we are the most easily intimidated and because the right wing hates us most. We're in for some dangerous times."

CBS has only one "commentator" and he is stationed in Washington. His name is Eric Sevareid. Off the record Mr. Sevareid had no difficulty in establishing he is a liberal.

This ritual denial of one's liberalism is not an accident. It is seen as a necessity by network newsmen who are well aware that to state otherwise leaves the networks open to a charge that they are liberal agencies—a charge which is equivalent to saying: Only liberal selective processes are operating.

The second and supportive myth is: *"The Myth of the Nonpartisan Middle."*

The purpose of this myth is to deny the existence and identity of liberal opinion when it is actually on the air. It does so by a primitive means:

The networks *rename* liberal opinion. It is called "middle" opinion or "center" opinion or "moderate" opinion.

Thus, former NBC news chief William McAndrew said (*TV Guide,* April 11, 1964): "The prevailing opinion of this network, I'd say, is moderate. We have the political spectrum interpreted by moderates."

Thus, Mr. McAndrew's then-assistant Julian Goodman, who is today president of NBC, says to his audience of broadcasters on June 23, 1970, ". . . television operates at the *center* of American life. As a result, it is always under pressure from the left and right." (Italics mine)

Thus, NBC's stellar newsman, John Chancellor, was quoted in *Broadcasting* Magazine, November 16, 1970, as declaring that most newsmen "are members of the *extreme center."* (italics mine)

The implication is thus smuggled in that by giving their position a nonideological label, it ceases to be a political position—that being in the "middle" of left and right is equivalent to being *nonpartisan.*

The networks have been so successful in gaining the acceptance of this spurious equation that it is now widely accepted by the nonreflective.

The equation of "middle" opinion with "nonpartisan" opinion is, of course, an absurdity.

Here, for example, is a set of opinions on Mr. Nixon—New Left, "middle," and conservative. All but one have already appeared earlier in this study:

New Left Opinion:

Richard Milhaus Nixon, you scumbunny, you creep, you clot of foetid pus,————of the Galaxy, you teaspoonful of————, infected————in the————of ————filthy chancre on the————of Eternity, flotsam and jetsam of the sea of life, sarcastic little————of borderline literacy, thornridden————on the————of the new century, infested sewer of the Woodstock nation, you greasy————, you————, corroded———— ———— ————, you viral plague, tertiary stage of Asiatic clap,————of the nuclear age, you drop of ————from the————of a pig,————, ————, ————, ————, ————, ————, honky devil you ————of the cancerous————, we anathematize you, we cut you off from the light, you filthy stench, you brain-damaged scumbunny, eater of dead babies,————, of————, a freight train should run up your nose, you————, may you be blighted in the eyes, and in the hands, and in the hair, and in the feet and the throat and the spine and liver and lights and————of you, you bum trip, you wrong number, bad rapper, day tripper, Mace-blister in the eye of our Generation, tomb-robber, leper, short circuit, redneck fag-stomper, fag, nag, skag, bag, drag bad dream, grease blot, you should————DIE!

> "Editorial" signed by the
> East Village Other staff, annotated
> and reproduced in *National Review,*
> June 23, 1970.

Two "Middle Opinions":

My observation of Nixon goes back a long way and I think it's important that people not forget the Tricky Dick that we used to talk about because there was significance in that phrase. It goes back to his behavior when he first entered politics, the kind of campaign he ran against Jerry Voorhis, against Helen Douglas. The fact that in the course of his whole career in politics he hasn't seemed to follow any consistent line, that he's been a man who seemed more interested in what public opinion polls were showing than in what basic principles were involved.

> George Ball, NBC, September 27, 1968

The public never sees the issues on which Mr. Nixon speaks, a man who deliberately misleads when trusted to lead. It's not too late for Mr. Nixon to tell us what he stands for, if anything. We know that he's playing a game. He tells us every day.

> Ramsey Clark, CBS, October 10, 1968

Conservative Opinion:

President Nixon is not . . . a panicky opportunist trying to prove himself a heroic statesman, a chronic trickster reverting to form . . . Mr. Nixon . . . is a man who dose not easily give way, whose political reputation was originally made by refusing to give way; by refusing to give way, moreover, to precisely those forces of political liberalism, ideological dissent and youthful idealism which are today once again ranging themselves against him in furious condemnation.

The original occasion, of course, was the case of the American traitor Alger Hiss, hero of the American Establishment, whom Mr. Nixon singlehandedly exposed, defying the whole massed weight of "informed" opinion which was convinced of his innocence.

I was in Washington during those years. Richard Nixon was the victim then of a sustained and vitriolic smear campaign. He was a social and political pariah, shunned and derided. Yet he refused to bend, and was eventually proved abundantly right, although never forgiven by those he proved wrong.

This was the beginning of the myth of "Tricky Dicky."

> Peregrine Worsthorne, *London Sunday Telegraph,* reprinted in *National Review,* August 11, 1970.

It is apparent that the "middle" opinions selected for broadcasting by network news departments are not "nonpartisan" at all. They are liberal opinion. It is also clear that liberal opinion on Mr. Nixon is simply a less colorful variant of the New Left opinion—to which it gave birth.

As former FCC Commissioner E. William Henry once said on this very issue in *TV Guide,* April 11, 1964: "The middle position isn't *no* position, it is *a* position." This primitive truth is what "The Myth of the Nonpartisan Middle" seeks to obscure.

In addition to this mythological denial of the existence of liberal reporters and liberal opinion, there is a third myth: *"The Myth of the Missing Intellectuals."*

This myth seeks to rationalize the absence of *non*-liberal opinion. Its thesis, often expressed off-the-record by network producers, is: "There are no intellectuals except liberal intellectuals. So don't blame *us* if we only put liberal opinion on the air."

This myth is pure "party line." In an essay on the role of the "intellectual" in America, *Time* Magazine, (May 9, 1969), writes:

> Americans have used the word [intellectual] for only about 60 years. It is frequently applied on the basis of fashion, folklore and snobbery. *An invisible admissions committee rules out most conservatives—except, perhaps, a William F. Buckley or a Milton Friedman. "Liberal" and "intellectual" are thought to meld nicely.* Among scientists, for example, Liberal J. Robert Oppenheimer met the test, but Conservative Edward Teller did not. If nothing else, Viet Nam has provided a handy screening device. Opposition to the war has clinched the intellectual standing of Senator J. William Fulbright and perhaps even of Dr. Spock. War supporters who have been drummed out of the fraternity include Dean Rusk, John Roche, and Eric Hoffer. As a crypto-opponent, Robert S. McNamara is slowly being reinstated, and the admissions committee is eyeing a most impressive candidate: General David M. Shoup, a Marine hero who calls the U.S. "a militaristic and aggressive nation." (Italics mine)

By such *political* standards, has it been proclaimed for years at the networks that only liberal "intellectuals" exist.

ABC-TV displayed the varied uses of this myth most blatantly during the campaign period.

Some months before the elections, news president Elmer Lower —the gentleman who allegedly does not know the political composition of his staff—discovered that this same staff was curiously lacking in conservatives and leftists. He announced, with some fanfare, a "spectrum" coverage, consisting of "guest commentators" from all points of the political spectrum. They included, of course, William F. Buckley, Jr. and James Kilpatrick—the token conservatives invariably employed by the networks as window dressing. Curiously enough, as the "spectrum" progressed, all one heard, with rare exceptions, was liberal opinion.

This odd phenomenon was investigated by reporter Robert Higgins and reported on in *TV Guide,* April 5, 1969, in an article entitled "It Fizzled When It Should Have Crackled."

In seeking to understand how a "spectrum" could consist primarily of liberal opinion, Mr. Higgins questioned producer Blaine Littell. Mr. Littell informed him that opinion from the New Left was missing because: "When we told them they had to be articulate in two minutes, they never came back." Conservative opinion was missing, he said, because: "There's a lack of conservatives who write and think for a living. Most conservatives are businessmen or farmers."

Mr. Higgins checked up on ABC. He queried "five of the most important and most publicized of the New Left intelligentsia": Professor Herbert Marcuse, author Abbie Hoffman, editors Paul Krassner and Jeff Schero, and film-maker Jim Morrison. "Not one had been approached by ABC," said Mr. Higgins.

He then questioned "nine of the most prominent and influential conservative authors and journalists": columnists John Chamberlain and Henry Taylor; *U.S. News and World Report* editor David Lawrence; *Human Events* editor Alan Riskin; authors Ralph De-Toledano and Victor Lasky; journalists Fulton Lewis III and Arthur Krock; and Pulitzer Prize winning novelist Allen Drury. "Not one had been approached by ABC," said Mr. Higgins.

Mr. Higgins then confronted ABC producer Littell with his findings and reported: "Under further questioning Blaine Littell admits this is true. The network, he says, has been 'hugging the middle' in its choice of commentators. Concedes he: 'We've gone after the common denominator.' "

Why were liberals the "middle" and the "common denominator" in a period when the majority of Americans were supporting Mr. Nixon and Mr. Wallace? Mr. Higgins didn't ask Mr. Littell and Mr. Littell did not say.

Thus, a network, by a skillful manipulation of "The Myth of the Nonexistent Liberal," "The Myth of the Nonpartisan Middle" and "The Myth of the Missing Intellectual," can end up with the incredible political anomaly of a liberal "spectrum."

A liberal "spectrum" which, during the 1968 Presidential campaign, emitted a tremendous volume of opinions on the campaign and its major issues.

These three mythologies are used consistently at all three networks to serve as a smokescreen around the liberal identity of its staff and its selective processes, and to camouflage the effective liberal ideological monopoly of the most powerful political medium of communication in the United States.

If the complex institutionalized evasions are astonishing, even more astonishing is the widespread belief at the networks that the results are invisible to the onlooker. Like the naked emperor parading through the streets in his invisible robes, the networks wrapped in their web of evasion cannot conceive that human eyes are witnessing them in their nudity.

There is some sense in which the men at the networks, like many "liberal intellectuals" today, have lost contact with reality.

Theodore White, author of *The Making of the President* series, said in *Newsweek*, September 8, 1969: "I regard the growing gap between the cult that dominates New York intellectual thought today and the reality perceived by thoughtful people elsewhere as a political fact of enormous importance and real danger."

It is a danger. Its nature and its magnitude have already become apparent, in the repeated explosions of anger by millions, even the majority, of Americans over network coverage. If the networks' vision of American "reality" remains divorced from "the reality perceived by thoughtful people elsewhere," one can expect repeated groundswells of rage. And it is already clear that politicians are using this rage as a battering ram.

It is not too difficult to anticipate that in a serious outbreak of anger by a substantial portion of the people, particularly if it is focused by articulate political leadership, the First Amendment could be trampled underfoot.

It is the networks' great sin that in their determination to hold on to an ideological monopoly they are exposing the United States to this danger.

In a hysterical period where, at the drop of a hat, charges of "conspiracy" fill the air, it is unsurprising that a persistent notion exists in the right-wing band of the American spectrum that a full-fledged political conspiracy is taking place in network news departments.

The material in this study—the open admissions and discussion of bias, the interminable confusions, and the incessant internal contradictions—should make it quite clear that this is not the case.

But the political uniformity of staffing, the almost universal dishonesty that followed the Vice President's Des Moines speech, the rationalized evasions and institutionalized mythologies that serve to cover up the existence of a liberal monopoly in the network news departments, indicate a tacit determination by a ruling intellectual elite to hold onto a position of influence in which it is now entrenched.

For at least a decade, Americans in huge numbers have been protesting network bias—to no avail. The networks' ultimate indifference to these charges is thus explained by ABC's Howard K. Smith: "The networks have ignored this situation, despite years of protest, because they have power. And you know what Lord Acton says about power. It subtly corrupts. Power unaccountable has that effect on people."

There is no conspiracy whatever in network news departments.

What we are seeing is: power lust.

Epilogue

It is not the purpose of this book to present detailed solutions to the bias problem, but a few words should be said on the subject before closing.

Perhaps the most striking single observation to be made on the subject is this: that for each of the three network myths used to conceal the liberal-interpretive stranglehold on nationwide newscasting, there is a directly corresponding solution to that very stranglehold.

The Myth of the Nonexistent Liberal: This myth exists to conceal the fact that *only* liberals have control of the selective and interpretive processes in the network news departments.

The corresponding solution is a simple denial of that myth, namely: *political labeling.*

Every publication in the land labels or identifies its editorial philosophy candidly and openly. *The New York Times* does not conceal its liberal identity. *The Chicago Tribune* does not conceal its conservative identity. *The Communist Daily World* does not conceal its Communist identity. There is no reason why network news departments should be allowed to keep producing an unlabeled product, and to maintain the pretense of a "nonpartisan" editorial identity.

The FCC should be pressed to analyze the bias patterns of the three network news services, and to announce to the nation that it is receiving three Democratic-liberal news services with identical editorial philosophies.

Ideally, this announcement should be made well before the Presidential election of 1972, so that the nation is properly alerted to the fact that it is receiving only one kind of political coverage in triplicate.

The Myth of the Missing Intellectuals: This myth rationalizes the absence from the screen of enlightened interpretation of national affairs by intellectuals *other* than liberals—the argument being that "they don't exist."

The corresponding solution is: *spectrum commentary*—political analysis and interpretation by intellectuals representing the full spectrum of American opinion.

Such intellectuals do, of course, exist—and they include professional journalists who are invariably to be found publishing and writing for newspapers and magazines at every polar point on the American political spectrum.

Pressure should be brought to bear on Congress, on the FCC and on the networks to institute such Spectrum Commentary immediately—of the authentic, not the ABC, variety. Journalistic representatives of the new libertarian right, the old right and of the new and old left should be regularly heard on the air interpreting national affairs along with liberals—all clearly identified. They should appear in proportions determined by their actual electoral significance—"proportional representation" being acceptable both to political logic and to the FCC.[1]

There is nothing particularly unique about spectrum commentary. It is commonplace in the free press where one consistently sees a group of columnists on the editorial page with identified and conflicting political viewpoints. Spectrum commentary was commonplace on radio for many years. It was *removed* from newscasting by the networks. It should be restored.[2]

The exclusive allocation of the political interpretive process to liberals should be stopped as rapidly as possible. Spectrum commentary would immediately neutralize the liberal monopoly on overt editorializing in network newscasting and would give the public the choice of political interpretations precisely as that choice exists in the free press.

The Myth of the Nonpartisan Middle: This myth rationalizes the monopoly of liberal selective processes in reporting by pretending that liberal selectivity alone is "nonpartisan" and "professional."

The corresponding solution is: *spectrum hiring*—the hiring of competent reporters from all other bands of the U.S. political spectrum in sufficient and representative numbers to create a genuine democratic mix in the network news departments.

---

[1]There can be no question, where access to the "publicly owned" airwaves is concerned, of differentiating between the political positions of which one approves or disapproves. Freedom of speech is the right of all citizens, whatever their political convictions may be, and however detestable, as in the case of advocates of totalitarian forms of government.

[2]Since January 4, 1970, CBS, in response to public pressures, has restored "spectrum" commentary to its *radio* network. This "spectrum" is of a curious nature: it allegedly contains no leftists. CBS offers a political "range" consisting of two conservatives, two "moderates," and two "liberals." Needless to say, the "moderates" are liberals (e.g., Stewart Alsop), and the "liberals" are leftists (e.g., Nicholas Von Hoffman).

The effect of spectrum hiring would be to put diversified selective processes and diversified opinion on the air. It would destroy "The Parallel Principle" by which reporters from one section of the spectrum create national and world opinion in the image of their own biases. The tendency towards such biased selectivity would still exist in each reporter, but such covert editorializing would be neutralized by the presence of men from all points of the spectrum. Assuming reasonable rotation of assignments, there would be an automatic mutual "policing" of each other's stresses and evasions —and the public would benefit by the additional coverage. Under such a system, no particular bias could take root or dominate.

The chief "argument" of the networks against spectrum hiring is an expression of righteous shock that any standard of hiring should be invoked other than "journalistic competence." This is an expression of purest hypocrisy, since network news departments habitually hire on such additional grounds as: personal attractiveness, age, voice quality, charm, ability to "project," sex, and skin color. Not one of these is rationally relevant to political interpretation, while the ideology of the interpreter *is* rationally relevant. It is precisely the willingness of the networks to consider so many totally irrelevant elements in hiring, while righteously refusing to consider the one which would undercut an ideological monopoly, which reveals their total insincerity.

The blunt truth is: current network hiring practices are nothing more or less than institutionalized political blacklisting. This blacklisting is automatically directed against journalists of the conservative and the far left persuasions. It should be terminated.

It is a significant fact that these spectrum solutions, or variants of them, have been repeatedly advocated by the groups—left and right of center—who have been systematically excluded for more than a decade from the interpretive and reportorial functions in network news departments. The most notable contemporary exponents of such solutions are former CBS vice president Frank Shakespeare, now head of the United States Information Agency, who has advocated spectrum commentary and spectrum hiring in the interests of Republicans and conservatives; and FCC Commissioner Nicholas Johnson, who has advocated a similar spectrum expansion, primarily in the interests of the New Left.

It is not a coincidence that men of such different political sympathies should arrive at the same ideas about how to improve the network news product. The common problem shared by the groups to whom they are most sensitive has led them logically to common solutions.

Nor is it a coincidence that these common solutions should inevitably challenge the three nuclear network myths, since these myths serve exclusively to camouflage the liberal interpretive monopoly and rationalize the exclusion of all other groups. It is actually inevitable that the "outsiders" solutions clash directly with these three entrenched myths.

This unity in the analytical process of the excluded groups—a unity which transcends their political differences—suggests a tactical solution to the bias problem that has never been undertaken: a unified attack on the network ideological monopoly by *all* excluded groups acting simultaneously.

The goal of a tactical alliance consisting of libertarians, conservatives, Republicans, and every variant of leftist, is not a simple one. Such unity could only be achieved if these groups provisionally ignored their partisan differences and focused exclusively on the fact of their joint victimization by blacklisting. They could make a practical delimited alliance on the basis of their common problem and conduct a systematic and integrated battle for access to the air under the Fairness Doctrine.

The very fact of unity among such disparate groups would of itself destroy the networks' ultimate rationalization—that criticism from the left and the right "proves" their "neutrality." Such unity would rip the cover off the arch-fact that the networks wish to evade—namely that all these groups are jointly excluded from the political interpretive process.

Needless to say, only a shared belief in the democratic process and a complete willingness to allow the public to be the ultimate judge of what political ideas and interpretations it will accept or discard, would permit such an alliance to function. If conservatives, rightists and libertarians refuse to act on behalf of radicals' and leftists' access to the airwaves and/or if radicals and leftists refuse to act on behalf of conservatives', rightists' and libertarians' access to the airwaves, they will remain divided, and will continue to be silenced by the entrenched liberal monopoly. In such a case they would deserve to be silenced.

There is strong evidence, however, that the excluded groups on the right and left are increasingly aware of their common problem today. And such an alliance based on the reciprocal acceptance of rights of all groups, under the Fairness Doctrine, is not an unrealistic project.

It is certain that there would be great dramatic impact in such an unlikely coalition, all elements of which simultaneously protested against the liberal monopoly in nationwide newscasting. Such an alliance could not long be ignored by the Congress or the FCC.

Nor could it be ignored by the people of this country. Indeed, it would have a profoundly educational effect. The degree to which great numbers of people in the United States have come to feel that "the system" is rigid and irresponsive, is already widely known in this country. What is not fully realized is the potent role played by an ideological monopoly in nationwide newscasting in intensifying this acute frustration.

The vision of an alliance of all excluded groups interpreting one major element of their frustration in common terms and asking for a common solution would be illuminating to the country. It would teach those who do not know it that an ideological monopoly does exist in network newscasting—and that it should be destroyed.

It should be said, of course, that the neutralization of this monopoly by spectrum commentary and spectrum hiring is not the ultimate solution. However improved the situation would be by such spectrum-expansion, it is still the "lesser evil" and not the ideal. At best, it would create an electic mix in triplicate that would fully satisfy no particular group, and we still would not see in nationwide newscasting the most significant function of political journalism: the competition between many news services, each of which offers a consistent and integrated approach to the news from a different political perspective.

The ideal solution is perfectly apparent, although infinitely difficult to achieve after decades of heavily rationalized government intervention into the broadcast medium. It is simply this: to create in broadcasting the identical system that exists in *all other* media of communication in the United States—the system which would totally expel government from its confines, and would allow the development of competing news services, each of which had the unbreached right to any political point of view it preferred.

This system, of course, is a private property system, totally sheltered by the First Amendment, in which the privately owned intellectual or ideological product is offered to the public for a fee. This is the system under which all other media in the United States operate today. It is the system which gives us maximum competition and maximum intellectual diversity. Most particularly, it gives each individual total control over the ideological commodity he consumes; it gives the collective public total control over the supply of such commodities by means of the "dollar vote"; and it gives the individual producer total First Amendment freedom from outside interferences in his mental processes. The First Amendment does not countenance "public" interference with individual thought or expression.

This, and only this, is the First Amendment system which has given us the incredible wealth of intellectual, ideological and artistic products we have in this country. It stands out in violent contrast to the monotonous, vacuous, ideological-one-note insipidity of standardized network broadcasting. Needless to say, such a reorganization of broadcasting would repudiate the very concept of "public ownership," which is the arch-justification for perpetual government intervention in this medium. It would be a revolution of the broadcast operation down to its very roots.[1]

In this context it is imperative to realize that when the networks cry out in impassioned voices for "First Amendment protection" they are *not* crying out for the First Amendment system as it operates in the free United States media.

The networks have systematically fought any innovation or technological developments—most notably pay TV and CATV— which would make it possible to bring such true First Amendment protection to the individual broadcaster and to the public. And nonlicensed entities themselves, they have systematically evaded, sanctioned or cooperated with every act of government intervention into the literary and news-dissemination freedom of the individual broadcaster.[2] This intervention included the total annihilation of the broadcaster's First Amendment rights in 1941, an FCC decision which totally forbade the broadcaster to air his political views for eight years. The prohibition was slightly modified by the Fairness Doctrine in 1949, when it was "discovered" that this had caused the intellectual death of the broadcasting medium.

---

[1] Those who are interested in more detailed exposition of how such a conversion could be made are advised to read the works of economist Milton Friedman; Professor R. H. Coase, "The Federal Communications Commission," *Journal of Law and Economics,* October 1959; A. S. DeVany, R. D. Eckert; C. J. Meyers, D. J. O'Hara, and R. C. Scott, "A Property System for Market Allocation of the Electro-Magnetic Spectrum: A Legal-economic-engineering Study," *Stanford Law Review,* June 1969.

[2] The chronic indifference of the networks to the First Amendment rights of broadcasters other than themselves has been repeatedly observed by members of the Federal Communications Commission— most notably by Newton Minow and E. William Henry, both former chairmen of the FCC. In his recent book, *How to Talk Back to Your TV Set,* published in March, 1970, Commissioner Nicholas Johnson echoes the charges of his predecessors, claiming that the networks are not interested in free speech, but in profitable speech. He cites the outstanding First Amendment case of the Pacifica stations, threatened with a loss of license for airing controversial opinion: Not one word of moral support came from any network news department.

Indeed, if the networks have a monopoly on nationwide newscasting today, it is precisely because they moved to fill the intellectual-ideological void created by this government-imposed frontal lobotomy on broadcasting.

The networks' urgent cries for "First Amendment protection" must be understood for precisely what they are: cries for protection of the monopoly that has grown up on the *ashes* of the First Amendment in broadcasting. It is the distorted status quo they now seek to protect—a status quo consisting of three versions of the same ideology in nationwide newscasting. The networks are *not* advocating the revolutionary casting out of government, the restoration of total First Amendment rights to each individual broadcaster in the land, and the placing of economic control directly in the hands of the public. But this is what the First Amendment means in the United States.

Because the painfully obvious solution to the broadcasting dilemma appears to be the most revolutionary solution, it is by no means widely accepted. Indeed, it is scarcely understood by many whose minds are dazed by the barrage of contradictory concepts which now regulate this tortured medium. The Supreme Court itself has fallen victim to this irrationality. It insists, today, that the First Amendment which allows bias and the Fairness Doctrine which forbids bias are "consistent" concepts; it insists that the First Amendment which denies the right of government to intervene in the activities of an intellectual medium, and the Fairness Doctrine which requires the government to intervene in an intellectual medium are "consistent" concepts. This supreme abandonment of logic now has the status of untouchable law.

Until a sufficiently large number of people in the United States grasp the hopeless irrationality of such schizophrenic regulation and trace the chronic problems of broadcasting to this irrationality, there is little hope that true First Amendment protection of this medium can be achieved.

In the vacuum that prevails, the only recourse open to the public is that "lesser evil," the Fairness Doctrine.

It should be fought for militantly and applied before the anger of the excluded groups takes an uncontrollable form. We are already seeing mob attempts to take over broadcasting station after broadcasting station. We are already seeing dynamiting. . . .

Such mob action and such violence are totally reprehensible. But it must be understood that the monopolistic practices of the networks are serving as provocateur. It is this monopolistic system which must be altered—a system which exists in defiance of the full-fledged political spectrum in this country and which mocks the very concept of a free competitive market of ideas. It is a system in which the American public has *neither* the First Amendment "dollar vote" control over the ideological material which is flooding into the nation . . . *nor* the political representation on the airwaves guaranteed by the Fairness Doctrine.

It is this double default which must be fought. And the first step of the arduous battle is to establish the fact that indeed an ideological monopoly does exist.

This is what I have established in this study. My methods are simple. Unquestionably they can be improved and refined. But simple as they are, they do prove that such an ideological monopoly exists.

To those Davids of all political persuasions who wish to fight rationally against the network Goliaths, I offer this study as a sling and a stone. To all of them—including those with whose political views I most profoundly disagree—do I dedicate this book.

EDITH EFRON
NEW YORK CITY
1971

Appendices

Appendix A

HANOI, North Vietnam, Dec. 13—At dusk a mist settles over Thuyen Quang Lake in the southern section of Hanoi and young couples sit close on benches along the shore, their bicycles parked against trees.

The sounds of a bamboo flute and a girl singing a heroic folk song drifts across the lake from a loudspeaker. At one end of the lake there are night food stalls selling bowls of noodles, fried chicken, green vegetables and red peppers. A few old women in black cotton trousers and padded jackets squat over baskets of tangerines and bananas, their wares lighted by tiny kerosene lanterns.

The mood of wartime Hanoi is determined but surprisingly natural and relaxed. There is no sense of panic or depression that the war has gone on for so many years. Instead the North Vietnamese, leaders and ordinary people alike, continue to seem confident that they will eventually win.

"Our situation is easy to understand," Maj. Pham Lam of the North Vietnamese People's Army liaison office explained to a visitor. "We are a small nation, but we insist on our independence. We will never give up until we are free.

"Of course we are suffering some hardships, we admit that. But we have been suffering them for 20 years already. We accept them. For we know that the Americans will get tired and go home."

As for the North Vietnamese leaders, they believe that they have been conciliatory and that it is President Nixon, with his plan for "Vietnamization" of the war, who is prolonging the fighting.

This was the major point stressed by three members of the Politburo of the Lao Dong (Communist) party in a series of interviews in which this reporter, who was traveling with the Cleveland industrialist Cyrus Eaton—Mr. Eaton is this reporter's grandfather—met with Premier Pham Van Dong, Foreign Minister Nguyen Duy Trinh and Le Duc Tho, political adviser to North Vietnam's delegation to the talks in Paris.

The capital in which they work, a city of 600,000 that was laid out by French architects with broad streets and lakes and which resembles Saigon or colonial African cities, was left almost untouched during the American bombing between 1965 and 1968. It is largely made up of administrative offices and private houses.

The bomb damage appears to have been concentrated in the industrial suburbs built by North Vietnamese since their independence in 1954.

According to the North Vietnamese, American reconnaissance planes continue to make occasional flights over Hanoi at very high altitudes. A visitor, surprised by a large explosion that shook the windows of the Foreign Ministry, was told that it had been caused by a Russian-built surface-to-air missile fired at an American plane.

There has been some speculation in the United States, based on hints in the North Vietnamese press, that with the end of the bombing in November last year and its ever-present reminder of the enemy morale has fallen. It was not possible for a visitor to find any concrete evidence to confirm the theory.

The North Vietnamese deny it, pointing out that they regard President Lyndon B. Johnson's decision to end the bombing as a great victory. Foreign diplomats in Hanoi, though they admittedly have only limited contact with the cautious Vietnamese, also say that they have been unable to find any substantial proof of a decline in morale.

A Western European diplomat who has experience both here and in Communist China believes that despite the war the political atmosphere in Hanoi is relaxed by comparison with that in Peking.

One example is the obviously friendly attitude toward American visitors and the absence of any anti-American campaign. No sign of hatred for Americans was encountered in a week in Hanoi and the surrounding countryside.

Instead, the North Vietnamese profess to make a distinction between the American people, who are considered basically good and sympathetic, and the Nixon Administration, which is regarded as hostile and aggressive. "Even our children make this distinction," said Nguyen Van Long, an interpreter, explaining why a group of school children all wanted to shake hands with a visiting American.

The three North Vietnamese leaders, in the interviews, emphasized that the program proposed by the National Liberation Front in Paris on May 8 was the only possible basis for a solution as far as they were concerned and that if the Americans withdrew it would not be viewed as a defeat or humiliation for them. The example of the French withdrawal from Algeria was cited.

The North Vietnamese profess to find it difficult to understand the argument that after such a large investment of men and money, the United States must at least have a face-saving way to withdraw or it will lose prestige.

"We have always wanted to end the war and have been conciliatory," Mr. Tho said at the interview in the ornate reception room of the Foreign Ministry's guest house. "For example, while we had insisted that all the bombing be stopped before we would enter negotiations, we agreed to go to Paris when Mr. Johnson had stopped only part of the bombing.

"But now Mr. Nixon wants to prolong the war. This can be seen from his plan for Vietnamization. He says he is going to withdraw only his combat troops and leave his support troops, aircraft, artillery and logistics, to help the Saigon Government. Even the combat troops will be withdrawn only step by step."

With a wide grin he noted that Senator J. W. Fulbright had accused the President of trying to prolong the war with his Vietnamization plan.

The two most important points in the Liberation Front's plan, in the view of the three leaders, are the withdrawal of American troops and the formation of a provisional coalition government to replace the present Government in Saigon.

They believe the plan to be conciliatory because it would allow anyone, "regardless of his past activities or political opinions," to take part in the coalition as long as he is in favor of peace, independence and neutrality for South Vietnam. It was made clear that no one who favored the continuing presence of American troops would be acceptable.

The North Vietnamese officials emphasized repeatedly that they hoped that their country and the United States could be friends in the way they now have good relations with the French, their former colonial overlords.

In answer to a question why the North Vietnamese Government has refused to disclose the names of American prisoners, an official of the Vietnam Committee for Solidarity with the American People replied that some names might be made public next week.

He said that Mrs. Cora Weiss of the Bronx, national co-chairman of the New Mobilization Committee to End the War in Vietnam, was in Hanoi negotiating for the disclosure of the names of 200 of the more than 400 men known to be prisoners. Mrs. Weiss is expected to leave Hanoi next Friday.

After so many years of strife—the Vietnamese fought the Japanese during World War II and the French from 1946 to 1954—the people seem to have become inured to war and to have overcome its hardships by accepting them as facts of their daily existence.

Most buildings in Hanoi badly need a fresh coat of paint; few houses have more than one bare electric bulb showing at night, and many residents must draw their water from communal taps on the street.

There are no private cars and very few motorcycles, a common sight in most Asian countries. Hanoi moves by bicycle. Day and night the streets are filled with crowds of silent bicycle riders.

The children, who were evacuated to the countryside during the bombing, have been brought back to the capital.

It is difficult to judge the human cost of the war. Officially the North Vietnamese do not admit that they have troops fighting in the South. Strangely, only two disabled men of military age, one missing an arm and one a leg, were to be seen during a week in North Vietnam.

Foreign observers here concur that it is rare to see wounded soldiers in Hanoi. They generally agree with the view of the American military that the infiltration trails through Laos and Cambodia are largely a one-way street and that few of the men—estimated at up to 150,000—who march south every year return.

But there is no visible shortage of manpower, and there are many young men in Hanoi who are not in uniform.

Perhaps most significant, the people here do not seem to measure things in a material way.

"The Vietnamese are in the grip of an idea," an Eastern European Communist official remarked at a gathering of the small diplomatic community. "North Vietnam is a state of mind. The people just don't care that the war is hurting them. They won't give up this idea of independence and to them that means driving out the Americans."

The following article appeared in *U.S. News & World Report* **on December 22, 1969, under the headline, "North Vietnam: Plight of Enemy":**

For the first time since the death of Ho Chi Minh last September, a fresh U.S. analysis of conditions in Communist North Vietnam is available.

The picture is one of "enormous" problems in the North, despite the report of President Nixon on December 8 that Red rulers in Hanoi still are resisting serious peace talks.

U.S. experts with access to both official intelligence and other sources of information make this assessment of the enemy's plight:

• Economically, conditions are bad in all respects but one. The exception is that Soviet and Chinese aid keeps pouring into North Vietnam and can be expected to continue as long as there is no new Chinese-Russian border crisis.

• Politically, the death of dictator Ho opened the door for a possible power struggle—based on old personal feuds and current differences over how to fight the war. Evidence so far is that the leaders are being careful to avoid a split in collective rule while the fighting continues.

• Militarily, Hanoi's current strategy is unchanged from the basic plan adopted last April, while Ho Chi Minh was still alive. That strategy: Pull back, build up—and strike hard once "enough" American troops have been withdrawn. This offensive now is expected within the next three months.

Hanoi's troubles. The list of problems facing North Vietnam is long.

Cumulative effects of the war are telling. American bombing ended more than a year ago, but few basic industrial plants have been rebuilt. Labor productivity is low. Repeatedly the regime complains openly about petty thievery, black-marketeering, other crimes.

Manpower and material resources are in short supply. As a result, there is a potentially divisive debate within North Vietnam's Politburo on whether to give priority to the war in the South or to the build-up of a "secure rear area" in the North.

"Individualism" is decried in official newspapers. This means putting personal desires above the needs of the State. Party, Government and Army newspapers charge that all types of people are guilty of this "sin."—soldiers, youth leaders, Government workers and even party officials.

Morale has been hurt because end of the bombing has not meant end of the war. Young men still are conscripted and disappear. North Vietnamese soldiers in the South are not permitted to write letters home.

War-weariness is growing among the people. One reason: Last year, for the first time, wounded began to be sent home from over-crowded field hospitals in Laos and Cambodia. For the first time Northerners began to see the lame, the halt and the blind—and to hear their tales of hardship in the South.

There is enough food, but it is mostly bad. For example, millet is mixed in with rice, about evenly.

Because the end of the bombing last year produced a letdown, the regime, in the last 12 months, has felt it necessary to campaign constantly for support and enthusiasm.

To American analysts, these unusual appeals and indoctrination campaigns mean Hanoi's leaders now are concerned that sagging morale and faltering zeal may become a serious problem.

Summing up. The over-all conclusion of this American study, however, is as follows:

Despite problems with the people, there is no evidence of any significant decline in either the will or the capability of the Hanoi regime itself to press on with the war in the South.

There are disagreements among Ho's successors on how best to fight the war, but these are not expected to split the Politburo, at least in the predictable future. Two reasons are given:

First, the plan for a new military-political onslaught this winter was adopted while Ho Chi Minh was alive. Presumably Ho endorsed the plan. Therefore, nobody now on the Politburo can be expected to take the political risk of countermanding what Ho endorsed.

Second, the war itself is a unifying force. While Hanoi's leaders disagree on many details, they agree that the South must be conquered.

Whether they can succeed is another question. More and more

American experts now doubt that they can. As these Americans see it:

In South Vietnam, the Communist military and political position is growing worse, while the Saigon Government is making headway in both fields. How solid this headway is remains uncertain.

One analyst says:

"While Saigon gains are steady and real, they also are tenuous so far. The gains are still vulnerable. They could be shot away if the Communists are willing to take the risks."

In action in the South, the Communists have been suffering ever-increasing casualties, even though they have recently avoided big-unit actions. During the third quarter of 1969, an average of 2,500 enemy troops were killed each week.

Infiltration, too, dropped off—perhaps because Hanoi decided to hold back and build up for a winter offensive. Whatever the reasons, the result was the first net drop of enemy troop strength in South Vietnam during the war.

Best U.S. estimates, cited in the study, are that enemy main-force units, North Vietnamese and Viet Cong, declined by about 40,000 men during the 12 months ended last September 30, and the number of Viet Cong guerrillas dropped by about 50,000.

Increased defections of both Viet Cong and North Vietnamese troops, as well as Viet Cong underground agents, helped cut enemy strength. As of November 15, there had been 42,147 defections by Red troops and agents—more than twice the total of any year except 1967, when the total was 27,178.

The missing agents. New highs also are being set in the number of underground enemy agents who defect or are killed or captured. A record of 1,800 was set in August, then exceeded by September's more than 2,000.

Most of these were low-level agents—but American experts say their loss seriously hampers Viet Cong operations.

Enemy troop morale also is found to be down, for several reasons. Loss of experienced and competent company-grade commanders is one. Another is increasing isolation of both Viet Cong and North Vietnamese troops from the people in the South, as the

Allies push into new territories. Other factors are continued rumors of peace, food shortages, dwindling hope of military victory, and the loss of Ho as a rallying symbol.

One well-placed American, commenting on the latest study, emphasizes:

"The important thing is that this picture of what is going on is not what we say, but what the North Vietnamese themselves are saying openly. In their system they have to say these things to get the word around. So we are not playing a guessing game on this."

Still, while there is agreement about the facts of what is happening in North Vietnam, there are disagreements on the interpretation of the facts.

Some experts think a power struggle already has broken out in Hanoi. Most do not. Some see indecision in the Hanoi leadership. Others disagree.

There are differing conclusions, too, about whether there is a "dove" faction in Hanoi that wants to negotiate—not for a real settlement but as a way to get the Americans out of the South quickly.

On one crucial point there is wide agreement:

The enemy is suffering weaknesses that can be exploited. The assessment is that if President Nixon is given time—in the face of domestic pressure to get out of Vietnam quickly—problems for the North will get worse.

The following interview with French journalist Pierre Darcourt appeared in *U.S. News & World Report* **on December 22, 1969, under the headline, "Buildings in Hanoi Crumble . . . Haiphong is Ruined, Ravaged":**

AT PARIS

Q Mr. Darcourt, do the North Vietnamese people generally support the war against the South?

A Remember, people in the North suffered terribly under the [American] air attacks. They lived like animals. Now that is ended, but at the same time the North is suffering heavy casualties in the South. Since the *Tet* offensive, nearly two years ago, more than 300,000 Northern troops—at a conservative estimate—have died in the South. There isn't a single family in the North that hasn't lost a husband or a son. And the war, still going on, is a drain on the North.

You find peasants complaining about sons dying on "foreign" soil. For four years, children were taken out of the cities to escape the air attacks and were separated from their families. Couples are separated. The Northerners no longer know the rhythm of life in peacetime.

When the Americans stopped bombing the North, that relieved a certain amount of tension, and this in turn created a morale problem. But that's not a decisive factor. The Government is still very solid.

Q Is the North recovering from the air attacks?

A Not really. Buildings in Hanoi are crumbling from a lack of maintenance. Almost everyone rides a bicycle or walks. Almost all of the few vehicles you see are Russian jeeps and cars and Chinese trucks. In the old Hotel Metropole, now called Hotel Reunification, foreign guests are advised to boil the water—even what they use to brush their teeth.

Only one hospital in Hanoi is still above ground. All the others are still in underground sites in the suburbs. Schools, too, are under ground.

French medical teams recently in the North say that, over all, the people are in good health as a result of a massive vaccination program and strict preventive measures against epidemics.

There is no industry to speak of, no production of chemical fertilizer. The steel plant is idle. There's a great shortage of coal. Gasoline is reserved for military transport.

Electricity is rationed in Hanoi and, in the summer, is available in homes for only an hour a day—from 8 to 9 in the evening. In the winter, electricity is on for an additional hour—from 7 to 9. Why? Because all the thermal power centers were knocked out. Small diesel generators are used instead.

Q Are food and other consumer items scarce?

A The people appear to be well nourished. The meat ration is about 500 grams—that's about a pound—a month. Rice is rationed at 24 pounds a month for all except the heavy manual workers, who get about 30 pounds.

It's impossible to find the simplest items—buttons, safety pins, paper, pens, wire and wool anywhere. A friend of mine said the most valuable present he could offer people when he left Hanoi was a ball-point pen. You can't even find chalk for blackboards in the schoolrooms.

Q What about other cities in the North? Are they in bad shape?

A Friends of mine who visited Haiphong said the city reminded them of Berlin in 1945. It's a ruined, ravaged city, but it's still the country's lifeline. On one day alone, they counted 13 ships moored in the harbor. Russian flour, Chinese rice and trucks, and Rumanian gasoline were piled up on the docks.

The trip from Hanoi to Haiphong, 61 miles by road, took five hours. Bombed bridges had not been repaired, and bomb holes in the road were simply filled with gravel.

Q Are there any signs that Hanoi expects the air war to start up again?

A Certainly they seem prepared for it. Along the main highways one sees antiaircraft guns in place with boxes of Soviet-made ammunition ready at hand. Soviet-made helicopters are parked in the underground shelters built into the banks of the high irrigation and flood-control dikes. Cars and trucks are camouflaged and their headlights have cat's-eyes to reduce visibility from the air. And none of the one-man air-raid holes in the cities and along the highways have been filled up.

However, there is this fact that shows they no longer fear a return of the air war—

During the years of the air war, the Government imposed a slogan: "If you are in love, don't take a fiancé. If you are a fiancé, don't get married. If you're married, don't have children." Now visitors report seeing an extraordinary number of pregnant women about, which obviously means they don't really expect more bombing.

Q Over all, did the bombings produce a lasting effect?

A North Vietnam is in ruins. I'd say the air war put the country back 20 years, and it is now almost entirely dependent on outside aid.

The Russians give around a billion dollars a year. Aid from China has been running at about 600 million each year for the last four years. But much of this has been lost in the war, and there is nothing to show for all the help.

The North Vietnamese are living on what you might call blood transfusions. The Russians supply heavy engineering equipment, and the Chinese food, consumer items and small arms. There is no new investment, no new industry, and their technicians went off to war. And with the economy at a subsistence level, the only trade is barter in the villages. That means black-market rings are found everywhere.

A North Vietnamese not long ago made this sad comment:

"We want France to send teachers and other technicians, but we cannot pay for their travel or their salaries. We produce just to survive. We export nothing. We are proud, but we are very, very poor."

Q Now that the bombing has ended—

A If anything, the bombing halt has complicated life—at least for the Government. Chinese aid is now more important than Russian aid, because Peking sends food—probably at least 400,000 tons of rice this year alone. So that makes the North more dependent on the Chinese. The North Vietnamese don't like that.

Contrast this with the South, where the U.S. has built modern ports, airfields and an extensive road network. Local industry is feeding off the war. And you eat well everywhere in the South; food is even wasted.

Along with this prosperity, you find Southerners who say the North Vietnamese troops do nothing but bring trouble with them. So they are betraying the Northerners—telling the Americans or the South Vietnamese military whenever North Vietnamese units come to their villages. That is new. Before, few villagers would betray the Viet Cong, because they were Southerners—even neighbors and relatives.

Any way you look at the situation, at least in my opinion, it is now impossible for the North to conquer the South by military force, even if the Americans leave. So the odds are that in the long run there will be some kind of deal between North and South.

Q Exactly how do you think the war will end?

A There certainly won't be a neat ending, in which one proceeds directly from fighting to peace. This is a political-military civil war involving two differing systems, and the issues between them aren't settled. The only possible end is a compromise among the Vietnamese themselves.

What happens next depends partly on the American program of Vietnamization. I'd rather call it the nationalization of the war. If it is successful, the North Vietnamese will be facing a trained force of at least a million men in the South.

Also, I'm convinced the South Vietnamese will continue to fight even if American combat troops are withdrawn. The fighting has created a feeling in the South, that they are a separate nation. Even Southerners who oppose the Thieu Government are nationalistic and are determined never to take orders from Hanoi. Furthermore, the National Liberation Front no longer has the power to claim the exclusive right to speak for all of South Vietnam.

So it's clear that the longer Hanoi waits to negotiate, the more its options are narrowed.

Q Could a settlement be made in the Paris talks?

A At most, these talks will reflect a deal made on the ground in Vietnam. It's easier to stop the shooting, as the Americans are trying to do, than to organize a peace. Only Vietnamese can do that.

Q Why won't Hanoi negotiate seriously?

A One reason is that the Northerners feel they cannot tolerate a strong, anti-Communist military regime in the South. They need a friendly regime in Saigon with which they can trade. Without the South's resources, Hanoi's only alternative—given its economic situation—is to turn to the Chinese. No Vietnamese wants to do that.

Q Are there other reasons why Hanoi won't negotiate?

A The men who run North Vietnam are men of blood and steel who have been fighting for 40 years. They are tough, dedicated Communists. They won a war against France. All they know is war.

Of course, there are intellectuals in the regime who are sent abroad occasionally as spokesmen, but the real leadership is a small clan—a kind of tough Mafia of ex-convicts who have killed and in turn have suffered torture.

Q Are there any influential Southerners in this group?

A The only Southerner in the Politburo is the Vice Premier. All the rest are Northerners.

An example of what I mean about the clan is Ton Duc Thang, the new President of North Vietnam. He is nominally Ho Chi Minh's successor, but actually, at 80 years of age, is largely a figurehead. But look at his record: He has been in the independence struggle for 50 years. In 1928, he was convicted by the French for murder, kidnaping and the first holdup of a river boat. He was in jail until 1945, trying to escape several times.

Hanoi's leaders are all tough types like that.

Q Have there been any changes in Hanoi since the death of President Ho Chi Minh?

A Oh, yes! Remember, Ho was a real organizer, as well as being a professional revolutionary trained by Moscow. He was pro-Russian, but he had the authority to form a Politburo that balanced off pro-Chinese and pro-Russian groups within the party. Neither group, I might add, is dovish.

At the risk of oversimplification, the pro-Russians may be called the pragmatists who are fully aware of the huge difficulties their country is in. Now that the Americans have stopped bombing the North, they want to keep the home front quieted down. The pro-Chinese Vietnamese, on the other hand, want absolute Communism without compromise.

Now that Ho is dead and there is no one of his stature to succeed him, obviously Hanoi finds it difficult to maintain the balancing act between pro-Russian and pro-Chinese groups. Sooner or later one group will come out on top.

Q How does that affect peace?

A Look at it this way: The Russians have done as much as they can to push negotiations for peace. The Chinese, I believe, see many advantages to them if the war goes on. As is often said, the Chinese will fight to the last Vietnamese. Why do the Chinese want the war to continue? As Peking sees it, the war in Vietnam keeps the Americans and Russians from making a deal—on a worldwide scale—at Red China's expense. So if the pro-Chinese group wins, a settlement is unlikely.

Q Does anyone in Hanoi want a quick end to the war?

A The North Vietnamese leaders privately admit they cannot win a military victory. They have a vital need for peace, and they want peace. But they feel their position is not strong enough militarily at the moment to negotiate. As long as they are inferior in military power, any settlement would require concessions on their part. They are not ready to do that, and, unfortunately for peace, this inferiority is growing.

(Copyright 1969, U.S. News and World Report, Inc.)

Appendix B

The following article appeared in *U.S. News & World Report* on February 2, 1970, under the headline, "The Carswell Nomination— New Direction for High Court":

Another move now has been made by President Nixon to re-shape the Supreme Court into a more "conservative" mold.

Federal Judge G. Harrold Carswell, 50, of Tallahassee, Fla., nom-inated by Mr. Nixon on January 19 to be an Associate Justice of the High Court, is described as a jurist whose philosophy is that of "balanced conservatism."

If confirmed by the Senate—and prospects for confirmation are rated by most Senators as bright—Judge Carswell, a member of the U.S. Court of Appeals for the Fifth Circuit, will take the seat vacated by the resignation last year of Associate Justice Abe Fortas.

Second choice. The President's original nominee for that seat,

Judge Clement F. Haynsworth, Jr., of South Carolina, was rejected by the Senate after bitter debate.

Judge Haynsworth was opposed by labor and civil-rights groups, but the key to his rejection was the feeling of some Senators that he had shown insensitivity to possible conflict between his private business interests and his judicial duties. Mr. Nixon determined to his own satisfacton that no such feeling could arise concerning Judge Carswell.

When he campaigned for the Presidency, Mr. Nixon promised that his appointments to the Supreme Court would shift it away from the "liberalism" and "judicial activism" that marked it during the 16 years in which Earl Warren served as Chief Justice. Mr. Nixon said he would choose jurists who were "strict constructionists"—meaning those who would interpret the law rather than write decisions that could be construed as making new law, breaking into areas of social and political reform reserved for the legislative branch.

Chief Justice Warren Burger, named by the President as Mr. Warren's successor, met the standards set by Mr. Nixon and so, according to White House officials, does Judge Carswell.

Shifting the balance. The main effect of Judge Carswell's appointment once it is approved by the Senate, will be a new balance of power on the side of judicial restraint rather than the "liberal activism" of the Warren years.

The Warren Court, dominated by "liberals," made sweeping changes in the political, social and economic life of the nation. It ordered desegregation of public schools, expanded the rights of Negroes, reapportioned State legislatures, banned any requirement of prayers in public schools, and dramatically enlarged the rights of suspects in criminal cases.

The new Court, it is felt, will have a "conservative" majority composed of Chief Justice Burger, Justices John M. Harlan, Byron R. White, Potter Stewart and Judge Carswell. The four "liberal" Justices, now to be a minority, are Hugo L. Black, William O. Douglas, William J. Brennan, Jr., and Thurgood Marshall.

With the reconstituted majority, it is believed that the Court will adhere more closely to precedents and be less inclined to reach out to decide controversial issues, leaving them to the two other branches of the Government.

No quick changes. The addition of Judge Carswell is not seen in Washington as a sign of any wholesale, abrupt retreat from the rulings of the Warren Court. But some changes with great impact are expected.

One big departure anticipated is in the area of crime. Several important decisions in this field were decided by a 5-to-4 vote under former Chief Justice Warren. A new majority made possible by Chief Justice Burger and Judge Carswell is considered likely to force a tougher attitude toward persons accused of criminal offenses.

Some possible results:

• A weakening or overruling of the *Miranda* decision requiring police to warn suspects of their constitutional rights before questioning.

• More latitude for the police to search for and seize evidence and to use electronic-surveillance devices. This would mean that fewer criminal convictions would be reversed on appeal because of technicalities.

• New precepts on the admissibility of confessions.

In the field of desegregation, the major rulings of the Warren Court were unanimous. There are indications now that this solid front is crumbling. The presence of Judge Carswell on the Court may weaken it further.

The changed Court may slow the pace of the expansion of the Federal Government's power over the States.

Choosing a nominee. According to Administration sources, the choice of Judge Carswell came about in this way:

Stung by rejection of Judge Haynsworth, the President was determined to name another Southerner. He sought a "strict constructionist," relatively young but with judicial experience, whose financial holdings were comparatively modest and uncomplicated and who would not be opposed by powerful special-interest groups.

Judge Carswell was found to fit the image. A native of Georgia, son of a Democratic politician, he once ran unsuccessfully for State office as a Democrat. After moving from Georgia to Florida in 1949, he entered private practice as a trial lawyer. In the 1952 presidential election, he was active in "Florida Democrats for Eisenhower," later switching his own political registration to Republican.

In 1953, President Eisenhower named Mr. Carswell United States attorney for the northern district of Florida and five years later he was appointed a U.S. district-court judge. In May, 1969, he was elevated by President Nixon to the U.S. court of appeals.

Judge Carswell, associates said, has had few business dealings since he entered public service. His net worth is estimated at about $200,000.

The record. A study of Judge Carswell's rulings shows this:

During the time he has been on the federal appellate bench, he has taken part in only one major decision—favoring the delay recommended by the Nixon Administration in desegregation of Mississippi schools. This unanimous ruling by the appeals court was overturned by the Supreme Court's October 29 "desegregate at once" decision.

As a jurist in a U.S. district court, Judge Carswell generally followed precedents set by the Supreme Court in desegregation cases, but when there was no precedent he took a "go slow" attitude or ruled against some forms of integration. The background material on Judge Carswell which was gathered for Mr. Nixon emphasized that "he has repeatedly enforced the constitutional and statutory rights of Negroes."

On January 21, it was disclosed that in a 1948 campaign speech Judge Carswell declared his belief in the "principle of white supremacy." In retrospect, the nominee said that the thought he expressed 22 years ago is now "abhorrent."

In criminal cases, examination of Judge Carswell's rulings supports the statement made in a background report to the President that the jurist "has indicated his concern that the right of society to convict and punish should not be lost sight of in an effort to protect the rights of the accused defendant."

But, the Administration officials said, balance was shown by Judge Carswell in ruling that a State court's refusal to allow a court reporter to take down the closing argument of an indigent defendant's lawyer was a violation of that defendant's right to the equal protection of the laws secured by the Fourteenth Amendment.

In a case concerning student disorders, Judge Carswell ruled that a university's disciplinary committee had the power to suspend students because a court had convicted them of contempt.

The nominee's attitude in labor cases is described by Administration officials as "even-handed." A point made was that while participating in eight cases involving the National Labor Relations Act, Judge Carswell voted five times to sustain the employer's position and three times to sustain the union's position. A spokesman for the AFL-CIO, which spearheaded the attack on Judge Haynsworth, said that Judge Carswell "doesn't appear to have a significant record in labor cases" and added that organized labor had no plans to oppose him. Civil-rights groups, however, have indicated opposition.

From a lawyer who has studied many of Judge Carswell's decisions comes this comment:

"His opinions are technically clear and to the point. He is not an outstanding judicial scholar, nor an innovator—but rather a technically competent practical-minded judge."

Pending business. Among Supreme Court decisions expected to be handed down this term—in some of which Judge Carswell may have an opportunity to demonstrate his convictions—are these:

Antitrust. Whether Great Northern and Northern Pacific railways should be permitted to combine with the Chicago, Burlington & Quincy Railroad in one of history's biggest rail mergers.

Crime. Cases hinging on the right to counsel at a preliminary hearing, electronic "bugging," confessions, double jeopardy and capital punishment.

State laws. Whether a State can bar Communist Party candidates from the ballot; constitutionality of State action against obscenity; legality of property-tax exemptions granted to churches and other religious organizations.

Draft cases. Clarifying action in connection with antiwar demonstrators and conscientious objectors.

Also on the docket are cases involving questions about welfare payments and whether the "one person, one vote" principle can be applied to small governing bodies.

At 50, Judge Carswell would be the youngest member of the Court. He expressed his reaction to the appointment in these words:

"I am overwhelmed at the responsibility that may lie ahead and hope I will be equal to the task."

(Copyright 1970, U.S. News and World Report, Inc.)

The following article appeared in *Time* on February 2, 1970, under the headline, "Once More, with Feeling":

"God Almighty, did I say that? It's horrible!"

That was the first reaction of George Harrold Carswell last week when confronted with a blatantly racist speech he had made 22 years ago. The revelation came only two days after Judge Carswell, 50, was named by President Nixon to fill the Supreme Court seat vacated last May by Abe Fortas.

The embarrassment seemed like a playback of the recent Clement Haynsworth episode. That time, Attorney General John Mitchell and the FBI had overlooked Haynsworth's financial dealings, which led to ethical questions and eventually Haynsworth's rejection by the Senate. This time, Mitchell & Co. had apparently been so concerned in checking the nominee's finances that they overlooked another bit of damaging information. The Administration's bungle was all the more ironic because the Senate, after the bruising Haynsworth battle, stood ready to accept virtually whomever President Nixon chose the second time. Taking full advantage of that license, Nixon picked Carswell, who, like Haynsworth, is a strict constructionist, an interpreter of the law rather than an innovator, and a Southerner, from Tallahassee, Fla.

Carswell had made the speech in 1948 during his unsuccessful campaign for a seat in the Georgia legislature. "I believe that segregation of the races is proper," Carswell, who was then 28, told an

American Legion gathering, "and the only practical and correct way of life in our states. I yield to no man in the firm, vigorous belief in the principles of white supremacy and I shall always be so governed."

Candidates, of course, often say things on the hustings better left unrecorded. But Carswell printed the speech in the Irwinton *Bulletin,* a home-town weekly newspaper that he had operated while he was a Duke University student. The browning copy was found last week by George Thurston, a newsman for the local CBS-TV station and TIME's Tallahassee stringer, who aired his findings. Chagrined, a Department of Justice spokesman lamely tried to explain why the FBI had not bothered to check the Carswell contributions to the *Bulletin:* "If an FBI man had stopped to fill his tank" in Irwinton, a town of 700 people, he would surely have caused talk and then the news of the nomination would have been disclosed.

After the initial shock, both Carswell and Attorney General Mitchell issued statements about the remarks "attributed" to the judge —seemingly a vague attempt to hint that Carswell had never made the speech, Carswell said: "I denounce and reject the words themselves [of the speech] and the ideas they represent. They're obnoxious and abhorrent to my personal philosophy." The statement concluded with the wry comment that "incidentally, I lost that election; I was considered too liberal."

Ambitious. At the time he was running for office, Carswell was two months out of Mercer University Law School, editing the paper and running a local telephone company that he had helped to finance. Ambitious, having fought in the Pacific as a Navy lieutenant during World War II, Carswell might have figured that it was time to leave rural Irwinton, and politics was a way to do it. When his political bid failed, Harrold and his wife Virginia moved to her home town of Tallahassee.

Carswell, a Democrat, was persuaded by a local newsman to take Eisenhower's side in a radio debate with an Adlai Stevenson backer. Soon he became known as Ike's advocate in Florida, and when the Republicans took office, Carswell was named a U.S. Attorney. He became a Republican, and in 1958 Eisenhower ap-

pointed him a federal district judge. Last spring, when Nixon and
Attorney General Mitchell were shopping for a Chief Justice to replace Earl Warren, Carswell figured prominently among the con-
tenders. After Warren Burger was named, Carswell was elevated to
the U.S. Court of Appeals for the Fifth District. Now, after serving
in that post for only six months, he will very likely become the
ninth and youngest member of the Supreme Court.

Crisp Style. In assessing his colleague, Chief Judge John R.
Brown of the Fifth Circuit says that Carswell has "the ideal combination of physical vigor and dynamic personality." He is not, says
Brown, "a neutral spirit." In contrast to his pleasant, gregarious
manner off the bench, Carswell's decision-writing style is crisp and
cautious. New York University Associate Law Professor Leroy
Clark, a black former Legal Defense Fund lawyer in Florida, calls
Carswell "very bright." But, adds Clark, "he was probably the
most hostile judge I've ever appeared before. He was insulting to
black lawyers; he rarely would let me finish a sentence."

As proof of Carswell's conservative civil rights record, Clark
refers to a Yale University Ph.D. thesis by Mrs. Mary Hannah
Curzan, a former political science student and wife of a Washington lawyer. Between 1953 and 1967, according to Mrs. Curzan's
thesis, Carswell ranked eighth among 31 Southern district judges in
rulings against blacks. Most observers agree that Carswell is less an
interpreter of the law than Haynsworth in every area, including
civil rights. While he was a district judge, 60% of his 23 civil rights
decisions were reversed by the Fifth Circuit Court. In 1963, he dismissed a complaint on behalf of blacks who were trying to attend a
Tallahassee theater; the Circuit Court reversed his ruling with the
biting comment, "These orders are clearly in error."

Among his decisons for civil rights plaintiffs was a 1962 order
that the rest rooms, counters and waiting rooms at Tallahassee air-
port be desegregated. In 1965, he ordered his own Tallahassee
barber to cut black customers' hair. Civil rights activists complained that these decisions were painfully slow, in contrast to his
quick handling of criminal litigation. But while the plaintiffs

thought he dallied, the whites in Tallahassee complained that he was moving too rapidly.

In most of his reversed decisions, Carswell had stuck closely to the letter of the law in ruling against civil rights plaintiffs. Thus, in a suit to desegregate the faculty of a former all-black school near Pensacola, Carswell reasoned that the Supreme Court's desegregation decisions in 1954 and 1955 referred only to students, not to faculty.

After becoming a circuit-court judge, he joined in granting a desegregation delay to five Southern states. It was a decision tacitly endorsed by Nixon's Southern strategist, John Mitchell. In mid-January, as Carswell and Mitchell were dining and discussing the impending appointment, the Supreme Court reversed Carswell's decision and told the states to desegregate by Feb. 1.

Upper Class. Carswell's decisions have reflected his close ties to the society in which he lives. As a member in good standing of Tallahassee's ruling class, he seldom misses one of the Cotillion Club's four annual formal dances. The Carswells have four children: two married, two in school, all living in the South. The judge lives on Lake Jackson, putters about in his ten acres, plays bridge, and in the fall has a reserved seat at Florida State University football games. Carswell's defenders wonder if, once removed from this parochial atmosphere and faced with broad constitutional questions, he would become less conservative.

His vote will not make much difference on school desegregation, the only major racial issue still to be settled. In the Supreme Court's recent rulings, six of eight Justices have voted that a maximum of eight weeks should elapse between decision and desegregation. Carswell's vote could, however, be crucial in criminal cases and those involving free speech and other First Amendment rights. Several free-speech and dissent cases were scheduled to be heard early in this term, but were postponed. This is a strong indication that the Justices were split 4-4; if confirmed, Carswell might be expected to side with conservative Justices.

Despite protests from black leaders, it seems likely that the Sen-

ate will confirm Carswell, even granting his white-supremacy remarks of more than two decades ago. No one wants another
Haynsworthian donnybrook, and much has changed—not the least
the attitudes of millions of other Americans about race—in America since 1948. Carswell wants to forget his past, just as many liberals have pleaded for their unreasoned remarks about Communism
some 20 years ago to be forgotten. Republican Leader Hugh Scott
seemed to sum up the Senate's attitude when he observed: "A wise
man changes his mind often and a fool never."

(Reprinted by Permission from *Time,* The Weekly Newsmaga-
zine; Copyright Time Inc., 1970.)

Appendix C

METHODOLOGY OF THE STUDY

The requirements for this analytical method are: a command of the English language; a detailed knowledge of the major positions and arguments on the political controversies to be studied; and a thorough mastery of the rules as set forth.

I. Basic Method:

1) All weekday news programs (7-7:30 P.M.) during the 1968 study period—from September 16 to November 4—were simultaneously tape-recorded. Three tape-recording machines were used —one for each network.

2) The tapes were transcribed by a typist, resulting in three transcripts of varying lengths: ABC—100,600 words; CBS— 115,500 words; NBC—107,000 words. See Section IV, below, for omissions.

3) The transcripts were coded. Each story has a date and a number, i.e., ABC 9/23/10—and is always referred to by that number in the study.

4) The issues to be analyzed were selected: the three Presidential candidates; the major campaign issues; the principal groups of the United States political spectrum.

5) Every story on these subjects was read and any statement of opinion pro or con on any of these issues was (a) excerpted, (b) classified under the appropriate subject heading, and (c) counted and compiled in opinion volumes.

6) There are 26 such volumes, each containing the opinion found on all networks on that issue—to wit:

Volume 1: Pro-Humphrey	Volume 13: Pro-Black Militants
Volume 2: Anti-Humphrey	Volume 14: Anti-Black Militants
Volume 3: Pro-Nixon	Volume 15: Pro-White Middle
Volume 4: Anti-Nixon	Class Majority
Volume 5: Pro-Wallace	Volume 16: Anti-White Middle
Volume 6: Anti-Wallace	Class Majority
Volume 7: Pro-US Policy on	Volume 17: Pro-Liberal
the Vietnam War	Volume 18: Anti-Liberal
Volume 8: Anti-US Policy on	Volume 19: Pro-Conservative
the Vietnam War	Volume 20: Anti-Conservative
Volume 9: Pro-US Policy on	Volume 21: Pro-Left
Bombing Halt	Volume 22: Anti-Left
Volume 10: Anti-US Policy on	Volume 23: Pro-Demonstrators
Bombing Halt	Volume 24: Anti-Demonstrators
Volume 11: Pro-Viet Cong	Volume 25: Pro-Violent Radicals
Volume 12: Anti-Viet Cong	Volume 26: Anti-Violent Radicals

II. Opinion

A. DEFINITION

In this study, an opinion is defined as any *passage* in the transcript of a network news program which communicates the pro or con views of an individual or group on the issues analyzed by the study.

An opinion will include some or all of the following elements:

—*Who* is expressing the opinion.
—*What* the opinion is.
—*Why* he holds that opinion (his reasons).
—*Actions* he takes that communicate that opinion.

B. NONEDITORIAL SOURCES:

All opinion, other than editorial, is classified in terms of four major sources:

—Public
—Politicians
—Candidates (Presidential and Vice Presidential)
—Foreigners

C. FORMS:

All noneditorial opinion is *overt,* and comes in only three forms: direct quote, paraphrase, and report.

1. Direct Quote:

A direct quote means: an opinion expressed directly by the individual who holds that opinion—invariably in an on-screen appearance.

Since the opinion is expressed in the first person, it will contain only the *what* and, perhaps, the *why* elements—i.e., the person's views and, perhaps, the reasons for which he holds those views.

Here is a typical example of a direct quote—an antiwar opinion expressed directly by a soldier named Michael Watts on ABC, 10/15/9, explaining why he is leading an organization called GI's for Peace:

> (Watts): *We are American citizens first. We are military men also, but as American citizens we feel that there are certain things we have to do. We are in the military because the country says we are in the military, therefore we are participating, more or less, in the war as military men. However we have a right and duty as American citizens to at least criticize what we feel are*

basic betrayals of the ideals on which America was
founded, and as American citizens, this is what we are
doing.

2. Paraphrase:

A paraphrased opinion is one in which an individual's or group's
opinion is summed up or recapitulated by the reporter. It is relayed
to the public in the third person.

Such paraphrased opinion will always include the *who* and *what*
elements—i.e., will always state the source of the opinion, and
what the opinion is. (It may or may not give the *why*, or reasons.)

Here are two typical examples of paraphrased antiwar opinion:

• On ABC, 10/8/7, the reporter summarizes an antiwar opinion by
an individual, New York's Paul O'Dwyer:

> (Network): *O'Dwyer refuses to support Vice President*
> *Humphrey because of the Vice President's stand on the*
> *war.*

• On NBC, 9/26/12, the reporter summarizes an antiwar opinion
by a group:

> (Network): *But the students demand more changes—*
> *they want an end to the war.*

3. Report:

A report on an opinion is a narrative, descriptive statement by
the reporter, relating the attitudes and actions of a group of people.
It, too, is relayed in the third person.

A report will always contain *who, what* and *action* elements.

Here is a typical example of a report on antiwar opinion aired on
ABC, 9/25/9:

> (Network): *In Washington, Pennsylvania, today, Sena-*
> *tor Edmund Muskie was faced with the same kind of*
> *shouting antiwar demonstrators that have bedeviled Vice*
> *President Humphrey during his campaign. About 50*
> *students from Washington and Jefferson College inter-*
> *rupted Muskie's speech by booing and chanting, "stop*
> *the war" . . . Senator Muskie had prepared a speech*

*on education for delivery this noon, but they wanted
brutal confrontation on the war.*

D. CLASSIFICATION PRINCIPLES:

1. When an opinion contains attack on, or praise of any subject or
issue analyzed by the study, it is classified as pro-issue or con-issue,
and filed under that heading.

2. When an opinion contains attack on or praise of more than one
subject or issue analyzed by the study, it is classified under every
heading to which it is relevant.

> *Thus: the paraphrased opinion by O'Dwyer, cited earlier, is classified as antiwar opinion and anti-Humphrey
> opinion, because O'Dwyer is attacking both.*

> *Thus: the report on antiwar demonstrators, cited earlier,
> would be classified as antiwar opinion and anti-Muskie
> opinion, were this study analyzing opinion on Muskie.*

3. When part of an opinion contains praise of or attack on a subject or issue analyzed by the study, and the rest contains praise of
or attack on a different subject—that part is classified separately.

> *Thus: the first sentence of the report on antiwar demon-
> strators is also classified as anti-Humphrey opinion—
> because it tells us about the shouting demonstrators that
> have bedeviled Vice President Humphrey during his
> campaign.*

4. There is no limit to the number of times an opinion may be sub-
divided and cross-indexed, but no opinion may be counted twice in
any given pro or con classification, or appear in both the pro and
con classification of the same issue.

5. Where editorial opinion is tightly integrated with the opinions
of another source, the opinion may be classified as coming from either source.

> *For illustrations of such integrated or overlapping opin-
> ion, see Chapter III, section 2, on George Wallace. It
> contains a whole series of anti-Wallace opinions in which
> public opinion and covert editorial opinion overlap. In*

this study, these were classified as public opinion—and
the editorial components are discussed separately, in the
content-analysis section.

E. EXCERPTING AND CUTTING PRINCIPLES

1. Save for the exception listed below, only complete sentences and unbroken or running passages are excerpted—those containing the opinion elements of: *who, what, why* and *actions.*

2. Direct quotes, which appear in the first person, must include the complete sentences or running passages which contain the *what* and *why* elements—i.e., the opinion and any reasons given by the speaker for holding that opinion.

3. Paraphrases, which appear in the third person, must include the complete sentences or running passages which include the *who, what* and *why* elements.

4. Reports, which appear in the third person, must include the complete sentences or running passages which include the *who, what, why* and *action* elements.

5. If the complete sentences or running passages containing these opinion elements also contain nonopinion material, it must be directly and narrowly relevant to the opinion itself.

"Relevant" is here defined as information that states: when, where, to whom, and under what circumstances the opinion was expressed.

> *Thus: the report on the opinion of antiwar demonstrat-*
> *ors, cited above, states when, where and to whom the*
> *opinion is directed; it also includes the tangential fact*
> *that Muskie had prepared a speech for delivery to the*
> *demonstrators, but was prevented from giving it by their*
> *antiwar protest. This is nonopinion material, but it is*
> *narrowly relevant to the opinion presented, and consti-*
> *tutes a circumstantial context.*

6. Cuts in complete sentences or passages are made in only one situation: where irrelevant material appears in a sentence or passage communicating opinion.

"Irrelevant" is here defined as any information *other* than: when, where, and to whom the opinion is expressed, and the circumstances surrounding its expression.

7. Such irrelevant material may be opinion on another issue being analyzed by the study. It, too, is then classified under a different heading, in accordance with all preceding principles.

8. All cuts of irrelevant material in single sentences must follow syntactic logic—i.e., cuts must be of subjects, predicates, clauses or phrases. The symbol for such *voluntary cuts* is the conventional one: . . .

9. Where background noise renders a few words unintelligible, this break in communication is marked (. . .), indicating an *involuntary cut*. In no case, in this study, did such cuts render opinion unclassifiable as pro or con.

Here is an example of an antiwar opinion, in report form, interrupted five times by static or noise. As will be seen, it is readily classifiable:

> ABC, 9/19/1 (Network): . . . *the crowds gathered in the main square at Boston (. . .) a majority of (. . .) demonstrators. (. . .) They shouted and shouted (. . .) because they were trying to make themselves heard. They even shouted down Mr. Kennedy himself, and as Vice President Humphrey started to speak, the shouts got louder, the gestures wilder . . . How this many peace demonstrators were out in this part of the city is not known at this time; someone made a mistake . . . The entire square is (. . .) by demonstrators all yelling for peace . . .*

(The voluntary cuts marked . . . indicate irrelevant material—i.e., direct quotes and paraphrases of the Kennedy and Humphrey speeches, all classified under other headings.)

F. COUNTING PRINCIPLES:

1. Every word of the opinion, sentence or passage is counted, excluding cuts.

2. In direct quotes, the name and any description of the speaker—placed in parentheses before the quote, i.e., (Watts)—is *not* counted as part of the opinion.

3. In paraphrases and reports, the names and descriptions of the individuals or group whose views are presented are part of the reporter's text, and *are* counted.

4. Paraphrases and reports delivered by reporters are preceded by an attribution in parentheses—(Network); this word is *not* counted.

5. Save for the exception below, if an opinion requires a wider context for intelligibility this context is included, italicized, but is *not* counted.

6. In an interview where the reporter's questions are required to understand the interviewee's answers, or are recapitulations of the intervewee's answers, the reporter's statements *are* counted—as paraphrased versions of the *interviewee's* opinion.

> THUS:
> (Reporter): *Do you consider yourself a Wallace sup-*
>   *porter?*
> (Citizen): *Oh, yeah. Sure.*
> (Reporter): *I believe you said it was because of your*
>   *feelings on the law-and-order issue?*
> (Citizen): *That's right.*

Every word spoken in this exchange is classified as pro-Wallace opinion from the *public,* and counted. The sources, in parentheses, are *not* counted.

III. Editorial Opinion:

A. OVERT EDITORIAL OPINION

An overt editorial opinion is a direct quote, with the reporter himself as source. All rules for identifying, classifying, excerpting and counting overt editorial opinion are identical to those listed above.

B. COVERT EDITORIAL OPINION, OR COVERT-OVERT MIXED

Covert editorial opinion, and mixtures of covert and overt, are more difficult to identify and classify than overt opinion. A textual analysis is required to name the implications, to demonstrate what the opinion is, and how it is to be classified.

Because such analyses are often very lengthy and because they are of many types, no prototype can be given here. The full set of analyses of editorial opinion prepared for this study is available to anyone who purchases the opinion volumes.

The principal standards used in making these analyses of editorial opinion can be defined, however. They are listed and illustrated in detail in Chapter V, entitled "Non-Partisan . . . ?" And the principles by which editorial opinion is classified specifically as a covert justification of violence are detailed in Chapter III.

IV. Omissions

Due to tape-recorder malfunction, three newscasts on ABC, and one on NBC were incomplete.

ON NBC: 10/7/68 was incomplete. Because of this, approximately 2% of the total number of words of opinion on NBC are missing, assuming consistency with the total NBC pattern.

ON ABC: 10/7/68, 10/11/68 and 10/14/68 are incomplete. Because of this approximately 7% of the total number of words of opinion on ABC are missing, assuming consistency with the total ABC pattern.

There is no reason to assume that the opinion which may have been aired on these days would have violated the bias pattern of the rest of the period studied. To postulate that it did, is to postulate that two tape recorders broke down briefly at precisely those moments in the seven-week period when the bias pattern was reversed. This is, of course, absurd. It is reasonable simply to posit that we are working with slightly smaller quantities of ABC and NBC opinion.

Appendix D

Pro-Humphrey

STORY #	SOURCE OF OPINION	ABC
9/17/1	Political	LBJ supports Humphrey as one to lead and heal the world.
	Political	LBJ supports Humphrey as fighter and patriot,

---

¹This summary, like all the summaries that follow, presents a brief condensation of every pro and anti opinion on the subject. In the case of all opinion save editorial, the original opinion was explicit. In the case of editorial opinion, the original may have been explicit, implicit, or a combination of both; the condensation process itself renders all explicit. Editorial opinion includes the opinion of both reporters and commentators. (All original opinions, as they appeared on the air, may be obtained by purchasing my research files.)

STORY #	SOURCE OF OPINION	**ABC**
		a man with courage, common sense and compassion.
9/18/7	Editorial	Reporter commiserates with "good old Hubert" because the "poor fellow" is being picked on by right and left, and attacks the motives of Humphrey's critics.
9/19/1	Political	Senator Edward Kennedy supports Humphrey.
	Political	Senator Edward Kennedy supports Humphrey.
	Political	Senator Edward Kennedy supports Humphrey.
9/20/4	Political	Theodore Sorenson supports Humphrey.
	Political	Steven Smith supports Humphrey.
9/20/5	Editorial	Reporter protects Humphrey by failing to transmit a Wallace attack, and only mentions the attack on Humphrey's opponent.
9/23/2	Public	Crowd supports Humphrey.
	Editorial	Reporter praises Humphrey's warmth and zest.
9/24/2	Public	Crowd supports Humphrey.
9/26/1	Political	George Ball supports Humphrey.
	Political	George Ball supports Humphrey as a man of exacting qualities of mind and spirit, of settled principles and clear vision, of perception and compassion, with understanding of the epic forces governing the world and the capacity to lead us to peace.
9/26/2	Political	Arthur Goldberg supports Humphrey.
9/27/2	Editorial	Reporters analyze Humphrey's conflicts with Nixon exclusively from a Humphrey-Democratic Party point of view.
9/30/2	Public	Crowd supports Humphrey.
10/1/4	Political	Arthur Goldberg and George Ball support Humphrey's position on Vietnam.
10/1/5	Political	Senator Fulbright praises Humphrey's speech on Vietnam.
	Political	Senator Edward Kennedy praises Humphrey's speech on Vietnam.
10/1/15	Editorial	Reporter praises Humphrey as a good and honorable man and expresses sympathy for Humphrey's tragic political dilemma.

STORY #	SOURCE OF OPINION	**ABC**
10/3/5	Public	Crowd supports Humphrey.
	Editorial	Reporter praises Humphrey's speeches as sharper and tougher, praises Humphrey himself as being tougher and more confident, and finds it "encouraging" that Negroes are supporting Humphrey.
10/3/6	Public	Democrats respond with support and cash after Humphrey's Vietnam speech.
10/7/4	Political	LBJ supports Humphrey.
	Public	ILGWU supports Humphrey.
10/8/7	Political	Democratic politician supports Humphrey.
10/9/6	Public	Crowds support Humphrey.
10/10/4	Political	LBJ supports Humphrey.
	Political	LBJ supports Humphrey.
10/10/7	Public	Crowds support Humphrey.
10/10/8	Editorial	Reporter praises Mrs. Humphrey as confident, enthusiastic, exuberant.
10/10/9	Editorial	Reporter praises Mrs. Humphrey as a woman of strong personality and independent convictions.
10/15/3	Public	College students support Humphrey.
10/21/5	Editorial	Reporters compare Humphrey favorably and lyrically to Nixon: Humphrey is spontaneous where Nixon is "mechanical"; Humphrey is beloved by the workers, the elderly, and minority groups while Nixon is supported by stupid racists. One reporter finds Humphrey to be "touching" and believes him to be the Democrats' "last best hope."
10/21/9	Editorial	Reporter praises Humphrey's "goodness of heart."
10/22/8	Political	Senator McGovern supports Humphrey.
10/28/3	Political	LBJ supports Humphrey.
10/29/1	Political	Senator Eugene McCarthy supports Humphrey.
	Political	Senator Eugene McCarthy urges followers to support Humphrey.
	Political	Senator Eugene McCarthy supports Humphrey because of his domestic positions and because

	SOURCE OF	**ABC**
STORY #	OPINION	
		Humphrey will try to reduce the arms race and the military tension of the world.
10/29/2	Political	LBJ supports Humphrey.
10/30/4	Editorial	Reporter portrays the Democrats as immensely enthusiastic about Humphrey.
10/30/11	Public	Negroes support Humphrey.
	Public	Abernathy says Negroes can elect President.
	Public	Negroes support Humphrey.
	Public	Southern Negroes support Humphrey.
	Public	Eighty-five percent of the Negroes support Humphrey.
	Public	Charles Evers is getting out the vote.
	Public	Negro minister supports Humphrey.
10/31/7	Public	Crowds support Humphrey.

	SOURCE OF	**CBS**
STORY #	OPINION	
9/17/4	Political	LBJ supports Humphrey, praises Humphrey as fighter and patriot.
	Public	Audience supports Humphrey's views on dissent.
9/17/19	Editorial	Reporter defends Humphrey the educator against jeering students.
	Political	LBJ supports Humphrey.
	Political	Senator Edward Kennedy supports Humphrey.
	Political	Senator Eugene McCarthy will support Humphrey.
9/18/6	Public	AFL-CIO supports Humphrey.
9/18/7	Political	LBJ supports Humphrey.
9/18/8	Public	Mexican farm workers support Humphrey.
9/19/1	Political	Senator Edward Kennedy supports Humphrey.
9/19/21	Editorial	Reporter justifies Humphrey's name-calling of Nixon.
9/20/3	Public	Crowd supports Humphrey.
9/20/10	Public	UAW officials support Humphrey.
	Public	AFL-CIO board supports Humphrey.

STORY #	SOURCE OF OPINION	CBS
9/26/1	Political	George Ball supports Humphrey.
	Political	George Ball supports Humphrey.
	Political	George Ball supports Humphrey.
9/26/2	Public	People increasingly support Humphrey.
9/27/3	Editorial	Reporter endorses Humphrey's intensity and aggression in attacking Nixon.
9/27/7	Political	George Ball supports Humphrey.
	Political	Ball predicts that McCarthy will endorse Humphrey.
10/1/4	Public	People responsive to Humphrey's Vietnam speech.
10/1/6	Editorial	Reporter praises Humphrey's Vietnam speech as dramatic and as unifying Democratic Party.
10/1/20	Editorial	Reporter praises Humphrey's speech as a move to peace, and portrays Humphrey as future peacemaker.
10/2/7	Political	Joan Kennedy supports Humphrey, says Edward Kennedy supports Humphrey.
10/2/18	Editorial	Reporter praises Humphrey by attacking Humphrey's opponents as law-and-order racists, portraying Humphrey as slightly overgenerous humanitarian who wants to abolish poverty.
10/4/12	Candidate	Muskie praises Humphrey as an impressive man.
10/9/13	Editorial	Reporter justifies Humphrey's name-calling of Nixon, criticizes polls showing Humphrey behind, portrays Humphrey as a political victim of Johnson and McCarthy, sympathizes with Humphrey's hurt, attacks McCarthy on Humphrey's behalf.
10/9/14	Political	Dr. Berman, Humphrey advisor, praises Humphrey's political sensitivity, strength, leadership qualities.
10/10/8	Editorial	Reporter elaborates poetically on public response to Humphrey.
10/11/15	Editorial	Reporter commiserates with Humphrey on a series of political "bad breaks."

STORY #	SOURCE OF OPINION	**CBS**
	Public	Majority of political reporters support Humphrey.
10/15/4	Public	Crowds support Humphrey.
10/18/3	Editorial	Reporter praises Humphrey's personal style.
10/22/5	Public	Crowd supports Humphrey.
10/24/1	Political	LBJ planning series of speeches for Humphrey.
10/25/4	Editorial	Reporter sympathizes with Humphrey who is "forced" to eat ethnic foods as a campaign technique.
10/28/5	Political	Senator McCarthy supports Humphrey.
10/28/16	Political	LBJ supports Humphrey.
10/29/1	Political	Senator McCarthy supports Humphrey.
	Political	Senator McCarthy supports Humphrey on domestic program and because Humphrey will cut down arms race.
10/29/2	Political	Senator McCarthy supports Humphrey.
11/1/4	Political	Paul O'Dwyer supports Humphrey.
11/4/2	Public	Crowd supports Humphrey.

STORY #	SOURCE OF OPINION	**NBC**
9/17/5	Political	LBJ supports Humphrey in name of world order.
	Editorial	Reporter praises Humphrey as handling self well.
	Public	People support Humphrey.
9/18/7	Public	Democratic Party member supports Humphrey on economic grounds.
9/19/1	Political	Senator Edward Kennedy endorses Humphrey.
	Political	Senator Edward Kennedy likes Humphrey.
9/19/2	Public	UAW President Walter Reuther supports Humphrey.
	Public	UAW President Walter Reuther supports Humphrey.
	Public	Delegates will support Humphrey.
9/20/12	Political	Steven Smith supports Humphrey.

STORY #	SOURCE OF OPINION	**NBC**
9/23/7	Public	United Auto Workers Union supports Humphrey.
9/26/1	Political	George Ball supports Humphrey because he has perception, compassion, can understand the epic forces at work in the world, and will guide the country to peace.
	Political	George Ball supports Humphrey.
9/27/5	Political	George Ball supports Humphrey.
9/27/6	Public	Democrats more enthusiastic for Humphrey.
10/1/4	Political	Senator McGovern supports Humphrey for breaking with administration on Vietnam war.
	Political	Senator McGovern supports Humphrey for breaking with administration on Vietnam war.
	Editorial	Reporter praises Humphrey's self-confidence.
	Public	Crowd supports Humphrey.
	Public	Public approves Humphrey's new war position.
10/4/2	Editorial	Reporter sympathizes with Humphrey's success.
	Public	Crowds support Humphrey.
	Public	Negro crowds support Humphrey.
10/9/4	Public	People support Humphrey.
10/10/2	Political	LBJ supports Humphrey.
	Public	ILGWU supports Humphrey.
	Political	LBJ praises Humphrey's understanding, imagination, commitment to freedom, love of country, capacity to do good.
10/16/6	Public	Popular support for Humphrey growing.
10/17/7	Public	Crowd supports Humphrey.
	Public	More people support Humphrey.
	Public	More people are responding to Humphrey.
	Public	Union man will support Humphrey.
10/21/7	Public	People are supporting Humphrey's campaign financially.
10/22/9	Political	Governor Connally and Senator Yarborough support Humphrey.
10/23/6	Political	Governor Connally and Senator Yarborough support Humphrey.

STORY #	SOURCE OF OPINION	**NBC**
	Political	Texas Democratic Party supports Humphrey.
	Public	Crowds for Humphrey grow.
	Public	Money for Humphrey coming in.
	Political	Mrs. LBJ (?) supports Humphrey as able, great Senator, great Vice President.
	Political	LBJ may campaign for Humphrey.
10/23/7	Public	Southern Negroes support Humphrey.
10/25/4	Public	California Democrats support Humphrey.
	Public	Kennedy supporters have joined Humphrey.
10/28/1	Public	Crowd supports Humphrey.
10/29/1	Political	Senator Eugene McCarthy supports Humphrey.
	Political	Senator Eugene McCarthy praises Humphrey for domestic positions and being likely to bring
10/29/2	Public	peace.
		Mrs. Coretta King supports Humphrey as
10/29/3	Public	being for racial and economic justice.
10/30/5	Public	Labor leaders support Humphrey.
		Woman defends Humphrey against fraud
10/30/6	Public	charge.
10/31/9	Political	Crowd supports Humphrey.
		Senator McCarthy strengthens endorsement of
	Political	Humphrey.
		Senator McCarthy asks followers to work for
11/4/3	Public	Humphrey.
	Editorial	Crowd supports Humphrey.
		Reporter sympathizes with Humphrey's "playful" and exuberant mood.

Pro-Nixon

STORY #	SOURCE OF OPINION	**ABC**
9/17/9	Editorial	Reporter supports Nixon's "healthy cynicism" towards Soviet Union after Czech invasion, and his temporary opposition to nuclear treaty.
9/19/3	Public	Conservative audience supports Nixon.

STORY #	SOURCE OF OPINION	**ABC**
9/20/2	Public	Crowd supports Nixon.
9/23/3	Public	Woman supports Nixon's "forgotten American" thesis, says lawful taxpayers are forgotten.
	Public	Man supports Nixon's "forgotten American" thesis, says there is little return for taxes.
9/25/13	Public	Bud Wilkinson expresses admiration of Nixon.
9/30/5	Public	Crowd supports Nixon.
9/30/6A	Public	Crowds support Nixon.
9/30/7	Public	Scripps-Howard papers support Nixon.
10/1/15	Editorial	Reporter supports Nixon's refusal to tip his hand on negotiations with North Vietnamese, says it is a good way to approach negotiations.
10/8/6	Public	Big cities and big states are supporting Nixon.
10/8/7	Politician	Javits supports Nixon because Nixon can end the war.
10/9/2	Editorial	Reporter praises Nixon's powers as a debater, declares he won debate with Kennedy in terms of pure debating considerations, sympathetically praises logic of Nixon's current refusal to debate.
10/10/6	Public	Walter Lippman supports Nixon for President.
10/21/9	Editorial	Reporter praises Nixon's "extraordinary political astuteness."
10/22/6	Public	Crowds support Nixon.

STORY #	SOURCE OF OPINION	**CBS**
9/17/3	Public	Crowd supports Nixon in home town.
9/18/8	Public	Nixon supporters drown out hecklers.
9/19/3	Public	Crowd supports Nixon.
	Editorial	Reporter praises Nixon for "staying on the high road" in his attack on Democratic Administration.
	Public	Young admirer throws roses at Nixon.
9/20/4	Public	Crowd supports Nixon.
9/30/4	Public	Crowd supports Nixon.

STORY #	SOURCE OF OPINION	CBS
10/3/7	Public	Crowd supports Nixon.
	Public	Crowd supports Nixon.
10/18/1	Editorial	Reporter sympathetically describes Nixon's "good-natured jabs" at his opponent.
10/28/10	Political	Eisenhower and wife support Nixon.
10/28/15	Political	Nixon assistant, Pat Buchanan, expresses confidence that Nixon will launch the country in new direction, start solving problems of the cities.
	Political	Nixon assistant, Raymond Price, is intensely loyal to Nixon.
	Political	Nixon assistant, Price, says Nixon is a man of great dimensions.

STORY #	SOURCE OF OPINION	NBC
9/16/12	Political	Senator Dirksen praises Nixon's calm way of campaigning.
9/17/6	Public	Home county supports Nixon.
9/18/6	Political	Representative Gerald Ford praises Nixon's campaign as effective.
9/20/1	Public	"The people" support Nixon.
9/26/9	Public	Republican voters support Nixon.
	Public	Republican voter says we need a new coach in game, supports Nixon who will give us a sound economy not based on war.
	Public	Republican voter supports Nixon as electable.
	Public	Republican voter predicts Nixon victory.
9/30/4	Public	Crowd supports Nixon.
10/3/3	Public	Crowd supports Nixon.
10/4/3	Editorial	Reporter describes Nixon's TV shows as an effective format.
10/9/2	Public	Crowd supports Nixon.
	Editorial	Reporter presents sympathetic description of Nixon as "serene and confident" in face of hecklers.

STORY #	SOURCE OF OPINION	**NBC**
10/14/4	Candidate	Agnew praises Nixon for winning his nomination by going to the people and discussing the issues.
10/16/7	Public	Crowd supports Nixon.
10/28/12	Political	State Senator David Stanley supports Nixon, expects him to find a responsible way to end the war.
10/30/7	Public	Crowd supports Nixon.

Anti-Humphrey

STORY #	SOURCE OF OPINION	**ABC**
9/16/3A	Editorial	Reporter criticizes Humphrey for talking too much.
9/16/6	Candidate	Agnew calls Humphrey soft on Communism.
	Candidate	Agnew charges Humphrey with an equivalent attack on Nixon as a "wobbler" on Vietnam.
9/17/3	Candidate	Nixon charges Humphrey with collusion with Wallace.
	Candidate	Nixon criticizes Humphrey.
	Candidate	Nixon charges Humphrey with inadequate understanding of crime problems.
9/17/9	Editorial	Reporter criticizes Humphrey for delusions about peaceful intentions of Soviet Union.
9/18/5	Candidate	Wallace attacks Humphrey as desperate.
9/18/7	Public	People not supporting Humphrey financially.
9/19/1	Public	Peace demonstrators denounce Humphrey.
9/20/5	Candidate	Wallace attacks Humphrey for succumbing to anarchists and their blackmail and for backing legislation violating individual rights.
9/24/3	Candidate	Nixon charges Humphrey and administration with driving down farm prices.
9/24/7	Editorial	Reporter opposes all three candidates.
9/25/9	Public	Antiwar demonstrators denounce Humphrey.

STORY #	SOURCE OF OPINION	ABC
	Public	Student attacks all three candidates as anti-justice and pro–law and order.
9/26/3	Editorial	Reporter criticizes Humphrey for lack of independence from Johnson and for saying the same old thing.
9/26/6	Candidate	Nixon charges violence surges forth with Johnson-Humphrey Administration.
9/27/1	Candidate	Nixon charges Humphrey with trying to build up Wallace.
	Candidate	Nixon calls Humphrey demand for debate kids' stuff.
9/27/2	Public	American people are repudiating Humphrey's liberal message.
9/30/1	Public	Hecklers disrupt Humphrey's speeches.
9/30/2	Editorial	Reporter says Humphrey denounces demonstrators as totalitarian out of personal pique because they try to interrupt him.
9/30/7	Public	Scripps-Howard newspapers oppose Humphrey.
10/1/1	Candidate	Nixon charges Humphrey with self-contradiction on bombing halt.
10/1/3	Editorial	Reporter critical because Humphrey didn't advocate unconditional bombing halt and for trying to dupe the press into believing that he did.
10/1/5	Political	Senator Dirksen and Congressman Gerald Ford attack Humphrey's speech as being inspired by partisan motivation.
10/1/15	Editorial	Reporter criticizes Humphrey's Vietnam speech for ambiguity and for appearing to play politics with the war.
10/2/4	Candidate	Wallace attacks Humphrey for giving the clenched fist salute of Communism.
10/2/5	Candidate	Agnew charges Humphrey with undercutting Paris peace talks, with aiding and abetting the enemy.
10/3/4	Political	Senator Dirksen accuses Humphrey of gambling with American lives.

STORY #	SOURCE OF OPINION	**ABC**
	Political	Senator Hruska says Humphrey's speech will cause casualties.
10/4/4	Public	Man opposes all three candidates.
	Public	Farm businessman says Humphrey has not offered a farm program.
	Public	Newspaper editor says people don't like Nixon or Humphrey.
	Editorial	Reporter charges both Nixon and Humphrey with failure to speak on the issues.
10/7/3	Candidate	Agnew criticizes Humphrey.
10/7/5	Editorial	Reporter criticizes Humphrey for shouting down demonstrators in contrast to Muskie who invites them to speak on the platform.
10/8/7	Political	Antiwar Democrat Paul O'Dwyer denounces Humphrey.
	Political	O'Dwyer opposes all three candidates.
10/9/6	Political	Senator Eugene McCarthy opposes Humphrey.
10/10/7	Public	Antiwar demonstrators heckle Humphrey.
10/15/2	Candidate	Nixon charges Humphrey with panicking and name calling.
10/15/5	Candidate	Agnew attacks Humphrey for rationalizing riots.
10/22/6	Candidate	Nixon criticizes Humphrey.
10/22/8	Editorial	Reporter criticizes Humphrey as a drag on George McGovern's kite.
	Political	Ex-governor of South Dakota criticizes Humphrey for ambiguous position on Vietnam.
10/22/12	Editorial	Reporter opposes all three candidates.
10/23/5	Candidate	Nixon charges Humphrey with inconsistency on bombing halt.
10/28/5	Candidate	Nixon charges Humphrey with trickery.
10/28/10	Editorial	Reporter attacks all three candidates.
10/29/5	Editorial	Reporter criticizes all three candidates, and charges Humphrey with "talking us to death."
10/30/5	Candidate	Nixon charges Humphrey with trying to throw election into the House.
11/1/8	Editorial	Reporter says Humphrey talks too much.
11/4/5	Candidate	Wallace criticizes Humphrey.

STORY #	SOURCE OF OPINION	CBS
9/16/4	Political	Lester Maddox opposes Humphrey.
9/17/3	Candidate	Nixon charges Humphrey with collusion in the South.
	Candidate	Nixon charges Democrats and Wallaceites with collusion.
9/17/4	Public	Upstate New Yorkers oppose Humphrey.
	Public	Student demonstrators deride Humphrey.
	Political	Democratic politician opposes Humphrey.
9/19/1	Public	Angry demonstrators oppose Humphrey.
9/19/3	Candidate	Nixon criticizes Humphrey as architect of current policies.
9/20/3	Editorial	Reporter says Humphrey is role playing.
9/24/9	Public	Antiwar hecklers oppose Humphrey.
9/25/7	Public	Student denounces all three candidates.
9/27/4	Candidate	Nixon criticizes Humphrey.
	Candidate	Nixon charges Humphrey with perpetuating old policies.
	Candidate	Nixon calls Humphrey's debate demands "kid stuff."
9/30/2	Political	Senator Hugh Scott criticizes Humphrey for hecklers.
	Political	Scott charges Humphrey with lack of leadership.
	Editorial	Reporter mocks Humphrey, sides with demonstrators, and portrays Humphrey as passive and impotent before them.
10/1/4	Public	Demonstrators heckle Humphrey.
10/1/6	Candidate	Nixon criticizes Humphrey's Vietnam speech as threatening negotiations.
	Candidate	Nixon charges Humphrey to clarify ambiguity of speech.
10/8/8	Candidate	Nixon criticizes Humphrey.
10/9/13	Public	Students oppose Humphrey, prefer Muskie.
10/10/3	Political	Senator Dirksen criticizes Humphrey for being willing to share debating platform with racist demagogue Wallace.
10/10/8	Public	Democrats not supporting Humphrey financially.

	SOURCE OF	**CBS**
STORY #	OPINION	
10/10/9	Candidate	Nixon charges union treasuries are being drained to support Humphrey.
10/11/15	Public	Democrats not supporting Humphrey financially.
	Editorial	Reporter criticizes Humphrey for talking too much and for slovenly ad-libbing of well-written speeches.
10/14/8	Candidate	Agnew charges Humphrey with ducking issues during primary.
	Candidate	Agnew calls Humphrey soft on Communism and apologizes.
10/15/5	Candidate	Nixon attacks Humphrey for employing tactics of fear and smear.
10/16/4	Editorial	Reporter ridicules Humphrey for receiving LBJ phone call near men's room.
10/18/1	Candidate	Nixon charges Humphrey with self-contradiction.
10/22/4	Candidate	Nixon criticizes Humphrey.
10/23/5	Candidate	Nixon attacks Humphrey as self-contradictory, as having the fastest, loosest tongue in American politics.
10/24/5	Candidate	Nixon charges Humphrey with avoiding issues.
	Candidate	Nixon charges Humphrey with evasion of Democratic failure.
10/24/6	Candidate	Nixon attacks Humphrey for loose talk on Vietnam.
10/29/3	Candidate	Nixon attacks Humphrey as architect of failing policy.
10/30/5	Public	*Chicago Tribune* charges Humphrey with graft.
10/31/8	Public	Students attack Humphrey.
	Public	Workers apathetic to Humphrey.

	SOURCE OF	**NBC**
STORY #	OPINION	
9/17/5	Public	Students demonstrate against Humphrey.
	Public	One student attacks Humphrey.

STORY #	SOURCE OF OPINION	**NBC**
	Public	Dissenters and demonstrators oppose Humphrey.
9/17/7	Candidate	Agnew charges Humphrey is soft on Communism, retracts.
	Candidate	Nixon stands by Agnew's charge.
9/18/7	Public	McCarthy supporter charges Humphrey with self-contradiction.
	Public	McCarthy supporter charges Humphrey with self-contradiction.
	Public	McCarthy supporter demands Humphrey repudiation of LBJ.
	Public	Cab driver criticizes Humphrey.
9/19/1	Public	Demonstrators jeer Humphrey.
	Public	Demonstrators shout at Humphrey.
	Editorial	Reporter says Humphrey talks too much.
	Public	Democrats are not financing Humphrey.
9/20/2	Public	Demonstrators heckle and boo Humphrey.
9/20/3	Public	Demonstrators disrupt Humphrey meetings, insult him.
9/23/6	Candidate	Agnew attacks Humphrey's federal spending record.
9/24/7	Candidate	Nixon attacks Humphrey's federal spending record.
9/25/2	Public	Student attacks all candidates.
9/25/3	Editorial	Reporter criticizes Humphrey for making crude bid for votes.
9/27/6	Public	People criticize Humphrey for not breaking with Johnson.
	Editorial	Reporter predicts permanent dependency of Humphrey on Johnson.
	Candidate	Nixon condemns Humphrey as formulator of Johnson policy.
	Candidate	Nixon charges Humphrey with building up Wallace.
	Candidate	Nixon charges Humphrey's debate demands are "kid stuff."
9/30/4	Public	Democrats refuse to work for Humphrey.
	Public	Antiwar demonstrators heckle Humphrey.

STORY #	SOURCE OF OPINION	**NBC**
10/1/3	Candidate	Nixon criticizes Humphrey for risking American lives by calling for bombing halt.
	Editorial	Reporter charges Humphrey with acting out of desperation.
10/1/4	Editorial	Reporter charges Humphrey with being a "drag" on dove candidates.
10/2/9	Candidate	Agnew charges Humphrey with undercutting Paris peace talks.
10/2/17	Political	Republicans charge Humphrey with lying.
10/4/3	Candidate	Nixon jokes about Humphrey's dragging campaign.
	Candidate	Nixon jokes about Humphrey's dragging campaign.
10/9/3	Editorial	Reporter calls for destruction of Democratic Party and advocates Humphrey's defeat.
10/9/4	Public	College students oppose Humphrey.
10/11/5	Candidate	Nixon attacks Humphrey for spending policy.
	Candidate	Nixon criticizes Humphrey.
	Candidate	Nixon criticizes Humphrey's vulnerability to hecklers.
10/14/4	Candidate	Agnew criticizes Humphrey for machine politics nomination.
10/15/8	Candidate	Nixon charges Humphrey with panicking and swinging wildly.
10/16/7	Candidate	Nixon charges people are two-to-one against Humphrey.
	Candidate	Nixon criticizes Humphrey.
	Candidate	Nixon directs scorn and ridicule at Humphrey.
	Candidate	Nixon criticizes Humphrey as architect of failing policy.
	Candidate	Nixon charges Humphrey with panicking and name-calling.
10/22/8	Candidate	Nixon charges Humphrey with deception in promising to raise Social Security benefits by 50%.
10/22/12	Public	Watts militant charges Humphrey with saying nothing and lacking soul.
	Public	Watts militant charges Humphrey with offering

STORY #	SOURCE OF OPINION	NBC
		Negroes a bigger crumb off the cake if they would act like white people.
	Public	Watts militant declares Humphrey as bad as Wallace.
10/24/4	Editorial	Reporter criticizes Humphrey as posturing as a peace candidate.
10/24/5	Candidate	Nixon attacks Humphrey's slaphappy economics.
10/30/5	Public	*Chicago Tribune* reports on alleged Humphrey graft.
10/30/6	Public	Crowds are apathetic to Humphrey.
10/30/7	Candidate	Nixon charges Humphrey with refusing to abide by the results of a popular vote.
10/30/8	Candidate	Agnew charges Johnson-Humphrey Administration with encouraging demonstrations.
10/31/10	Editorial	Reporter charges Humphrey with trying to justify himself to the "young."
	Public	College students heckle Humphrey.

Anti-Nixon

STORY #	SOURCE OF OPINION	ABC
9/16/3A	Editorial	Reporter explains Nixon victory by defending Democrats as too advanced for the country. He portrays Nixon as an unkindly automaton; as overconfident; as a former hard-core anti-Communist who attacked liberals as Communist sympathizers.
9/16/6	Candidate	Humphrey calls Nixon a "wobbler" on Vietnam.
9/17/3	Editorial	Reporter calls Nixon an evader on the issues.
9/17/5	Candidate	Muskie calls Nixon an evader on the issues.
9/18/5	Candidate	Wallace criticizes Nixon.
9/18/6	Candidate	Humphrey charges Nixon with playing politics with nuclear weapons, with equivocating, with inviting disaster.

STORY #	SOURCE OF OPINION	ABC
9/19/3	Public	Demonstrators disrupt Nixon's speech.
9/20/2	Editorial	Reporter minimizes Nixon triumph in Philadelphia.
9/20/3	Candidate	Humphrey charges Nixon with self-contradiction, says anti-Communist "old" Nixon is at war with "new" Nixon.
9/20/5	Editorial	Reporter transmits attack on Nixon to the advantage of Humphrey.
9/24/2	Candidate	Humphrey charges Nixon with stalling nuclear treaty and with having antilabor record.
	Candidate	Humphrey attacks Nixon as an instrument of big business with racist alliances and charges him with duplicity.
9/24/6	Candidate	Muskie criticizes Nixon.
	Editorial	Reporter endorses Muskie criticism of Nixon, presenting the criticism as evidence of Muskie's seriousness and forthrightness.
9/24/7	Editorial	Reporter attacks all three candidates, advocates the viewers vote for none.
9/25/9	Public	Student attacks all three candidates as being for law and order and not for "justice."
9/25/13	Editorial	Reporter charges Nixon with fear of being interviewed on TV; with being intellectually intimidated by reporters; with wanting control over his intellectual outlets; with hiding in controlled panel shows; with cold-bloodedly marketing himself.
9/26/1	Political	George Ball advocates defeat of Nixon.
	Political	George Ball charges Nixon with lamentably lacking exacting qualities of mind and spirit, principles and clear vision, perception, compassion, and the capacity to understand the epic forces at work in the world.
9/26/5	Editorial	Reporter defines Nixon's "forgotten American" theme as code talk which "massages the prejudices" of the white middle-class American against the young, the poor and the black.

STORY #	SOURCE OF OPINION	ABC
9/26/6	Editorial	Reporter attacks Nixon as unattractive to young people and as winning them only by default; denies the existence of young Republicans; says Nixon cannot communicate with "youth"; minimizes Nixon's statements.
9/27/1	Candidate	Humphrey charges Nixon with contrived performances; with manipulating audiences by means of balloons and confetti; with contempt for the intelligence of the voter; with a lack of ideas; with fear of debating.
9/27/2	Editorial	Reporters analyze campaign issues from the Humphrey-Democratic Party point of view; suggest Nixon is being supported by a racist "country"; justify Humphrey's ambiguities, while criticizing Nixon's ambiguities.
9/30/5	Candidate	Wallace attacks Nixon.
9/30/5. 6A	Editorial	Reporter compares Nixon rallies to show business; contradicts Nixon on significance of his crowds; says Nixon's crowds are politically meaningless; says Nixon's crowds have no rational political reason to support him; says Nixon is lying about the size of his crowds.
10/2/6	Candidate	Muskie attacks Eisenhower-Nixon Administration, says the economy was stagnant and unemployment increased under their leadership.
10/2/7	Editorial	Reporter charges Nixon with overconfidence; with being a posturer; a pseudostatesman and a pseudophilosopher.
10/3/5	Candidate	Humphrey attacks Nixon.
10/4/1	Candidate	Humphrey attacks Nixon, criticizes him on nuclear treaty.
	Candidate	Humphrey charges Nixon with lack of leadership and lack of interest in building world peace.
10/4/4	Public	Man criticizes Nixon.
	Public	Businessman criticizes Nixon for not formulating farm policy.

STORY #	SOURCE OF OPINION	ABC
	Editorial	Reporter criticizes Nixon for not making himself clear on the issues.
10/7/4	Candidate	Humphrey says Nixon does not speak out on the issues, contradicts himself in North and South, can't be trusted.
10/8/13	Editorial	Reporter says Nixon is a racist because he doesn't condemn Wallace voters morally.
10/9/6	Candidate	Humphrey charges Nixon with floating balloons, not ideas.
10/9/7	Candidate	Wallace charges Nixon with collusion with Gallup poll.
10/9/8	Public	Hecklers interrupt Nixon.
10/9/9	Editorial	Reporter portrays Nixon and Mrs. Nixon as cold, slightly false, and neurotically isolated from people.
10/10/3	Candidate	Muskie calls Nixon a man of little faith; charges him with refusing to debate.
10/10/4	Political	LBJ attacks Richard Nixon.
	Political	LBJ says Nixon is divisive, is trying to set Americans against each other in mutual fear and suspicion; charges Nixon with being opposed to aid to education, Medicare and vital progressive legislation.
10/10/9	Editorial	Reporter portrays Mrs. Nixon as a charming robot without an independent mind as compared to Mrs. Humphrey and other Democratic First Ladies with "strong personalities" and "independent convictions."
10/16/1	Editorial	Reporters say that Nixon, if elected, will be an obstacle to peace because of his anti-Communist background, reporter defends LBJ from Republican charges of political motivation in bombing halt negotiations.
10/17/4	Editorial	Reporters say election of Nixon is obstacle to peace, that Nixon may continue hardline policy and escalate the war for four more years.
10/21/5	Editorial	Reporter describes Nixon as mechanical,

STORY #	SOURCE OF OPINION	ABC
		robotic man, calculating, posturing and without emotion; who is putting on a "Broadway show" for a campaign with balloons and pretty girls; who talks generalities at political rallies; who has been overconfident; and whose followers are shallow and closed-minded.
10/22/6	Editorial	Reporter devotes half his story on Nixon's triumphant Ohio campaign tour to a small piece of trash thrown at Nixon in Springfield; he says Nixon's air of confidence in Ohio is a pose.
10/22/7	Candidate	Humphrey charges Nixon with refusal to debate, with a record that is against the people.
10/22/12	Editorial	Reporter attacks all candidates; says Nixon and Humphrey inspire no confidence or enthusiasm; are not big enough for the role of President.
10/24/6	Candidate	Humphrey charges Nixon with attacking nuclear treaty.
10/25/6	Political	Clark Clifford denies the truth of Nixon's security gap charges.
10/25/7	Candidate	Humphrey denies the truth of Nixon's security gap charges.
	Editorial	Reporter supports Humphrey's charges and elaborates on them extensively, attacking Nixon as one who can't be trusted, who tells lies, who risks the security of the country, and from whom one should not buy a used car.
10/28/5	Candidate	Humphrey charges Nixon "will put on the most desperate and cynical display of political irresponsibility ever made in America."
10/28/10	Editorial	Reporter attacks all three candidates.
10/29/1	Political	Senator Eugene McCarthy opposes Nixon.
10/29/2	Editorial	Reporter charges Nixon with falsity.
10/29/5	Editorial	Reporter charges Nixon with "being a cheerleader at his own rally."
10/30/5	Public	Students protest Nixon's refusal to debate, his Madison Avenue image, his evasion of the issues.

	SOURCE OF	**ABC**
STORY #	OPINION	
	Editorial	Reporter says Nixon is weak and fearful before hecklers; that Nixon says the same things all the time.
10/30/6	Editorial	Reporter attacks Nixon's campaign as a blend of promises and balloons; says the promises will not be kept; he attacks Nixon as posturing, experiencing nagging fears of failure, being in extreme conflict from holding in the desire to go for his enemy's jugular; he says Nixon's nature is to go after his enemy with a club or a meat axe. In sum, he attributes to Nixon the psychology of a murderer.
10/30/8	Candidate	Muskie charges Nixon with refusing to debate, says he will lose the election because of it.
10/30/11	Editorial	Reporter portrays Nixon as anti-Communist and racist, says this is why all blacks oppose him.
10/31/7	Candidate	Muskie charges Nixon's period in office had three recessions and high unemployment.
11/4/4	Editorial	Reporter attacks Nixon's speeches as freeze-dried bits of bland pap; says Nixon oratory is uninspired and slick; describes Nixon rallies as manipulative in which audience response is controlled; says Nixon's campaign is devoid of excitement and passion.
11/4/5	Candidate	Wallace attacks Nixon.

	SOURCE OF	**CBS**
STORY #	OPINION	
9/16/4	Political	Lester Maddox opposes Nixon.
9/17/3	Editorial	Reporter ridicules Nixon's entry into rally; discounts crowd response as meaningless; discounts crowd response as hysterical; discounts crowd response as inevitable for Nixon's birthplace; discounts crowd response as a result of manipulation; compares rally to football game; says Nixon is a boring, anticlimactic presence

STORY #	SOURCE OF OPINION	CBS
		at his own rally; criticizes Nixon as overconfident.
9/17/7	Political	Maryland's treasurer, Joseph Tydings, attacks Nixon for not taking a stand on gun control.
9/17/19	Editorial	Reporter levels personal attack on Nixon as "unyoung, unhandsome, unsexy"; finds it "deeply unsettling" to see Nixon adored by screaming and jumping female teenagers.
9/18/6	Public	Labor leader George Meany attacks Nixon's labor record.
9/18/7	Candidate	Humphrey attacks Nixon on nuclear treaty.
	Candidate	Humphrey attacks Nixon for playing political games with nuclear weapons.
9/18/8	Public	Mexican grape workers boo and heckle Nixon.
9/19/3	Editorial	Reporter denies significance of crowd response to Nixon; charges Nixon with evasion of issues.
9/19/21	Editorial	Reporter argues with Nixon on Humphrey's behalf by reviewing a series of events in which people at home and abroad have attacked Nixon; reporter retransmits Humphrey's wisecracks at Nixon and justifies Humphrey's personal invective while discounting Nixon's political courtesy.
9/20/3	Candidate	Humphrey charges Nixon with evading a debate, taking both sides of issues, and with taking positions as firm as jello.
9/20/4	Editorial	Reporter attacks Nixon's campaign techniques; discounts repeated triumphs in city after city; discounts the convictions of Nixon's supporters and campaign contributors; discounts the significance of Nixon radio-TV statements; criticizes Nixon as devious for evading the press.
9/23/2	Candidate	Humphrey attacks Nixon as resistant to social change, as opposed to social legislation, as a cold warrior.
9/24/9	Candidate	Humphrey attacks Nixon for concealing his plan to end war.
9/25/7	Public	Leftist student attacks all candidates.

STORY #	SOURCE OF OPINION	**CBS**
9/25/12	Editorial	Reporter says Nixon has a rancorous streak; says Nixon is overconfident; suggests he is a liar.
9/26/1	Political	George Ball criticizes Nixon for lack of ability.
	Political	George Ball attacks Nixon's character; says Nixon lacks principles and is a danger to country.
9/26/3	Editorial	Reporter discounts significance of Nixon's white middle-class youth audience; criticizes Nixon's hard-core anti-Communist past; says Nixon is appealing to race prejudice of the middle-class young people; says Nixon is counting on race prejudice in white middle-class majority to win; suggests Nixon is a racist.
9/27/3	Candidate	Humphrey criticizes Nixon for evading debate.
	Editorial	Reporter cites Humphrey's charges that Nixon is evasive, avoiding debate, endorses them by describing Humphrey's spontaneity, passion and strength as he makes these charges. (This report is aired before Humphrey has made the speech containing the charges.)
9/27/7	Political	George Ball attacks Nixon.
	Political	George Ball attacks Nixon as cynical and irresponsible.
	Political	George Ball predicts Eugene McCarthy will come out against Nixon because it is the responsible thing to do.
9/27/18	Editorial	Reporter argues with Nixon on Humphrey's behalf, rebuts Nixon charge that Humphrey is perpetuating Johnson's foreign policy.
9/30/2	Candidate	Humphrey says his opposition is "low."
	Candidate	Humphrey says Nixon doesn't tell the truth.
9/30/3	Public	Unnamed people criticize Nixon for membership in golf club which allegedly discriminates against Negroes and Jews; Nixon resigns.
9/30/4	Candidate	Wallace says Nixon says different things in the North and South.
10/2/6	Candidate	Humphrey attacks Nixon.

	SOURCE OF	**CBS**
STORY #	OPINION	
10/2/18	Editorial	Reporter links Nixon with Wallace as law-and-order racist candidate, in contrast to overgenerous humanitarian Humphrey.
10/3/7	Editorial	Reporter links Nixon with Wallace as law-and-order racist candidate; suggests Nixon is a hypocrite, devoid of principles; says Nixon and Wallace appeal to same group of failures and malcontents.
10/4/12	Candidate	Muskie attacks Nixon as being opposed to education for American children.
	Editorial	Reporter endorses Muskie's attack on Nixon by praising Muskie before and after the attack as morally courageous and respected.
10/9/13	Editorial	Reporter justifies Humphrey's personal attacks on Nixon, and retransmits one such attack while discounting Nixon's politer manner of campaigning.
10/11/13	Candidate	Muskie charges Nixon with fear of debating; says Nixon is unsure of his potential for leadership.
	Candidate	Humphrey charges Nixon with contradicting his former approval of debates.
10/14/8	Candidate	Humphrey equates Nixon's naming of Agnew to Emperor Caligula's naming his horse to the Roman Council.
	Editorial	Reporter describes Nixon as inhuman, comparing him to a computing machine who is programmed by a programmer.
10/15/5	Editorial	Reporter charges that Nixon "prevents" reporters from recording his statements.
10/16/13	Political	Ramsey Clark charges Nixon with deliberately misleading Americans on law and order.
	Political	Ramsey Clark attacks Nixon with appealing to fear and hatred, with fabricating straw men, with deliberately misleading, with standing for nothing, with playing a game, with being a wrecker, an egotist, nonhumane, and untrustworthy.

	SOURCE OF	**CBS**
STORY #	OPINION	
10/17/1	Editorial	Reporter says Nixon, if elected, would be an obstacle to peace.
10/17/7	Editorial	Reporter criticizes Nixon for attacking the press in 1962.
10/18/1	Public	Young Democrats criticize Nixon for refusing to debate.
10/18/3	Candidate	Humphrey criticizes Nixon.
10/21/11	Candidate	Humphrey charges Nixon's law-and-order position with being a cover for racism.
	Candidate	Humphrey charges Nixon with being ignorant of crime issues.
10/22/4	Editorial	Reporter says Nixon's whistle-stop tour is an emotional failure.
	Public	Someone throws a small piece of debris at Nixon.
10/23/4	Candidate	Wallace charges Nixon with contradicting himself.
10/23/6	Candidate	Humphrey charges Nixon with compromising on principles and on human rights.
10/24/6	Editorial	Reporter attacks Nixon on behalf of Humphrey after a strong Nixon attack on Humphrey's four-year record of failure: He says Nixon is emotionally false; that he is playing the hero; that his crowds are unenthusiastic; that he is making personal attacks on Humphrey; that he was a hard line anti-Communist when younger who attacked the patriotism of opponents; that his campaign has a core of falsity contrived by Madison Avenue; that he pretends to be supported by youth; that his campaign promises are oversimplified and self-contradictory; that he has not yet convinced his supporters to vote for him.
10/24/9	Candidate	Humphrey charges Nixon's delays on nuclear treaty as indefensible, unconscionable, uncondonable.
	Candidate	Humphrey attacks Nixon for playing on fears

STORY #	SOURCE OF OPINION	**CBS**
		of American people about Communism and Communist aggression.
10/25/1	Political	Lawrence O'Brien, Humphrey's campaign manager, accuses Nixon of making vicious and false accusations without taking responsibility for his words.
10/25/2	Political	Clark Clifford denies truth of Nixon charge of security gap.
	Political	Clark Clifford denies truth of Nixon charge of security gap.
	Political	Clark Clifford denies truth of Nixon charge of security gap.
10/25/4	Candidate	Humphrey denies truth of Nixon charge of security gap and attacks Nixon as militarist.
10/28/8	Candidate	Humphrey attacks Nixon as opposed to Social Security and federal aid to education.
10/28/15	Editorial	Reporter describes Nixon and staff as squares who don't conform to liberal-left cultural standards; mocks their "forgotten American" crusade; compares Nixon and staff to inhuman computers.
10/28/16	Editorial	Reporter argues with Nixon on behalf of Humphrey, denies Republican charges that Johnson is playing politics with the peace negotiations to defeat Nixon.
10/29/1	Political	Senator Eugene McCarthy repudiates Nixon because of his comments on the security gap.
10/30/7	Editorial	Reporter criticizes Nixon for not debating.
	Public	Students criticize Nixon for not debating and for unclarity of positions.
	Public	Students walk out on Nixon silently.
10/31/8	Candidate	Humphrey charges Nixon with trickery.

STORY #	SOURCE OF OPINION	**NBC**
9/16/12	Editorial	Reporter "explains" Nixon's commanding lead

	SOURCE OF	**NBC**
STORY #	OPINION	

		with a joke that minimizes Nixon's strength and evades Democratic weaknesses.
9/18/7	Public	Cab driver opposes Nixon.
9/19/2	Public	Union leader Walter Reuther attacks Nixon.
9/20/1	Editorial	Reporter suppresses intensity of Nixon's triumph in Democratic Philadelphia as reported by two other networks, and devotes whole story to "proving" that it was not a success at all, that the crowds were not for Nixon.
9/20/2	Candidate	Humphrey attacks Nixon's position as being as firm as wobbly gelatin.
	Public	Someone boos Nixon.
9/20/3	Public	Hecklers insult Nixon.
9/23/6	Editorial	Reporter attacks "old" Nixon for "travelling the low road" of anti-Communism.
9/23/7	Candidate	Humphrey attacks Nixon as evasive.
9/24/7	Candidate	Humphrey charges Nixon with refusing to debate him.
9/25/2	Public	Student attacks all candidates as being for law and order and against "justice."
9/26/1	Political	George Ball attacks Nixon as lacking perception, compassion, understanding of epic forces in the world.
9/27/5	Political	George Ball attacks Nixon as Tricky Dick, given to attacking liberals as Communist sympathizers, inconsistent, cynical, shallow, and shockingly irresponsible.
	Editorial	Reporter endorses Ball's attack on Nixon.
9/27/6	Candidate	Humphrey attacks Nixon as opposed to various forms of social legislation, says he has a "miserable conservative reactionary record."
10/1/3	Editorial	Reporter criticizes as evasive Nixon's refusal to make public his tactical plans for Vietnam.
10/2/9	Candidate	Muskie charges Nixon with evasion on bombing halt.
10/4/2	Candidate	Humphrey charges Nixon with evasion.
10/4/3	Editorial	Reporter charges Nixon with malicious con-

STORY #	SOURCE OF OPINION	NBC
		duct to Humphrey; with posturing as a winner; with using commercial gimmickry and fakery to win his support.
10/8/5	Candidate	Curtis LeMay charges Nixon with being influenced by the liberal wing of the Republican Party.
	Candidate	Curtis LeMay charges Nixon with making deals with Republican left wing.
10/9/2	Editorial	Reporter charges Nixon with uttering bromides.
10/9/3	Editorial	Reporter describes Humphrey as "lesser evil" than Nixon.
10/9/4	Candidate	Humphrey attacks Nixon as representing the status quo and a step backward.
10/9/5	Candidate	George Wallace attacks Nixon for being in collusion with pollsters.
10/10/2	Political	LBJ attacks Nixon for opposing progressive legislation and calling for delay in adopting nuclear treaty.
10/11/4	Candidate	Humphrey charges Nixon with refusing to debate.
10/11/5	Editorial	Reporter debates Nixon's view of his success, says Nixon crowds are bored with and don't like Nixon, and that even when they cheer it's only because of "applause lines" in Nixon's speeches.
10/14/5	Candidate	Muskie criticizes Nixon as ignoring those who demand equal opportunity.
10/16/6	Candidate	Humphrey compares Nixon to Sally Rand, hiding behind balloons, and to a wind-up doll that hides; he charges him with evading the issues.
10/16/7	Editorial	Reporter charges Nixon with cruel mockery of Humphrey; suggests he is a liar or a hypocrite for saying that he isn't going in for name-calling; reminds people Nixon is refusing to debate Humphrey.
10/16/9	Political	Ramsey Clark attacks Nixon as ignorant on

STORY #	SOURCE OF OPINION	NBC
		crime issues and as appealing to fear and hate in the electorate.
	Editorial	Reporter endorses Clark attack on Nixon; assures the electorate it has no reason to fear or hate "hippies and Yippies"—denying any lawlessness or violence in these groups.
10/18/9	Editorial	Reporter attacks Nixon for not giving complex speeches on economic, international, legal issues at his rallies; for not explaining in detail how he will solve the nation's problems; for "hiding" these serious analyses from the people by giving them on the radio.
10/21/4	Candidate	Humphrey attacks Nixon for being opposed to various pieces of social legislation and for hypocrisy on this subject in election years.
10/22/12	Public	Black militant charges Nixon with WASP prejudice against Negroes, with trying to hold Negroes down economically.
	Public	Black militant says it would be suicidal to vote for Nixon who hates Negroes.
10/23/6	Candidate	Humphrey charges Nixon with cheap politics.
10/24/5	Editorial	Reporter says Nixon audiences don't really like Nixon but they are responding to theatrical gimmicks like Pavlovian dogs.
10/24/8	Candidate	Wallace suggests Nixon is a liar.
10/25/3	Political	Defense Secretary Clifford denies the truth of Nixon's charge of a U.S. security gap in relation to the USSR.
10/25/4	Candidate	Humphrey charges Nixon with playing politics with national security.
10/28/1	Candidate	Humphrey charges Nixon with trying to win election with a big Madison Avenue budget and advertising and PR techniques.
10/29/1	Political	Eugene McCarthy criticizes Nixon for security gap charges.
10/29/2	Public	Mrs. Coretta King attacks Nixon and Wallace jointly as antagonistic to racial and economic justice.

	SOURCE OF	**NBC**
STORY #	OPINION	
10/29/3	Candidate	Humphrey says that Nixon smells up the air.
10/29/5	Editorial	Reporter says that Nixon rallies are monotonous, including the audience's cheers.
10/30/7	Public	University students heckle Nixon in song.
10/31/9	Political	Senator Eugene McCarthy attacks Nixon.
	Political	McCarthy attacks Nixon for advocating nuclear parity; says he has a militaristic attitude; says Nixon can't distinguish between the pale horse of death and the white horse of victory.
11/1/9	Editorial	Reporter portrays Humphrey as advocating peace, brotherhood and unity and Nixon as representing militarism and banality.
11/4/9	Political	Democrats charge Nixon campaign with violating law requiring filing of expenses by certain date.

Appendix E

Pro-Wallace

STORY #	SOURCE OF OPINION	ABC
9/16/4	Political	Lester Maddox supports Wallace.
9/19/5	Public	Crowds support Wallace.
	Public	Group of individuals supports Wallace.
	Public	Man supports Wallace.
	Public	Three men support Wallace.
9/19/6	Public	General Edmund Walker supports Wallace.
	Public	Crowd supports Wallace, including Democrats.
9/20/5	Public	Crowd supports Wallace.
9/26/4	Political	Romney compliments Wallace's personality.
9/30/5	Public	Crowd supports Wallace.
10/2/4	Public	Crowd supports Wallace.
	Public	Crowd supports Wallace.

	SOURCE OF	**ABC**
STORY #	OPINION	
10/9/2	Editorial	Reporter praises Wallace's qualities as a debater.
10/11/1	Public	Arkansas supports Wallace.
10/17/8	Public	People cheer Wallace.
10/21/9	Editorial	Reporter praises Wallace's charisma.
10/25/9	Public	Crowd supports Wallace.
	Public	Crowd supports Wallace.
10/28/7	Public	Wallace's mother praises Wallace.
	Public	Old school friend praises Wallace.
10/31/6	Public	Crowd supports Wallace.
10/31/8	Public	Union men support Wallace.
	Public	Union men support Wallace.
	Public	Union men support Wallace.
	Public	Union men support Wallace.
	Public	Union men support Wallace.
11/4/5	Public	Significant portion of country supports Wallace.

	SOURCE OF	**CBS**
STORY #	OPINION	
9/16/4	Political	Lester Maddox supports Wallace.
9/17/6	Political	Convention supports Wallace.
	Public	Advance man supports Wallace.
	Political	Delegates support Wallace.
9/18/6	Public	Union men support Wallace.
9/20/10	Public	Union men support Wallace.
	Public	Millions of voters support Wallace.
	Public	Labor supports Wallace.
	Public	Union man supports Wallace.
	Public	Union man supports Wallace.
	Public	Union man supports Wallace.
	Public	Union men support Wallace.
	Public	Union men support Wallace.
	Public	Law-and-order union men support Wallace.
	Public	Union man supports Wallace.

STORY #	SOURCE OF OPINION	**CBS**
	Public	Union men deny Wallace is a racist.
	Political	Wallace's campaign manager denies Wallace is a racist.
	Political	Wallace's campaign manager denies Wallace is a racist.
	Political	Wallace's campaign manager praises Wallace.
	Public	Union men support Wallace.
	Public	Man supports Wallace.
	Public	Anti-bussing woman supports Wallace.
	Public	Man supports Wallace.
	Public	Woman supports Wallace.
	Public	Man supports Wallace.
	Public	Union men support Wallace.
9/25/8	Public	White middle-class suburbanites support Wallace.
9/30/4	Public	Crowds support Wallace.
10/1/8	Public	Crowds support Wallace.
10/7/1	Public	Public heavily supports Wallace.
10/23/4	Public	Individual supports Wallace.
10/25/5	Public	Crowd supports Wallace.
	Public	Crowd supports Wallace.
10/30/8	Public	Crowd supports Wallace.
11/4/5	Political	Lester Maddox supports Wallace.
	Public	Crowd supports Wallace.

STORY #	SOURCE OF OPINION	**NBC**
9/16/5	Political	Governor Maddox supports Wallace.
9/18/7	Public	Law-and-order cab driver supports Wallace.
9/18/10	Public	People support Wallace all over country.
9/19/2	Public	Union men support Wallace.
9/23/8	Public	People contribute to Wallace campaign.
9/30/4	Public	Crowds support Wallace.
10/2/7	Public	Workers support Wallace.
10/8/4	Public	Workers support Wallace.
	Public	Union members support Wallace.

	SOURCE OF	**NBC**
STORY #	OPINION	
10/9/5	Public	Crowds support Wallace.
10/15/6	Public	Technical workers support Wallace.
10/17/7	Public	Law-and-order union man supports Wallace.
10/17/8	Public	School children support Wallace.
	Public	Crowd supports Wallace's law-and-order position.
10/23/4	Public	Ethnic working-class voters support Wallace.
10/25/7	Public	Crowd supports Wallace.
10/29/6	Public	Crowd supports Wallace.
10/30/9	Public	Crowd supports Wallace.
	Public	Crowd supports Wallace.
10/31/7	Public	Crowd supports Wallace.

Anti-Wallace

	SOURCE OF	**ABC**
STORY #	OPINION	
9/19/6	Editorial	Reporter criticizes Wallace as a threat to freedom and justice, as one who uses fear to pervert the passions and pervert the logic of human beings.
9/20/8	Editorial	Reporter criticizes George Wallace as the ultimate danger that the violent militants could bring on the nation.
9/24/2	Candidate	Humphrey criticizes Wallace as antilabor.
9/24/6	Candidate	Muskie criticizes Wallace as untruthful.
	Editorial	Reporter endorses Muskie's attack.
9/24/7	Editorial	Reporter criticizes all three candidates, advises people not to vote.
9/25/9	Public	Student criticizes all three candidates as law-and-order candidates against justice.
9/26/4	Public	Romney criticizes Wallace as a racist.
9/30/5	Public	Group criticizes Wallace.
9/30/7	Public	Scripps-Howard newspapers criticize Wallace.
10/2/3	Candidate	Humphrey criticizes Wallace as arousing prejudice and fear.

STORY #	SOURCE OF OPINION	ABC
	Candidate	Humphrey criticizes Wallace.
	Candidate	Humphrey criticizes Wallace for politics of fear and racism, for being supported by Ku Klux Klan, White Citizens Council, John Birch Society, Minutemen and anti-Semites.
10/2/4	Public	Many hecklers attack Wallace.
	Public	Hecklers compare Wallace to Hitler.
	Candidate	Humphrey attacks Wallace comparing him to Adolf Hitler.
	Public	Hecklers attack Wallace as bigot, racist, white supremacist.
	Public	Hecklers attack Wallace, wear Ku Klux Klan robes.
	Public	Hecklers attack Wallace with Nazi war salutes.
	Public	Hecklers defy police, destroy Wallace literature.
10/3/5	Candidate	Humphrey criticizes Wallace on grounds of LeMay nuclear statement.
10/4/1	Candidate	Humphrey criticizes Wallace and LeMay for nuclear stand.
	Candidate	Humphrey criticizes Wallace and LeMay as favoring brute force at home and catastrophic force abroad.
	Candidate	Nixon criticizes Wallace for threatening to run over protesters.
10/4/4	Public	Man criticizes all candidates.
	Public	Farmer criticizes all candidates for failing to discuss farm program.
	Editorial	Reporter criticizes all candidates for not speaking on the issues.
10/7/3	Candidate	Agnew urges voters not to waste votes on Wallace.
10/7/4	Candidate	Humphrey attacks Wallace for appealing to fear.
10/8/5	Public	Crowd heckles Wallace.
10/8/13	Candidate	Humphrey attacks Wallace as a racist.
	Candidate	Nixon says a vote for Wallace is a waste.

	SOURCE OF	**ABC**
STORY #	OPINION	
10/10/4	Political	LBJ attacks Wallace.
	Political	LBJ attacks Wallace as divisive and engendering fear.
10/10/6	Editorial	Reporter criticizes Wallace for threatening to run over dissenters.
10/15/4	Public	Hecklers unnerve Wallace by cheering him.
10/17/8	Public	Hecklers exhaust Wallace, who cancels appearances.
10/17/9	Editorial	Reporter attacks Wallace as demagogue, racist, rabble-rouser.
10/22/5	Public	Hecklers throw eggs, fruit and vegetables at Wallace; he is hit by apple core.
10/22/12	Editorial	Reporter criticizes all candidates.
10/23/6	Public	Hecklers throw sticks, stones, eggs, apple core, tomatoes, for three days in a row.
	Editorial	Reporter criticizes Wallace for violence at Wallace rallies.
	Public	Hecklers pelt Wallace with stones and fruit; object hits Wallace in the face.
10/24/3	Political	Kennedy asks voters to repudiate Wallace.
	Political	Kennedy attacks Wallace as leader of haters and wreckers, of forces of suspicion and repression, for racism, brutality and hate.
10/25/9	Public	Hecklers attack Wallace.
	Public	Group protests Wallace.
	Editorial	Reporter attacks Wallace for racism and violence at his rallies.
10/28/7	Editorial	Reporter attacks Wallace as a racist.
	Public	Wallace's brother describes him as "mean as hell."
10/28/10	Editorial	Reporter criticizes all three candidates.
10/29/5	Editorial	Reporter criticizes Wallace for threatening to run over protesters.
10/30/7	Public	College students heckle Wallace.
10/30/11	Public	Black men are opposed to Wallace.
10/31/6	Public	Demonstrators disrupt Wallace rally, throw rocks.

	SOURCE OF	**ABC**
STORY #	OPINION	
10/31/8	Public	Union member criticizes Wallace.
	Public	UAW editor calls Wallace a big farce.
	Public	Union literature attacks Wallace's labor record.
	Public	Union members turning against Wallace.
10/31/12	Editorial	Reporter criticizes Wallace, compares him to smelly albatross.
11/4/5	Public	Jeers and fights meet Wallace in almost all cities.

	SOURCE OF	**CBS**
STORY #	OPINION	
9/17/3	Candidate	Nixon criticizes Wallace's attempt to throw race into the House.
9/17/19	Editorial	Reporter criticizes Wallace's campaign as based on mass fear and mass anger.
9/18/6	Public	AFL-CIO warns against Wallace.
9/20/10	Public	Union bosses criticize Wallace.
	Public	AFL-CIO President George Meany attacks Wallace as a demagogue.
	Public	Union man criticizes Wallace's economic record in Alabama.
	Editorial	Reporter calls Wallace a "threat."
9/25/7	Public	Leftist student criticizes Wallace.
9/26/5	Editorial	Reporter refers to Wallace as "this man Wallace" and finds his law-and-order theme "disturbing."
	Political	Senator Eugene McCarthy attacks Wallace for preaching fear and hate.
9/30/4	Public	"Dissenter" throws an egg at Wallace.
	Public	Man opposes Wallace.
10/1/4	Candidate	Humphrey criticizes Wallace.
	Candidate	Humphrey criticizes high taxes and low standard of living in Alabama under Wallace.
	Candidate	Humphrey attacks Wallace as an apostle of hate and racism.
10/1/8	Public	Hecklers jeer Wallace.

	SOURCE OF	**CBS**
STORY #	OPINION	
10/2/18	Editorial	Reporter criticizes Wallace for putting his wife in governorship; criticizes Wallace for national law-and-order position when Alabama leads nation in murder and manslaughter.
10/4/10	Candidate	Humphrey attacks Wallace's swing vote.
	Candidate	Humphrey attacks Wallace ticket for endorsing irresponsible and deadly dangerous politics.
10/15/3	Public	Hippies heckle Wallace by cheering him.
	Editorial	Reporter openly enjoys Wallace's "congenial" tormentors, finds attacks "comical."
10/17/10	Candidate	Muskie attacks Wallace as a threat to our society, attacks Wallace as demagogue.
	Editorial	Reporter endorses Muskie.
10/22/6	Public	"Hecklers" throw rocks and tomatoes at Wallace.
10/23/4	Public	Black-power demonstrators throw objects at Wallace.
10/24/3	Political	Senator Edward Kennedy opposes Wallace, asks Kennedy supporters in labor groups to repudiate Wallace.
	Political	Senator Kennedy criticizes Wallace as leader of haters, wreckers and forces of suspicion and racism, and brutal repression of Negroes.
10/24/4	Political	Paul O'Dwyer criticizes Wallace as a hate-monger.
10/25/5	Public	Crowds protest Wallace.
10/29/6	Editorial	Reporter criticizes Wallace for delivering a "vulgar" attack on news media.
10/30/8	Public	Heckling, jeering, protesting, fighting break up Wallace rally.
10/30/12	Public	Most upper-middle-class Americans reject Wallace.
10/31/10	Political	Kentucky ex-governor Happy Chandler criticizes Wallace as lacking training in foreign affairs, for Wallace's attitude toward race relations and for choosing Curtis LeMay.
11/4/5	Public	Hecklers and blacks jeer Wallace.

STORY #	SOURCE OF OPINION	**NBC**
9/19/2	Public	UAW President Walter Reuther attacks Wallace for appealing to fear and frustration; compares Wallace with Hitler.
9/25/2	Public	Antiwar student criticizes Wallace.
9/26/5	Political	Romney attacks Wallace as a racist who would destroy this country.
9/30/4	Public	Group opposes Wallace.
	Public	Crowd smaller for Wallace than for Nixon.
10/2/6	Candidate	Humphrey attacks Wallace's campaign as based on strategy of hate, bringing nation to brink of civil disorder.
10/2/7	Public	Hecklers jeer Wallace.
	Public	Blacks heckle Wallace, break up speech.
10/4/2	Candidate	Humphrey attacks Wallace for inflaming fear, frustration and prejudice, for repression, bigotry and hate.
10/4/3	Candidate	Nixon attacks Wallace for threatening to run over protesters with his car.
10/9/4	Candidate	Humphrey attacks Wallace as representing repression and fear.
10/9/5	Public	Union man criticizes Wallace for Alabama labor conditions.
	Public	Crowd apathetic to Wallace.
	Public	Crowd apathetic to Wallace.
	Public	Hecklers jeer and boo Wallace.
10/10/2	Political	LBJ attacks Wallace for empty rhetoric and the appeals to emotion, as a false prophet of fear.
10/14/5	Candidate	Muskie attacks Wallace for seeking to build a wall between haves and have-nots.
10/15/6	Public	Hippies heckle Wallace by cheering him.
	Public	Crowds not enthusiastic for Wallace.
10/17/7	Candidate	Humphrey attacks Wallace as a union-buster who's against workers' compensation and education.
10/17/8	Public	Hecklers drive Wallace to exhaustion.
	Public	Children heckle Wallace.
	Public	Hecklers throw empty drink cans at Wallace.

STORY #	SOURCE OF OPINION	**NBC**
10/18/6	Public	Popular attack on Wallace "overwhelming."
10/22/10	Public	People heckle Wallace "mercilessly."
	Public	Someone throws an apple core at Wallace.
10/22/12	Public	Black militant from Watts criticizes Wallace as "barking" type black men know.
	Public	Black militant from Watts criticizes Wallace as a WASP who is trying to keep blacks in their economic place.
10/23/3	Public	Hecklers drown Wallace out.
	Candidate	Muskie attacks Wallace.
	Public	College students and black militants attack Wallace.
	Public	College students and black militants throw objects at Wallace.
	Public	Protest demonstrators against Wallace ceaseless.
10/23/4	Candidate	Muskie attacks Wallace as a power-hungry divider, sponsor of hate.
10/24/9	Political	Senator Kennedy attacks Wallace, urges voters to repudiate him.
	Political	Senator Kennedy attacks Wallace as standing for division and suppression, for segregation, for brutal repression of Negroes, for hate.
10/25/7	Public	Bands of jeering young people oppose Wallace.
	Public	Thousands of pickets demonstrate against Wallace.
10/28/4	Public	Hecklers boo and jeer Wallace; someone throws a rock at him.
10/29/6	Public	Wallace's popularity is dropping.
10/30/9	Public	A thousand people heckle Wallace.
	Public	Violence breaks out at Wallace rally, drives him away; "violence has become the signature of his campaign."
10/31/8	Public	Demonstrators attack Wallace, throw "things" at him.

Appendix F

Pro-LBJ Vietnam War Policy

	SOURCE OF	**ABC**
STORY #	OPINION	
9/26/1	Political	James Wiggins supports Vietnam policy.
9/30/12	Political	James Wiggins supports Vietnam policy.
10/9/3	Political	LBJ defends his Vietnam policy.
10/10/4	Political	LBJ defends his Vietnam policy.

	SOURCE OF	**CBS**
STORY #	OPINION	
10/9/5	Political	LBJ defends his Vietnam policy.

	SOURCE OF	**NBC**
STORY #	OPINION	
		0

Anti-LBJ Vietnam War Policy

STORY #	SOURCE OF OPINION	**ABC**
9/19/1	Public	Peace demonstrators oppose the war.
9/25/9	Public	Students oppose the war.
9/26/7	Public	Students oppose the war.
9/30/12	Editorial	Reporter opposes the war.
	Political	Senator Fulbright opposes the war.
10/1/5	Political	Senator Fulbright opposes the war.
10/8/7	Political	O'Dwyer opposes the war.
	Political	Senator Jacob Javits opposes the war.
	Political	Paul O'Dwyer opposes the war.
	Political	Javits opposes the war.
	Political	Paul O'Dwyer opposes the war.
	Political	Eugene McCarthy opposes the war.
	Political	Javits opposes the war.
	Political	Javits opposes the war.
	Political	Paul O'Dwyer opposes the war.
10/8/9	Public	Nine pacifists oppose the war.
10/9/8	Public	Hecklers oppose the war.
10/10/7	Public	Demonstrators oppose the war.
10/11/1	Editorial	Reporter opposes the war.
	Political	Senator Fulbright opposes the war.
10/15/9	Public	Soldiers oppose the war.
	Public	Soldiers oppose the war.
	Public	Soldiers oppose the war.
	Public	Soldiers oppose the war.
	Public	Soldiers oppose the war.
10/16/9	Public	Soldier opposes the war.
10/22/10	Foreign	Tokyo students oppose the war.
10/28/8	Political	Dick Gregory opposes the war.
	Foreign	Actress Vanessa Redgrave opposes the war.
	Political	Socialist Workers Party opposes the war.
	Political	Peace and Freedom Party opposes the war.
	Political	Freedom and Peace Party opposes the war.
	Political	Socialist Labor Party opposes the war.
	Political	Communist Party opposes the war.
10/28/10	Editorial	Reporter opposes the war.
10/30/11	Public	Black militants oppose the war.

STORY #	SOURCE OF OPINION	**CBS**
9/16/8	Editorial	Reporter opposes the war.
	Political	Ohio Senate candidate John Gilligan opposes the war.
9/18/5	Public	Leaders of Chicago demonstrators oppose the war.
9/19/1	Public	Demonstrators oppose the war.
9/24/9	Public	Hecklers oppose the war.
9/25/7	Public	Students oppose the war.
9/26/1	Political	George Ball opposes the war.
9/27/18	Editorial	Reporter opposes the war.
10/2/10	Public	Demonstrators oppose the war.
10/4/12	Public	Students oppose the war.
10/4/13	Public	Organizer of Chicago convention disorders opposes the war.
10/7/5	Political	Senate doves oppose the war.
	Political	Senator Morse opposes the war.
10/9/5	Editorial	Reporter opposes the war.
10/9/14	Political	Dr. Berman, Humphrey advisor, opposes the war.
10/22/13	Editorial	Reporter opposes the war.
10/31/11	Political	Eldridge Cleaver opposes the war.
	Political	Socialist Labor candidate opposes the war.
	Political	Socialist candidate opposes the war.
	Political	Socialist Worker Party candidate opposes the war.

STORY #	SOURCE OF OPINION	**NBC**
9/18/7	Public	Connecticut matron opposes the war.
9/25/2	Public	Students oppose the war.
9/26/12	Public	Columbia student opposes the war.
9/30/3	Public	Demonstrators oppose the war.
10/1/9	Public	Demonstrators oppose the war.
10/3/12	Editorial	Reporter opposes the war.
10/3/17	Public	Protest leader opposes the war.
10/8/7	Public	Soldier opposes the war.
10/22/5	Foreign	Japanese leftist students oppose the war.

	SOURCE OF	**NBC**
STORY #	OPINION	
10/23/8	Public	SDS head Tom Hayden opposes the war.
	Public	President of Yale opposes the war.
10/23/14	Public	Artists oppose the war.
10/28/13	Foreign	British demonstrators oppose the war.

Pro-U.S. Policy on Bombing Halt

	SOURCE OF	**ABC**
STORY #	OPINION	
9/30/1	Political	LBJ opposes unconditional bombing halt.
10/1/4	Political	LBJ, Rostow, Rusk oppose unconditional bombing halt.
10/4/6	Political	LBJ and Rusk oppose bombing halt.
10/22/2B	Foreign	Thieu opposes unconditional bombing halt.

	SOURCE OF	**CBS**
STORY #	OPINION	
9/16/8	Political	Ohio Republican William Saxbe opposes bombing halt.
9/26/19	Political	"The generals in Vietnam and the Secretary of State" oppose unconditional bombing halt.

	SOURCE OF	**NBC**
STORY #	OPINION	
10/22/3	Foreign	South Vietnam President Thieu opposes unilateral military concessions and unconditional bombing halt.
10/28/12	Political	Iowa State Senator David Stanley opposes unilateral military concessions and unconditional bombing halt.

Anti-U.S. Policy on Bombing Halt

	SOURCE OF	**ABC**
STORY #	OPINION	
9/23/8	Foreign	U Thant opposes U.S. bombing.
10/1/3	Candidate	Humphrey aides oppose U.S. bombing, advocate unconditional bombing halt.
10/1/4	Political	Arthur Goldberg and George Ball oppose U.S. bombing, advocate unconditional bombing halt.
	Political	Averill Harriman opposes U.S. bombing, advocates unconditional bombing halt.
	Editorial	Reporter opposes U.S. bombing, advocates unconditional bombing halt.
10/4/6	Political	Ambassador Cyrus Vance opposes U.S. bombing, advocates unconditional bombing halt.
10/8/7	Political	Senator Jacob Javits opposes U.S. bombing.
	Political	Senator Jacob Javits opposes U.S. bombing.
10/9/3	Foreign	Xuan Thuy, North Vietnamese negotiator, opposes U.S. bombing.
10/11/3	Editorial	Reporter opposes U.S. bombing, advocates unconditional bombing halt.
10/25/3	Foreign	Xuan Thuy opposes U.S. bombing, advocates unconditional bombing halt.
10/28/1	Foreign	Hanoi radio opposes U.S. bombing, advocates unconditional bombing halt.
	Foreign	Soviet Premier Kosygin opposes U.S. bombing.
10/30/1	Foreign	Xuan Thuy opposes U.S. bombing.
10/31/4	Foreign	Xuan Thuy opposes U.S. bombing, advocates unconditional bombing halt.
11/1/12	Editorial	Reporter opposes U.S. bombing.

	SOURCE OF	**CBS**
STORY #	OPINION	
9/16/2	Political	Humphrey advisor opposes U.S. bombing.

	SOURCE OF	**CBS**
STORY #	OPINION	
9/23/6	Foreign	U Thant opposes U.S. bombing.
9/26/1	Political	George Ball opposes U.S. bombing.
9/25/22	Editorial	Reporter opposes U.S. bombing.
9/26/19	Public	People advising Humphrey oppose U.S. bombing, advocate unconditional bombing halt.
	Political	The President's Paris negotiators oppose U.S. bombing, advocate unconditional bombing halt.
	Editorial	Reporter opposes U.S. bombing, advocates unconditional bombing halt.
9/30/13	Foreign	U Thant opposes U.S. bombing.
10/1/20	Editorial	Reporter opposes U.S. bombing, advocates unconditional bombing halt.
10/28/2	Foreign	Soviet Premier Kosygin opposes U.S. bombing.
10/30/1	Editorial	Reporter opposes U.S. bombing, advocates unconditional bombing halt.

	SOURCE OF	**NBC**
STORY #	OPINION	
9/23/2	Foreign	U Thant opposes U.S. bombing.
10/10/12	Political	George McGovern opposes U.S. bombing.
	Editorial	Reporter opposes U.S. bombing.
10/18/1	Foreign	Xuan Thuy, North Vietnamese negotiator, opposes U.S. bombing.
	Editorial	Reporter opposes U.S. bombing.
10/24/2	Foreign	Xuan Thuy, North Vietnamese negotiator, opposes U.S. bombing.
10/28/7	Foreign	Soviet Premier Kosygin opposes U.S. bombing.
10/28/12	Political	Iowa Governor Hughes opposes U.S. bombing.
10/30/1	Foreign	Xuan Thuy, North Vietnamese negotiator, opposes U.S. bombing.
10/30/4	Foreign	Indira Ghandi, Prime Minister of India, opposes U.S. bombing.

Pro-Viet Cong

STORY #	SOURCE OF OPINION	
		ABC
10/11/3	Editorial	Reporter justifies Viet Cong savagery by blaming the U.S. for dropping the atomic bomb on nonwhite people.

CBS
0

NBC
0

Anti-Viet Cong

ABC
0

CBS
0

NBC
0

Appendix G

Pro-Liberal

Anti-Liberal

ABC

STORY #	SOURCE OF OPINION	
9/27/2	Public	The country is repudiating liberalism.
10/25/9	Candidate	Wallace criticizes liberal establishment.
10/30/10	Candidate	Curtis LeMay criticizes liberals.
10/31/12	Candidate	Wallace's constituency is anti-liberal.

CBS

STORY #	SOURCE OF OPINION	
10/21/11	Candidate	Wallace criticizes liberals and left wingers in media who equate law and order with racism.

NBC

STORY #	SOURCE OF OPINION	
10/8/5	Candidate	Curtis LeMay criticizes the liberal wing of the Republican Party.
10/15/12	Public	New Leftist Jack Newfield criticizes liberals for centralization and bureaucracy.
	Public	Conservative William Rusher criticizes liberals for statist policies.
10/22/12	Public	Black militant mocks liberal "guilt."
	Public	Black militant criticizes liberals for making money out of poverty projects.

Pro-Conservative

ABC

STORY #	SOURCE OF OPINION	
9/27/2	Public	The country is embracing conservatism.

CBS

STORY #	OPINION	
	0	

STORY #	SOURCE OF OPINION	**NBC**
10/8/5	Candidate	Curtis LeMay advocates conservative adminis-tration.
10/15/12	Public	Conservative William Rusher advocates order.

Anti-Conservative

STORY #	SOURCE OF OPINION	**ABC**
9/16/3	Candidate	Humphrey attacks extremists of the right for violence.
9/27/2	Editorial	Reporter attacks conservatives as racists for ad-vocating law and order.
10/10/7	Candidate	Humphrey attacks radical right as rude.
10/25/10	Editorial	Reporter attacks rightists as stupid.

STORY #	SOURCE OF OPINION	**CBS**
9/16/1	Candidate	Humphrey attacks extremists of the right for violence.
10/3/7	Editorial	Reporter links Nixon conservatives and Wallace supporters as being the same group (racists) and for being malcontents seeking a scapegoat.

STORY #	SOURCE OF OPINION	**NBC**
9/17/8	Public	Attorney William Kunstler attacks rightists for plotting against black militants.
	Editorial	Reporter attacks rightists as racists, militarists and law-and-order advocates.
9/17/9	Editorial	Reporter attacks rightists as racists and law-and-order advocates.
9/20/5	Public	Berkeley teacher criticizes conservative Gover-nor Reagan for opposing Black Panther El-dridge Cleaver.

STORY #	SOURCE OF OPINION	**NBC**
	Editorial	Reporter criticizes conservative Governor Reagan for opposing Black Panther leader Eldridge Cleaver.
10/3/11	Public	Dore Schary declares that the right is the cause of black militancy and racist violence.

Appendix H

Pro-White Middle Class

STORY #	SOURCE OF OPINION	**ABC**
9/23/3	Candidate	Nixon defends law-abiding, tax-paying American majority.
	Public	Woman defends law-abiding, tax-paying American majority.
	Public	Man defends law-abiding, tax-paying American majority.

CBS
0

NBC
0

Anti-White Middle Class

STORY #	SOURCE OF OPINION	ABC
9/23/3	Editorial	Reporter attacks middle class as prosperous, self-pitying and mediocre.
9/24/11	Public	University member attacks middle class as materialistic.
	Editorial	Reporter attacks middle class as mindless compared to protesting groups.
9/26/5	Editorial	Reporter attacks white middle-class America as racist, haters of youth, poor and blacks.
10/10/9	Editorial	Reporter attacks middle-class American electorate as mediocre, hostile to intellectual values.
10/21/5	Editorial	Reporter attacks white middle class as racist, intellectually shallow.
10/28/10	Editorial	Reporter criticizes white majority as conscienceless.

STORY #	SOURCE OF OPINION	CBS
9/25/8	Editorial	Reporter attacks white middle class as racist.
9/26/3	Editorial	Reporter attacks white middle class as racist.
10/14/8	Editorial	Reporter attacks white middle class as racist, selfish and mentally limited.
10/28/15	Editorial	Reporter attacks white middle class as selfish, culturally limited, mentally limited.

STORY #	SOURCE OF OPINION	NBC
9/16/8	Editorial	Reporter holds white middle class responsible for black crime.
9/17/8	Editorial	Reporter attacks white middle class as authoritarian-racist-militaristic for advocating law and order against black crime.
9/18/1	Editorial	Reporter criticizes "wealthy upper middle class" for its law-and-order position.

STORY #	SOURCE OF OPINION	**ABC**
	Editorial	Reporter attacks "the American people" as "violent."
9/18/4	Editorial	Reporter holds lawful white middle class responsible for black crime.
10/4/7	Editorial	Reporter attacks white middle class and majority of Americans for willingness to sacrifice "freedom" for law and order—the "freedom" being the black freedom to riot and commit acts of violence.
10/22/12	Editorial	Reporter attacks majority of white voters for law and order—equating it to racism and police breakdown in discipline.
	Public	Black militant attacks racism of all candidates and "white America."
10/23/9	Public	Black "prototype" attacks "white America's" racism.
	Public	Black militant attacks "white America's" racism.
	Editorial	Reporter attacks white middle-class suburban racism.

Appendix I

Pro-Black Militants

STORY #	SOURCE OF OPINION	ABC
9/16/14	Editorial	Reporter finds burning, looting and rioting amusing and mocks those who take such "amateur" crimes seriously in the face of organized crime.
10/15/5	Candidate	Muskie expresses sympathy for rioting blacks, says we must meet black demands.
10/15/6	Public	Black militant demands control of schools.
10/17/10	Public	Two black athletes conduct Black Panther protest at Olympics.
	Public	Black militant explains symbolism of his black gloves, black scarf and black socks.
	Public	Black militant says he represents black America.

STORY #	SOURCE OF OPINION	**ABC**
	Editorial	Reporter expresses sympathy for Black Panther demonstrators.
10/18/7	Public	Two black athletes conduct Black Panther demonstration at Olympics.
	Public	Another black athlete rumored sympathetic to black-militant demonstrators.
10/18/8	Editorial	Reporter defends Black Panther demonstrators at Olympics.
10/22/11	Editorial	Reporter defends Black Panther demonstrators at Olympics and justifies their demonstration on the grounds of black poverty.
10/23/8	Public	Black militant says he's anti-Semitic if Jews are antiblack.
	Public	Black educator demands black control of schools.
	Public	Sympathetic whites support blacks in their efforts to control schools.
10/25/13	Public	Professor of sociology says Black Panthers are trying to channel black rage in creative ways, charges white oppression.
	Public	Black Panther Huey Newton says Black Panthers will go to war to win control of their communities, and intend to abolish all political parties but Black Panthers.
10/28/8	Political	Dick Gregory appeals to black and white and young to solve nation's racial problem.
	Political	Gregory refers to police clubbing and gassing demonstrators.
	Political	Gregory attacks the major parties.
	Public	Hippie attacks Democratic and Republican Parties, supports Cleaver's party.
	Editorial	Reporter describes Cleaver as a source of hope to New Left hippies.
10/30/11	Public	Black militants encourage boycott of election as protest against tokenism in civil rights.
	Public	Ralph Abernathy says blacks can elect the next President.

	SOURCE OF	**ABC**
STORY #	OPINION	
	Public	Charles Evers criticizes many black leaders, says they haven't thrown bombs, burned buildings, or done anything, and they should go out and get the Negro registered.

	SOURCE OF	**CBS**
STORY #	OPINION	
9/18/3	Public	Cleaver advocates shooting of businessmen, politicians, career military, police, decision-makers, profit-makers.
	Editorial	Reporter sanctions Cleaver's calls for mass murder as "revolutionary" thought and attacks those who would prevent Cleaver from teaching at Berkeley as "censors."
9/25/7	Public	Student advocates more black power in the ghettos.
9/26/14	Public	Black-power student union in Boston high school riots for rights to wear African dress.
	Political	Boston politician endorses Black Panther demand.
	Public	Black student protests on behalf of African dress.
	Editorial	Reporter defends black racism and justifies black riot as expression of black identity and pride.
9/27/12	Public	Black militant threatens violence to get control of schools.
	Public	Black militants demand control of local schools.
	Public	Black militant demands control of local schools.
	Public	Rhody McCoy, black administrator, demands control of local schools.
	Public	Black militant threatens to set fires if there's another teachers' strike.

STORY #	SOURCE OF OPINION	CBS
10/18/12	Public	Pro-black militant teachers give a course in slavery, the textbook author, Malcolm X.
10/18/16	Public	Athletes Tommy Smith and John Carlos conduct Black Panther protest at Olympics.
10/24/11	Public	Students riot to force Berkeley to hire Cleaver as teacher.
10/24/12	Public	Smith and Carlos hold Black Panther demonstration during playing of national anthem.
	Public	Black-power athlete is hailed by black community.
	Public	Black militant condemns Olympics.
	Public	Black athlete acclaims black militants as heroes.
	Public	Black athlete denies that national anthem represents him, threatens that black militants will set city aflame if there is no change.
	Public	Black students join black athletes in Black Panther salute.
	Editorial	Reporter describes black-power militants as heroes three times in story, lionizes black militant who threatens to fire the city.
10/25/8	Public	Black Panther expresses black rage.
	Public	Black Panther attacks white oppression.
	Public	Black Panther attacks white oppression.
	Public	Commission witness attacks American racism.
10/31/11	Political	Eldridge Cleaver calls all Presidential candidates pigs.
	Political	Cleaver calls for coalition with whites in Peace and Freedom Party.
	Political	Dick Gregory jokes about black looters.
	Political	Cleaver denounces police as pigs.
	Political	Gregory calls for higher pay for policemen to discourage busting black heads.
	Editorial	Reporter supports Eldridge Cleaver, portraying him as integrationist.
11/4/13	Public	Black Panther hijacks plane.

	SOURCE OF	**NBC**
STORY #	OPINION	
9/16/8	Public	Police chief blames black crime on poverty and racism, not on black criminals.
	Editorial	Reporter equates Black Panthers, Negroes and criminal Negroes, creates a black criminal stereotype, and blames the crime of that stereotype on poverty and white prejudice.
9/17/9	Editorial	Reporter demands that black lawlessness not be subjected to law enforcement, calls it racist to demand that Negroes obey the law.
9/20/5	Public	Cleaver calls for black armies to drive white dogs out of black communities—with no limit on violence.
	Public	Berkeley professor defends Cleaver's right to teach under "academic freedom."
	Editorial	Reporter portrays Cleaver as "enthusiastic" fighter for Negro rights, supports the view that academic freedom requires hiring Cleaver.
9/23/12	Editorial	Reporter endorses Cleaver as a "noted black nationalist," defends his right to teach under academic freedom.
10/3/11	Public	Dore Schary blames black-militant violence on the racism of the radical right.
10/9/10	Public	Witness blames race riots on poverty, advocates the understanding of the "alienated," and condemns those who are morally critical of rioters and criminals.
10/15/9	Candidate	Muskie interprets black riots as expression of search for personal dignity, pride and self-respect.
10/21/10	Foreign	Foreign newspapers defend Black Panther athletes who demonstrated at Olympics.
	Public	Four Black Panther athletes demonstrate at Olympics.
	Editorial	Reporter supports Black Panther athletes.
10/21/11	Editorial	Reporter endorses black militants in New York school strike and transmits their veiled threat of violence.

	SOURCE OF	**NBC**
STORY #	OPINION	
10/22/12	Editorial	Reporter endorses black militants from Watts as speaking for all Negroes.
	Public	Watts militant attacks three Presidential candidates, challenges white America, and predicts disaster for the black community.
	Public	Other Watts militant attacks whites for killing all the leaders of the black community, opposes three candidates as racists, delcares blacks will not stop fighting.
10/23/9	Editorial	Reporter endorses Watts black militant as voice of all Negroes.
	Public	Watts militant charges police with prejudice and shooting blacks, demands money for blacks to run their own communities, condemns white America's racist attitudes.
10/24/11	Public	Students riot to get Eldridge Cleaver hired as teacher.
10/25/8	Public	Black Panther leader Huey Newton threatens civil war by blacks to gain control of their communities.
	Public	Sociology professor testifies on anger and poverty in black communities, charges white oppression.
	Public	Witness supports black militant's charges.

Anti-Black Militants

	SOURCE OF	**ABC**
STORY #	OPINION	
9/16/3	Candidate	Humphrey attacks black militants for violence.
9/20/7	Political	Reagan opposes Cleaver appointment.
9/20/8	Editorial	Reporter attacks black militants for violence.
10/1/11	Political	FBI criticizes foreign influences in black nationalist movement.
10/17/10	Public	Public boos black militants at Olympics.
10/18/7	Public	U.S. Olympic Committee penalizes black-power demonstrators.

	SOURCE OF	**ABC**
STORY #	OPINION	
	Public	Black athlete unsympathetic to black-power demonstrators.
	Public	Black athlete indifferent to black-power demonstrators.
10/18/8	Editorial	Reporter agrees black-power athletes broke Olympic rules.
	Public	American public opinion opposed to black-power athletes.
10/22/11	Public	American public opinion opposed to black-power athletes.
10/23/8	Political	Lindsay criticizes black extremists for anti-Semitism.
	Public	Teacher charges militants with anti-Semitism, and with teaching race hatred.
	Public	Teachers charge militants with anti-Semitism and race hatred.
	Public	Teachers union charges blacks with teaching racism.
10/25/13	Public	Hoffer protests black-militant rage as unjustified.
10/30/16	Editorial	Reporter criticizes black-power militants for hatred in the face of progress.
10/31/8	Public	Union men angry at "the colored."
	Public	Union man criticizes arsonists and looters.
	Public	Union man attacks black militants for shooting policemen and fireman.

	SOURCE OF	**CBS**
STORY #	OPINION	
9/16/1	Candidate	Humphrey attacks black-militant violence.
9/18/3	Public	Man #1 criticizes Eldridge Cleaver as unqualified academically.
	Public	Man #2 criticizes Eldridge Cleaver as unfortunate choice.
9/19/15	Public	University regents trying to block Cleaver's appointment.
9/20/10	Public	Working men critical of black militants.

STORY #	SOURCE OF OPINION	**CBS**
	Public	Working men critical of Negroes who want income without work.
	Public	Working man critical of mess created in Resurrection City at expense of taxpayer.
9/27/12	Public	Middle-class parents protest black militants dictating school board policy.
	Public	Teachers union's Albert Shanker protests black militants violation of board of education rules.
10/17/14	Public	White teachers antagonistic to Negro school board.
10/18/16	Public	U.S. Olympic team dismisses two black militants for Black Panther gesture.
10/25/8	Public	Hoffer protests Black Panther rage as unjustified.
10/28/7	Candidate	Nixon protests black-militant intimidation of New York teachers.

STORY #	SOURCE OF OPINION	**NBC**
9/16/8	Public	Policeman protests black-militant abuse of police.
	Public	Policeman protests black-militant abuse of police.
9/18/7	Public	Cab driver protests black-racist abuse and muggings.
9/19/7	Public	Unnamed sources protest Berkeley hiring of Black Panther Eldridge Cleaver.
9/19/16	Political	Philadelphia police commissioner protests black-militant destructiveness and arson.
9/20/5	Political	Governor Reagan protests Black Panther Eldridge Cleaver's advocacy of racism and violence.
10/4/7	Political	Delaware governor charges fear caused by black-militant rioting.
	Public	Delaware citizens protest incipient black-militant violence.

STORY #	SOURCE OF OPINION	**NBC**
	Public	Delaware citizen protests black-militant sniping.
	Public	Delaware citizen protests incipient black-militant violence.
	Public	Delaware citizen grateful for National Guard presence.
	Political	Delaware governor says law and order is top issue in campaign.
10/9/10	Political	Senator McClellan protests black-militant blackmail and violence and giving U.S. funds to black-militant gangs.
10/15/9	Candidate	Muskie protests black extremists and haters.
10/18/11	Public	U.S. Olympic Committee protests black-power demonstration during U.S. flag salute.
10/21/10	Public	U.S. Olympic Committee protests black-power demonstration.
10/21/11	Public	New York teacher protests black-militant harassment of teachers.
10/25/8	Public	Eric Hoffer protests black-militant rage as unjustified.

Appendix J

Pro-Left

STORY #	SOURCE OF OPINION	**ABC**
10/1/10	Editorial	Reporter mocks House Un-American Affairs Committee, supports Yippies.
10/3/8	Editorial	Reporter asserts Yippie innocence of charges of violence and intentions to bomb buildings, kill police and assassinate politicians.
10/28/8	Political	Socialist Labor Party attacks capitalism.
	Foreign	Actress Vanessa Redgrave supports Socialist Workers Party, attacks war.
	Political	Socialist Workers Party attacks capitalism and war.

	SOURCE OF	**ABC**
STORY #	OPINION	
	Political	Socialist Workers Party member advocates revolution.
	Political	Communist Party candidate advocates black liberation.
	Editorial	Reporter describes goals of all left-wing parties as peace and justice.

	SOURCE OF	**CBS**
STORY #	OPINION	
9/25/7	Editorial	Reporter describes previously identified leftists as "enthusiastic" group of "students."
10/7/1	Editorial	Reporter describes left-wing student movement as one of the biggest institutions in the country.
10/31/11	Political	Cleaver attacks all candidates as pigs.
	Political	Cleaver attacks white power structure but advocates collaboration with "sympathetic whites."
	Political	Cleaver advocates black and white coalition in Peace and Freedom Party.
	Political	Dick Gregory makes jokes about black looting.
	Political	Eldridge Cleaver attacks police as pigs.
	Political	Dick Gregory asks higher pay for police.
	Political	Dick Gregory asks higher pay for police.
	Political	Socialist Labor candidate calls for true socialism.
	Political	Socialist Labor candidate attacks U.S. social and economic system.
	Political	Socialist Workers Party candidate attacks capitalist imperialism.
	Political	Communist Party candidate advocates a communist state that reflects American democracy.

	SOURCE OF	**NBC**
STORY #	OPINION	
9/19/5	Candidate	Muskie says radicals are honest "teenagers" and we should trust them.

	SOURCE OF	**NBC**
STORY #	OPINION	
	Editorial	Reporter says radicals are "young people" and we should trust them.
9/23/6	Editorial	Reporter opposes criticism of Communists.
9/26/12	Public	Radical student says Columbia students are moving left.
	Public	Radical student criticizes Columbia war research.
	Public	Radical student criticizes Columbia war research.
	Public	Columbia president praises students' sound ideas.
	Editorial	Reporter advocates Columbia's meeting radical demands.
10/15/12	Public	New Leftist Jack Newfield advocates temporary "disorder" for sake of "change."
10/23/8	Public	SDS head Tom Hayden blames student violence on establishment war.

Anti-Left

	SOURCE OF	**ABC**
STORY #	OPINION	
9/16/3	Candidate	Humphrey attacks extremists of the left for violence.
10/1/11	Political	FBI attacks New Left and SDS as main force behind violence, planning sabotage and destruction.
	Political	FBI attacks foreign influence in black nationalist movement.
10/3/8	Political	Undercover investigator of Yippies charges Yippies with plans to kill policemen and candidates.
10/10/7	Political	Humphrey criticizes the left as "noisy."

STORY #	SOURCE OF OPINION	**CBS**
9/16/1	Candidate	Humphrey attacks extremists of the left for violence.
10/21/11	Candidate	Wallace attacks liberal and left-wing media for equating law-and-order stand with racism.
10/31/11	Political	E. Harold Mung, Presidential candidate of the Prohibition Party, attacks Communism.

STORY #	SOURCE OF OPINION	**NBC**
9/18/2	Public	Columbia University officials will take disciplinary action against some SDS students.
9/19/5	Candidate	Muskie criticizes young radicals who give up on the system because they're not instantly successful.
9/26/12	Public	Columbia University member criticizes SDS and radical left for bothering other students.
	Public	Columbia President Cordier criticizes students' demand for instant success.
10/8/5	Candidate	Curtis LeMay attacks Republican left wing.
10/9/5	Candidate	Wallace criticizes presence of Communists in defense plants.
10/15/12	Public	Conservative William Rusher attacks indulgence of madness on the left.
10/24/10	Candidate	Curtis LeMay attacks several newsmen as left-wingers.

Appendix K

Pro-Demonstrators†

STORY #	SOURCE OF OPINION	**ABC**
9/24/11	Editorial	Reporter supports demonstrators (demonstrators politically unidentified).
	Public	Student supports demonstrators (demonstrators politically unidentified).
9/25/9	Public	Student heckler attacks US political system (demonstrators politically unidentified).

---

†In this section, opinions are summarized only as they deal with attacks on the US political system and the "Establishment"; with violence; and with the identity of the "demonstrators."

	SOURCE OF	**ABC**
STORY #	OPINION	
9/26/5	Editorial	Reporter supports demonstrators (demonstrators politically unidentified).*
9/30/2	Editorial	Reporter supports demonstrators (demonstrators politically unidentified).*
10/7/5	Editorial	Reporter supports demonstrators (demonstrators politically unidentified).
10/8/10	Editorial	Reporter supports demonstrators (demonstrators politically unidentified.)*
10/9/6	Candidate	Humphrey supports demonstrators (demonstrators politically unidentified).
10/24/8	Editorial	Reporter supports demonstrators (demonstrators politically unidentified).*
10/24/9	Public	Student protest leader supports demonstrators (demonstrators politically unidentified).*
	Editorial	Reporter supports demonstrators (demonstrators politically unidentified).
10/29/5	Editorial	Reporter supports demonstrators (demonstrators politically unidentified).
10/30/9	Editorial	Reporter supports demonstrators (demonstrators politically unidentified).

	SOURCE OF	**CBS**
STORY #	OPINION	
9/30/2	Candidate	Humphrey supports demonstrators (demonstrators politically unidentified).
	Editorial	Reporter supports demonstrators (demonstrators politically unidentified).*
10/4/12	Candidate	Muskie supports demonstrators (demonstrators politically unidentified).
	Editorial	Reporter supports demonstrators (demonstrators politically unidentified).
10/14/8	Editorial	Reporter supports demonstrators (demonstrators politically unidentified).

---

*Editorial rationalization of violence; for summaries, see Chapter III, section on "Demonstrators."

	SOURCE OF	**CBS**
STORY #	OPINION	
	Editorial	Reporter supports demonstrators (demonstrators politically unidentified).*
10/15/3	Editorial	Reporter supports demonstrators (demonstrators politically unidentified).
10/23/9	Public	Leader of student demonstrations at Berkeley attacks establishment violence (demonstrators politically unidentified).

	SOURCE OF	**NBC**
STORY #	OPINION	
9/23/12	Public	Activist student attacks U.S. political system (self-described radical, socialist, supporter of Eldridge Cleaver's Peace and Freedom Party).
	Editorial	Reporter supports demonstrators (demonstrators politically unidentified).
9/25/2	Public	Hecklers attack U.S. political system (demonstrators politically unidentified).
10/3/12	Editorial	Reporter supports demonstrators (demonstrators politically unidentified).*
10/8/11	Public	Student attacks U.S. political system (demonstrators politically unidentified).
	Public	Student attacks U.S. political system (demonstrators politically unidentified).
10/14/4	Editorial	Reporter supports demonstrators (demonstrators politically unidentified).*
10/16/9	Editorial	Reporter supports demonstrators (demonstrators politically unidentified).*
10/23/8	Public	Tom Hayden, of the SDS, attacks establishment violence (demonstrators politically unidentified).
10/23/14	Public	Artists attack establishment violence; condemn brutal repression of demonstrators (demonstrators politically unidentified).

*Editorial rationalization of violence; for summaries, see Chapter III, section on "Demonstrators."

	SOURCE OF	**NBC**
STORY #	OPINION	
10/30/10	Political	Ribicoff attacks establishment violence against "demonstrators" (demonstrators politically unidentified).
	Political	Ribicoff attacks establishment violence against "demonstrators" (demonstrators politically unidentified).
	Political	Ribicoff attacks establishment violence against "demonstrators" (demonstrators politically unidentified).
	Public	Man congratulates Ribicoff for his defense of "demonstrators" (demonstrators politically unidentified).
	Political	Ribicoff attacks Chicago police for brutality against "demonstrators" (demonstrators politically unidentified).

Anti-Demonstrators

	SOURCE OF	**ABC**
STORY #	OPINION	
9/16/6	Candidate	Agnew attacks demonstrators for violence (demonstrators politically unidentified).
9/18/2B	Political	J. Edgar Hoover attacks demonstrators for violence (demonstrators politically unidentified).
9/19/1	Candidate	Humphrey attacks demonstrators (demonstrators politically unidentified).
9/20/8	Editorial	Reporter attacks demonstrators for violence (demonstrators politically unidentified).
9/24/11	Public	Students attack demonstrators (demonstrators politically unidentified).
	Public	Student attacks demonstrators (demonstrators politically unidentified).
9/25/9	Public	Rally speakers attack demonstrators (demonstrators politically unidentified).
9/26/5	Editorial	Reporter attacks demonstrators (demonstrators politically unidentified).

STORY #	SOURCE OF OPINION	**ABC**
9/30/2	Candidate	Humphrey attacks demonstrators for violence (demonstrators politically unidentified).
10/2/4	Candidate	Wallace attacks demonstrators (demonstrators politically unidentified).
10/2/7	Candidate	Nixon attacks demonstrators for violence (demonstrators politically unidentified).
10/8/10	Editorial	Reporter attacks demonstrators (demonstrators politically unidentified).
10/15/4	Candidate	Wallace attacks demonstrators for violence (demonstrators politically unidentified).
10/15/5	Candidate	Agnew attacks demonstrators for violence (demonstrators politically unidentified).
10/17/8	Candidate	Wallace attacks demonstrators (demonstrators politically unidentified).
10/22/5	Candidate	Wallace attacks demonstrators (demonstrators politically unidentified).
10/24/9	Public	Policeman attacks demonstrators for violence (demonstrators politically unidentified).
10/24/12	Editorial	Reporter attacks demonstrators (demonstrators politically unidentified).
10/25/9	Candidate	Wallace attacks demonstrators (demonstrators politically unidentified).
10/30/9	Candidate	Agnew attacks demonstrators (demonstrators politically unidentified).
10/31/8	Public	Union man attacks demonstrators for violence (demonstrators politically unidentified).

STORY #	SOURCE OF OPINION	**CBS**
9/16/1	Candidate	Humphrey attacks demonstrators for violence (demonstrators politically unidentified).
9/17/4	Candidate	Humphrey attacks demonstrators (demonstrators politically unidentified).
9/18/2	Political	J. Edgar Hoover attacks demonstrators for violence (demonstrators politically unidentified).

STORY #	SOURCE OF OPINION	**CBS**
9/19/1	Political	Senator Edward Kennedy attacks demonstrators for violence (demonstrators politically unidentified).
	Candidate	Humphrey attacks demonstrators (demonstrators politically unidentified).
9/19/3	Candidate	Nixon attacks demonstrators (demonstrators politically unidentified).
9/20/10	Candidate	Wallace attacks demonstrators (demonstrators politically unidentified).
	Public	Working men attack demonstrators (demonstrators politically unidentified).
	Public	Union men attack demonstrators (demonstrators politically unidentified).
	Public	Union man attacks demonstrators (demonstrators politically unidentified).
9/24/9	Candidate	Humphrey attacks demonstrators for violence (demonstrators politically unidentified).
10/14/8	Candidate	Agnew attacks demonstrators for violence (demonstrators politically unidentified).
	Public	Middle-class whites attack demonstrators for violence (demonstrators politically unidentified).
10/16/11	Public	Chicago organization attacks demonstrators for violence (demonstrators politically unidentified).
10/21/11	Candidate	Wallace attacks demonstrators for violence (demonstrators politically unidentified).
10/22/13	Editorial	Reporter attacks demonstrators for violence (demonstrators politically unidentified).
10/23/9	Public	Hoffer attacks demonstrators (demonstrators politically unidentified).
10/30/7	Candidate	Nixon attacks demonstrators for violence (demonstrators politically unidentified).

STORY #	SOURCE OF OPINION	**NBC**
9/18/1	Political	J. Edgar Hoover attacks demonstrators for violence (demonstrators politically unidentified).

	SOURCE OF	**NBC**
STORY #	OPINION	
9/19/1	Political	Senator Edward Kennedy attacks demonstrators for violence (demonstrators politically unidentified).
9/19/20	Political	Georgia officials attack demonstrators for violence (demonsrators politically unidentified).
9/20/2	Candidate	Humphrey attacks demonstrators (demonstrators politically unidentified).
9/20/3	Political	Lawrence O'Brien attacks demonstrators (demonstrators politically unidentified).
9/30/3	Candidate	Humphrey attacks demonstrators (demonstrators politically unidentified).
10/3/17	Political	Undercover agent attacks demonstrators for violence (demonstrators politically unidentified).
10/8/11	Political	Senator Kennedy attacks demonstrators (demonstrators politically unidentified).
10/10/13	Political	Ex-governor of South Dakota attacks demonstrators for violence (demonstrators politically unidentified).
10/14/4	Candidate	Agnew attacks demonstrators for violence (demonstrators politically unidentified).
10/15/10	Candidate	Agnew attacks demonstrators for violence (demonstrators politically unidentified).
10/18/6	Candidate	Wallace attacks demonstrators (demonstrators politically unidentified).
10/23/5	Candidate	Agnew attacks demonstrators (demonstrators politically unidentified).
10/23/8	Public	Hoffer attacks demonstrators (demonstrators politically unidentified).
10/24/11	Public	"Berkeley University" member attacks demonstrators for violence (demonstrators politically unidentified).
	Editorial	Reporter attacks demonstrators (demonstrators politically unidentified).
10/25/7	Candidate	Wallace attacks demonstrators (demonstrators politically unidentified).
10/30/8	Candidate	Agnew attacks demonstrators (demonstrators politically unidentified).

	SOURCE OF	**NBC**
STORY #	OPINION	
10/30/10	Political	Ed May, Connecticut state senator, attacks demonstrators (demonstrators politically unidentified).
10/31/8	Candidate	Wallace attacks demonstrators (demonstrators politically unidentified).

Appendix L

Opponents of Nixon and Agnew

STORY #	SOURCE OF OPINION	**ABC**
9/19/3	Public	The reporter calls Nixon opponents "demonstrators."
9/25/9	Public	The reporter calls a Nixon opponent a "student."
10/9/8	Public	The reporter calls Nixon opponents "hecklers."
10/30/5	Public	The reporter calls Nixon opponents "students."

STORY #	SOURCE OF OPINION	**CBS**
9/18/8	Public	Nixon opponents are described by the reporter as "Mexican grapeworkers."

STORY #	SOURCE OF OPINION	CBS
10/18/1	Public	The reporter describes Nixon opponents as "young Democrats."
10/22/4	Public	Debris is thrown at Nixon. The reporter attributes it to "someone."
10/30/7	Public	The reporter describes Nixon opponents as "students."

STORY #	SOURCE OF OPINION	NBC
9/20/2	Public	Nixon is booed. The reporter attributes it to "someone."
9/20/3	Public	Nixon is insulted by "hecklers."
10/22/12	Public	The reporter describes a Nixon opponent as a "black militant."
	Public	The reporter describes a Nixon opponent as a "black militant."
10/30/7	Public	The reporter describes Nixon opponents as "university students."

Opponents of Humphrey and Muskie

STORY #	SOURCE OF OPINION	ABC
9/19/1	Public	The story reports on a wild mob assailing Humphrey. The reporter describes them as "peace demonstrators."
9/25/9	Public	A mob assails Muskie. The reporter describes them as antiwar demonstrators.
9/30/1	Public	The story reports on the disruption of Humphrey's campaign speeches. The reporter ascribes it to "hecklers."
10/10/7	Public	Humphrey is abused in New York City. The reporter calls it "heckling" and then ascribes it to "antiwar demonstrators."

	SOURCE OF	**CBS**
STORY #	OPINION	
9/17/4	Public	Opponents deride Humphrey. The reporter describes them as "costumed demonstrators."
9/19/1	Public	A thousand people shout at Humphrey. The reporter describes them as "young," "detractors" and "demonstrators."
9/24/9	Public	Opponents of Humphrey are described by the reporter as "anti-Vietnam hecklers."
10/1/4	Public	The reporter refers to "a few unfriendly signs" in the crowd.
10/9/13	Public	The reporter refers to critics of Humphrey as "students."

	SOURCE OF	**NBC**
STORY #	OPINION	
9/17/5	Public	The reporter calls Humphrey opponents "dissenters and demonstrators."
9/19/1	Public	Reporter calls Humphrey opponents "crowds."
9/20/2	Public	Reporter calls Humphrey opponents "hecklers."
9/30/3	Public	The reporter refers to the "demonstrators" who have been "heckling" Humphrey throughout his campaign.
10/9/4	Public	The reporter calls Humphrey opponents "college students."

Opponents of Wallace and LeMay

	SOURCE OF	**ABC**
STORY #	OPINION	
9/30/5	Public	A group opposes Wallace. They are described by the reporter as "protesters."
10/2/4	Public	Groups denounce Wallace as a Hitler and a white supremacist. They are described by the reporter as "hecklers."

	SOURCE OF	ABC
STORY #	OPINION	
10/8/5	Public	Groups abuse Wallace. They are described by the reporter as "hecklers."
10/15/4	Public	Groups jeer and cheer Wallace. They are described by the reporter as "hecklers."
10/22/5	Public	People throw objects at Wallace; the reporter calls them "hecklers."
10/23/6	Public	People throw objects at Wallace; the reporter calls them "hecklers."
10/17/8	Public	The reporter describes Wallace's "nightly battle" with "hecklers."
10/25/9	Public	People oppose Wallace in New York City. The reporter calls them a "protest group."
10/30/7	Public	A group pickets Wallace, wearing black armbands and carrying black signs. The reporter calls them "college students" and "hecklers."
10/31/6	Public	A group disrupts Wallace rally; throws rocks. Reporter calls them "demonstrators."
11/4/5	Public	The reporter refers to jeers and fights that have met Wallace in all cities, but identifies no one as jeering and fighting.

	SOURCE OF	CBS
STORY #	OPINION	
9/30/4	Public	Crowd protests Wallace; one throws object at Wallace. The reporter calls him a "dissenter."
10/1/8	Public	The reporter describes opponents of Wallace as "hecklers."
10/15/3	Public	The reporter describes member of a crowd of Wallace opponents as a "hippie heckler."
10/22/6	Public	A crowd throws objects and rocks at Wallace; the reporter calls them "hecklers" and "black-power demonstrators."
10/23/4	Public	A crowd throws objects and rocks at Wallace; the reporter calls them "hecklers" and "black-power demonstrators."

	SOURCE OF	**CBS**
STORY #	OPINION	
10/25/5	Public	Three thousand police are "sorely challenged" at a Wallace rally. The reporter describes the group as "protesters."
10/30/8	Public	Opponents of Wallace precipitate a fight and cut short his speech. The reporter calls them "protesters."
11/4/5	Public	Opponents of Wallace are described by the reporter as people "of other persuasions," "black people," and "Nixon supporters."

	SOURCE OF	**NBC**
STORY #	OPINION	
9/25/2	Public	Opponent of Wallace is called a "stop-the-war demonstrator."
9/30/4	Public	Opponents of Wallace are described by the reporter as "anti-Wallaceites."
10/2/7	Public	Opponents of Wallace are described by the reporters as "hecklers, mostly Negroes."
10/9/5	Public	People jeering and booing Wallace are described by the reporter as "hecklers."
10/15/6	Public	People jeering at Wallace are called "protesters in hippie garb" and "hecklers."
10/17/8	Public	Wallace cancels his appearances, the reporter says, because he is "beset by hecklers."
10/18/6	Public	Opponents of Wallace engage in what the reporter calls "overwhelming protest."
10/22/10	Public	Opponents throw objects at Wallace; reporter calls them "hecklers."
10/23/3	Public	Opponents throw objects at Wallace; reporter calls them "hecklers" and "college students."
10/25/7	Public	Reporter calls jeering bands who pursue Wallace "young people."
10/28/4	Public	Member of crowd throws rock at Wallace; reporter calls him "someone."

	SOURCE OF	**NBC**
STORY #	OPINION	
10/30/9	Public	Reporter describes Wallace opponents as "hecklers."
10/31/8	Public	Reporter calls Wallace opponents "hecklers."

Opponents of all Three Presidential Candidates

	SOURCE OF	**ABC**
STORY #	OPINION	
9/25/9	Public	A young person attacks all three candidates as racist. The reporter describes him as an "anti-war student."
10/29/5	Public	Mob assaults on Presidential candidates are a new and disturbing phenomenon that emerged in the 1968 campaign. In this story, the reporter refers to them casually by saying "heckling" is a "national pastime."

	SOURCE OF	**CBS**
STORY #	OPINION	
9/18/5	Public	Plans to "picket" the three Presidential candidates are announced by a group described by the reporter as "leaders of demonstrators who battled Chicago police during the Democratic convention."
9/25/7	Public	The reporter describes a student who opposes all three candidates as a "leftist."

	SOURCE OF	**NBC**
STORY #	OPINION	
9/25/2	Public	A student attacks all candidates as racist and advocates an election boycott. He is described by the reporter as a "stop-the-war demonstrator."

Appendix M

Antiwar Groups

STORY #	SOURCE OF OPINION	ABC
9/19/1	Public	The story reports on a wild mob assailing Humphrey. The reporter describes them as "peace demonstrators."
9/25/9	Public	A young person attacks all three candidates as racist. The reporter describes him as an "antiwar" student.
	Public	A mob assails Muskie. The reporter describes them as antiwar demonstrators and calls it "bedeviling."

STORY #	SOURCE OF OPINION	**ABC**
9/26/7	Public	A group of students assails Muskie. The reporter calls it an "antiwar demonstration."
10/8/9	Public	Nine people are charged with burning draft board records. The reporter calls them "pacifists," and quotes their defense counsel who compares them to Socrates and Jesus.
10/9/8	Public	Nixon is booed by people shouting "peace"; reporter calls them "hecklers."
10/10/7	Public	Humphrey is absued in New York City. The reporter calls it "heckling" and then ascribes it to "antiwar demonstrators."
10/15/9	Public	Story reports on an antiwar rally by a group called "G.I.'s for Peace." One wanted to burn the American flag. The reporter describes him as a "would-be marcher."
10/16/9	Public	A soldier opposes the war.
10/20/8	Foreign	Actress Vanessa Redgrave opposes the war.
10/30/11	Public	Black militants oppose the war.

STORY #	SOURCE OF OPINION	**CBS**
9/18/5	Public	"Leaders" of Chicago "demonstrators" oppose the war.
9/19/1	Public	"Demonstrators" oppose the war.
9/24/9	Public	Opponents of Humphrey are described by the reporter as "anti-Vietnam hecklers."
9/25/7	Public	A "leftist" student opposes the war.
10/2/10	Public	"Demonstrators" oppose the war.
10/4/12	Public	Opponents of Muskie are described by the reporter as "stop-the-war students" and "young restless hecklers."
10/4/13	Public	Robert Greenbrandt (?) testified at a Congressional hearing that he met with Viet Cong agents behind the Iron Curtain at a time when he was planning what the reporter describes as

STORY #	SOURCE OF OPINION	**CBS**

the "antiwar protests in Chicago." He himself is described by the reporter as "an organizer of the Chicago convention disorders."

STORY #	SOURCE OF OPINION	**NBC**
9/18/7	Public	A Connecticut matron opposes the Vietnam war.
9/25/2	Public	The reporter calls Muskie opponents "hecklers" and describes one opponent of all three candidates as a "stop-the-war demonstrator."
9/26/12	Public	A Columbia "student" opposes the war.
9/30/3	Public	A "demonstrator" opposes the war.
10/1/9	Public	The story reports on a House Un-American Activities Committee hearing on the Chicago riots and on the attendance of antiwar demonstrators. He describes Jerry Rubin as "one of their leaders."
10/3/17	Public	The story reports on the House Un-American Activites Committee hearings on the Chicago riots. The reporter describes the witness as an "antiwar protest leader."
10/8/7	Public	A soldier opposes the war.
10/23/8	Public	The reporter quotes the testimony of Henry Mayer who says the Violence Commission should not be investigating student violence but violence in Vietnam. The reporter describes Mayer as a "witness" from the University of California. (According to CBS, 10/23/9, *Pro-Demonstrators*, he was "a leader of the 1966 student demonstrations at the University of California at Berkeley.")
	Public	Thomas Hayden of the SDS opposes the war.
	Public	The president of Yale opposes the war.
10/23/14	Public	A group of artists opposes the war.

Appendix N

Editorial Sanctioning of Violence

NETWORK	OPINION CATEGORY	STORY #
ABC (11)	Anti-Conservative	9/27/2
	Pro-Black Militants	9/16/14
		10/28/8
	Pro-"Demonstrators"	9/26/5
		9/30/2
		10/8/10
		10/24/8
		10/24/9
	Anti-Wallace	10/22/5
		10/23/6
		10/31/6

NETWORK	OPINION CATEGORY	STORY #
CBS (9)	Pro-Black Militants	9/18/3
		9/26/14
		10/24/12
		10/31/11
	Pro-"Demonstrators"	9/30/2
		10/14/8
	Anti-Wallace	9/30/4
		10/22/6
		10/23/4
NBC (17)	Anti-Conservative	9/17/8
	Pro-Black Militants	9/16/8
		9/17/9
		9/20/5
		9/23/2
		10/21/11
	Pro-"Demonstrators"	10/3/12
		10/14/4
		10/16/9
NBC	Anti-White Middle Class	9/17/8
		9/18/4
		10/4/7
		10/22/12
	Anti-Wallace	10/17/8
		10/22/10
		10/23/3
		10/31/8

Appendix O

I. Number of words spoken for and against the candidates which express the opinion of reporters alone, **on three networks combined.**

Reporter Opinion on Nixon

	FOR	AGAINST	RATIO
ABC	488	5398	11 : 1 against Nixon
CBS	42	2791	67 : 1 against Nixon
NBC	23	1501	65 : 1 against Nixon

Reporter Opinion on Humphrey

	FOR	AGAINST	RATIO
ABC	2014	1499	1.3 : 1 for Humphrey
CBS	1069	242	4.4 : 1 for Humphrey
NBC	67	421	6.0 : 1 against Humphrey

Reporter Opinion on Wallace

	FOR	AGAINST	RATIO
ABC	96	1074	11 : 1 against Wallace
CBS	0	298	298 : 0 against Wallace
NBC	0	0	0 : 0 against Wallace*

II. Number of words spoken for and against the candidates by all sources excluding reporters—namely: the number of words spoken by candidates, politicians, and public—on three networks combined.

Candidates-Politicians-Public on Nixon

	FOR	AGAINST	RATIO
ABC	381	2095	5.5 : 1 against Nixon
CBS	278	2509	9.0 : 1 against Nixon
NBC	408	2733	6.8 : 1 against Nixon

Candidates-Politicians-Public on Humphrey

	FOR	AGAINST	RATIO
ABC	2204	2070	1.1 : 1 for Humphrey
CBS	1319	1841	1.4 : 1 against Humphrey
NBC	1785	2244	1.3 : 1 against Humphrey

Candidates-Politicians-Public on Wallace

	FOR	AGAINST	RATIO
ABC	1257	2299	1.8 : 1 against Wallace
CBS	1079	984	1.1 : 1 for Wallace
NBC	1041	1821	1.7 : 1 against Wallace

---

*This result is due to the classification problem explained in Chapter III, Section on "Candidate Wallace." NBC reporters communicated anti-Wallace opinion by sanctioning violence against him repeatedly. These editorial opinions were integrated with narrative reports on public opinion, were classified as public opinion, and were not counted twice. Thus there *was* strong anti-Wallace bias on the part of network reporters. For the precise opinions, see Chapter III.

III (a). Number of words spoken for and against a set of controversial issues by reporters alone **on the three networks combined.**

Reporters on US Vietnam War Policy

	FOR	AGAINST	RATIO
ABC	0	57	57 : 0 against US VN Policy
CBS	0	117	117 : 0 against US VN Policy
NBC	0	14	14 : 0 against US VN Policy

Reporters on US Policy on Bombing Halt

	FOR	AGAINST	RATIO
ABC	0	485	485 : 0 against US BH Policy
CBS	0	181	181 : 0 against US BH Policy
NBC	0	104	104 : 0 against US BH Policy

Reporters on Viet Cong

	FOR	AGAINST	RATIO
ABC	81	0	81 : 0 for the VC
CBS	0	0	0 : 0 opinion on VC
NBC	0	0	0 : 0 opinion on VC

III (b).

Reporters on Black Militants

	FOR	AGAINST	RATIO
ABC	1012	390	2.6 : 1 for BM
CBS	435	0	435.0 : 0 for BM
NBC	754	0	754.0 : 0 for BM

Reporters on "The White Middle-Class Majority"

	FOR	AGAINST	RATIO
ABC	0	671	671 : 0 against WMC
CBS	0	258	258 : 0 against WMC
NBC	0	662	662 : 0 against WMC

Reporters on Liberals

	FOR	AGAINST	RATIO
ABC	77	0	77 : 0 for liberals
CBS	0	0	0 : 0 opinion on liberals
NBC	101	0	101 : 0 for liberals

Reporters on Conservatives

	FOR	AGAINST	RATIO
ABC	0	141	141 : 0 against conservatives
CBS	0	45	45 : 0 against conservatives
NBC	0	189	189 : 0 against conservatives

III (c).

Reporters on the Left

	FOR	AGAINST	RATIO
ABC	365	0	365 : 0 for the left
CBS	79	0	79 : 0 for the left
NBC	210	0	210 : 0 for the left

Reporters on "Demonstrators"

	FOR	AGAINST	RATIO
ABC	1205	417	2.9 : 1 for demonstrators
CBS	369	19	19.0 : 1 for demonstrators
NBC	629	24	25.0 : 1 for demonstrators

Reporters on Violent Radicals

	FOR	AGAINST	RATIO
ABC	0	0	0 : 0 opinion on VR
CBS	0	0	0 : 0 opinion on VR
NBC	0	0	0 : 0 opinion on VR

IV (a). Number of words spoken for and against a set of controversial issues by all sources excluding reporters—**namely: the number of words spoken by candidates, politicians and public—on three networks combined.**

Candidates-Politicians-Public on US Vietnam Policy*

	FOR	AGAINST	RATIO
ABC	413	1419	3.5 : 1 against US VN Policy
CBS	287	534	1.9 : 1 against US VN Policy
NBC	0	1003	1003.0 : 0 against US VN Policy

Candidates-Politicians-Public on US Policy on Bombing Halt*

	FOR	AGAINST	RATIO
ABC	165	419	2.5 : 1 against US BH Policy
CBS	36	226	6.0 : 1 against US BH Policy
NBC	147	710	4.8 : 1 against US BH Policy

Candidates-Politicians-Public on Viet Cong

	FOR	AGAINST	RATIO
ABC	0	0	0 : 0 opinion on VC
CBS	0	0	0 : 0 opinion on VC
NBC	0	0	0 : 0 opinion on VC

---

*These figures do *not* include candidate opinions on the war. They were almost nonexistent; or nonclassifiable, in the case of Mr. Humphrey.

IV (b).

Candidates-Politicians-Public on Black Militants

	FOR	AGAINST	RATIO
ABC	1040	756	1.4 : 1 for BM
CBS	1143	742	1.5 : 1 for BM
NBC	2912	1383	2.0 : 1 for BM

Candidates-Politicians-Public on "The White Middle-Class Majority"

	FOR	AGAINST	RATIO
ABC	142	60	2.3 : 1 for WMC
CBS	0	0	0 : 0 opinion on WMC
NBC	0	406	406.0 : 0 against WMC

Candidates-Politicians-Public on Liberals

	FOR	AGAINST	RATIO
ABC	0	112	112 : 0 against liberals
CBS	0	120	120 : 0 against liberals
NBC	0	474	474 : 0 against liberals

Candidates-Politicians-Public on Conservatives

	FOR	AGAINST	RATIO
ABC	8	65	8.0 : 1 against conservatives
CBS	0	39	39.0 : 0 against conservatives
NBC	88	123	1.4 : 1 against conservatives

IV (c).

Candidates-Politicians-Public on the Left

	FOR	AGAINST	RATIO
ABC	136	280	2.0 : 1 against the left
CBS	550	183	3.0 : 1 for the left
NBC	648	602	1.1 : 1 for the left

Candidates-Politicians-Public on "Demonstrators"

	FOR	AGAINST	RATIO
ABC	196	1024	5.2 : 1 against demonstrators
CBS	240	1285	5.4 : 1 against demonstrators
NBC	1076	1449	1.3 : 1 against demonstrators

Candidates-Politicians-Public on Violent Radicals

	FOR	AGAINST	RATIO
ABC	0	208	208 : 0 against VR
CBS	0	0	0 : 0 opinion on VR
NBC	0	73	73 : 0 against VR

ABOUT THE AUTHOR

Edith Efron is an analyst of network programming trends and problems. She has been on the staff of *TV Guide* for ten years and her studies of coverage patterns in network news are used as texts in university communications courses across the country.

This analysis of network bias was undertaken privately by Miss Efron on a grant from The Historical Research Foundation. It was not influenced by nor does it express the policy of *TV Guide*.

Miss Efron has been a staff writer on *The New York Times Magazine,* Managing Editor of the Special Editorial Departments of *Look* Magazine, and Central American correspondent for *Time* and *Life* Magazines. Her articles on political, literary and cultural subjects have appeared in many major publications, have been used in overseas publications by the State Department, and have appeared in various anthologies. At the invitation of President Dumarsais Estimé of Haiti, in 1951, Miss Efron organized and headed the first journalism school at the Université d'Haiti, and assisted in the modernization of the Haitian press.

*   *   *

Clytia Chambers, who assisted the author in every aspect of the research study on which this book was based, is a Creative Services Executive and writer at Hill and Knowlton, Inc. She was formerly Associate Director of Research for The Council for Financial Aid to Education.